R.A. Markus's new and accessible work is the first full study of
Gregory the Great since that of F.H. Dudden (1905) to deal with
Gregory's life and work as well as with his thought and spirituality.
With his command of Gregory's works and of the entire Latin
tradition from which he came, Markus portrays vividly the daily
problems of one of the most attractive characters of the age. Gregory's
culture is described in the context of the late Roman educational
background and in the context of previous patristic tradition. Markus
seeks to understand Gregory as a cultivated late Roman aristocrat
converted to the ascetic ideal, caught in the tension between his
attraction to the monastic vocation and his episcopal ministry, at a
time of catastrophic change in the Roman world. The book deals
with every aspect of his pontificate: as bishop of Rome, as landlord of
the Church lands, in his relations to the Empire, and to the Western
Germanic kingdoms in Spain, Gaul, and, especially, his mission to
the English. Thus *Gregory the Great and his world* promises to be a major
contribution to the study of late antique society.

GREGORY THE GREAT
AND HIS WORLD

GREGORY THE GREAT
AND HIS WORLD

R.A. MARKUS

CAMBRIDGE
UNIVERSITY PRESS

PUBLISHED BY THE PRESS SYNDICATE OF THE UNIVERSITY OF CAMBRIDGE
The Pitt Building, Trumpington Street, Cambridge CB2 IRP, United Kingdom

CAMBRIDGE UNIVERSITY PRESS
The Edinburgh Building, Cambridge CB2 2RU, United Kingdom
40 West 20th Street, New York, NY 10011–4211, USA
10 Stamford Road, Oakleigh, Melbourne 3166, Australia

First published 1997

Printed in the United Kingdom at the University Press, Cambridge

Typeset in Monotype Baskerville

A catalogue record for this book is available from the British Library

Library of Congress cataloguing in publication data

Markus R. A. (Robert Austin), 1924–
Gregory the Great and his world/R. A. Markus
p.   cm.
Includes bibliographical references and indexes.
ISBN 0 521 58430 2 (hardback) – ISBN 0 521 58608 9 (paperback)
1. Gregory I, Pope, ca. 540–604.   2. church history – Primitive and early
church, ca. 30–600.   I. Title
BX1076. M37 1997
270.2′092–dc21   97-11308   CIP
[B]

ISBN 0 521 58430 2 hardback
ISBN 0 521 58608 9 paperback

CP

To Elizabeth Livingstone

implebatque actu quidquid sermone docebat
('he fulfilled in his actions what he taught in his words')
from Gregory's epitaph

Contents

Preface

In this book I am trying to portray Gregory in his proper setting. Gregory
lived in late sixth-century Rome, with a brief spell in Constantinople. His
world was sixth-century Europe. We live, however, in several worlds: not
only the world we see and hear and act in and upon; but also the world of
our imagination, perceptions, representations and ideas. The worlds we
live in are not separate; they interpenetrate unpredictably. In calling this
book *Gregory the Great and his world* I had all these in mind. To come to grips
with his work, we need to place him firmly in both his worlds: the social
reality and the intellectual and imaginative construct.

There is, of course, a large literature on Gregory.[1] The most complete
attempt to carry out a project akin to the one I have set myself is Homes
Dudden's, now ninety years old.[2] His book remains the classic account, at
any rate in English.[3] The first two parts of the book, devoted to Gregory's
life before his pontificate and the account of his pontificate, need revision
in the light of ninety years of historical scholarship. But many of his narratives of chains of events are masterpieces of unravelling untidy strands,
and I have often been helped by them. Dudden's Books I and II remain the
best narrative history available of Gregory's pontificate. I record here my
general debt, and would refer the reader to them for fuller accounts of
episodes I have not discussed in detail. Of the episodes which he has
traced in full I shall discuss only those which matter to my argument; and
generally not as fully as does Dudden. I devote more space to themes
where research and the shifting perspectives of modern scholarship have
moved furthest since he wrote.

Homes Dudden's Book III, on Gregory as the 'fourth doctor of the Latin
Church', has worn less well. Now, however, we have the distinguished and

---

[1] For a complete bibliography covering the years 1890–1989, see Godding, *Bibliografia*.

[2] Dudden, *Gregory the Great.*

[3] I would single out Erich Caspar's two chapters (4 and 5) in the second volume of his *Geschichte des
Papsttums* as the only other serious and successful account of his pontificate.

sympathetic accounts of Gregory's mind by Dom Robert Gillet, by Claude Dagens and by Carole Straw, written from very different perspectives, and with very different objectives, but all three hard to improve on.[4] Why do I not content myself with putting together their work on Gregory's culture, his spirituality, his inner world, with a revised version of Homes Dudden's account of his outer world?

That, perhaps, would have been the more modest, the more useful, certainly the easier thing to do. I have nevertheless chosen to portray Gregory in a landscape sketched in a perspective of my own choosing. I have done so because I have become convinced in the course of many years' work on the history of Christianity from the fourth century to the sixth that the cast of his mind can be understood only when we have taken the measure of the intellectual and spiritual shift that took place between the Christianity of, say, Augustine, Jerome and Ambrose, and that of Gregory. That I have tried to do in my book, *The end of ancient Christianity*, conceived, when I set out on writing it, as a Preface to what was to be the present book.[5] That study outgrew its original scope; but in doing so it has only confirmed my view that to understand Gregory we need to see him as belonging to two worlds at once, or rather as a *Grenzgestalt*[6] between them: the world of Ambrose, Augustine, John Cassian and their contemporaries, and the world of his medieval successors.

After an introductory chapter on Gregory's biography in its historical setting I sketch (chapters 2–5) Gregory's intellectual and spiritual landscape; but I do so by signposting its principal landmarks, not by plotting all its details. Its contours stand out in sharper relief when placed in the context of the Latin patristic tradition which I sketch as required and as briefly as I can; for the background often referring the reader to the fuller discussion in my *The end of ancient Christianity*. I do not wish to appear to attempt anything like a systematic exposition of Gregory's thought; for that, in as far as it can be done, I refer the reader to Carole Straw's book. I attempt something far more modest: to assemble, from some characteristic or suggestive utterances, a set of pointers towards the way he thought about matters that concerned him. If this is bound to be fragmentary and impressionistic, my hope is that it will, nevertheless, highlight some important facets of his mind. The chapters that follow (6–12) deal with Gregory's activities in the various spheres of his concern.

---

[4] Gillet, 'Grégoire le Grand'; Dagens, *Saint Grégoire le Grand*; Straw, *Gregory the Great*.

[5] Markus, *The end*, xi.

[6] Erich Caspar has designated Gregory as a *Grenzgestalt*, in rather a different, though equally true sense, between the Roman and the Germanic worlds: see his *Geschichte*, 2, 306–514, especially 408.

To convey something of the flavour of his mind, I have quoted Gregory's words freely. When either the richness of meaning, or the obscurity, or the striking quality, of Gregory's expression seemed to require quotation of his words or phrases in Latin, I have given the Latin text either in parentheses or in the footnotes, always, however, providing some English translation. A few technical words, such as titles of rank or office, I have left in Latin and listed in the glossary. For the reader who may wish to pursue further any of the themes touched on, I have made it a habit to give references to some of the more interesting relevant passages in Gregory's writings which I do not discuss in the text. I have not thought it useful to go in detail over ground that has been well covered either by myself or by others. In such cases I have been content to summarise earlier work, giving the necessary references. In particular, I have generally given narrative accounts in a largely condensed form, with references which will enable readers interested in the detail to follow them up. Nor have I been able to sketch the histories of the Germanic kingdoms, still less their diplomatic relations, except to the extent that is essential for the purpose of expounding Gregory's activities. References in the notes are given in abbreviated form. The details will be easily found in the lists of sources and works referred to.

I began working on Gregory the Great around 1960, when I first started to teach a 'Special Subject' on his age in the Liverpool University School of History. I left Liverpool in 1974, and had no further opportunity to teach such a course. In 1992–93, however, I was allowed to give a semester's doctoral course as visiting Professor at Notre Dame University. We are all aware how much our work owes to our students: they not only help us to sharpen the problems and sometimes, to glimpse the answers, or bring us back to earth when we have been reading between the lines from too great a height; but it is often the work of the seminar that brings the slow revelation of the shape of the subject, of a sense of what is important and what is not. For this, and much else, I want to thank my students, both at Liverpool and at Notre Dame.

I came across Michael Fiedrowicz's rich and meticulously careful work, *Das Kirchenverständnis Gregors des Grossen. Eine Untersuchung seiner exegetischen und homiletischen Werke* (1995) too late in the course of writing my own book to make as good use of it as I should have liked. I wish to thank Paul Meyvaert for generous help; also Claire Sotinel and Ian Wood, who have given good advice on chapters 9 and 11 respectively. My beloved wife has had to put up with Gregory almost as long as she has had to put up with me. She has, moreover, heroically read the whole book in draft. Her labour and the many improvements resulting from it are the least of the things I have to thank her for.

In dedicating the book to Elizabeth Livingstone I wanted, in the first place, to express my gratitude to a generous friend. The dedication is also intended to honour her as the great facilitator of patristic studies during the second half of our century: the person to whom my generation of scholars active in work on early Christian history and religion owes more than to anyone else.

Two important publications appeared too late to be taken into account in the book. One is the Notre Dame Symposium (1993) on Gregory the Great (*Gregory the Great. A Symposium*, ed. J. C. Cavadini (Notre Dame, 1995 (*sic*, for 1996)). I have been able to refer (p. 128) only to the contribution by Paul Meyvaert, of which I had a typescript before publication. The other is the paper by Dom Adalbert de Vogüé, 'L'auteur du Commentaire des Rois attribué à saint Grégoire: un moine de Cava?', which appeared in January 1997 (*Revue Bénédictine* 106 (1996) 319–31). The latter has raised serious doubts about the authenticity of the Commentary on I Kings. Pending further study and discussion, it is now not safe to rely on this Commentary to establish Gregory's views. This discovery affects the argument of this book only to a limited extent. For most of the points on which I have referred to this work, texts can easily be found in Gregory's other writings to support the views ascribed to him, though sometimes in slightly different terms. There are two exceptions, on which I should warn the reader: one is Gregory's discussion of the value of secular studies (*I Reg.* v.84; cf. chapter 3, n. 20), which, if not authentic, must suggest that Gregory was somewhat less favourably inclined towards these than this paragraph would suggest. The other is the passage in which the *Rule* of St Benedict is quoted (*I Reg.* IV.70; cf. chapter 5, n. 6), which merely clinches the view that Gregory knew the *Rule*, which is highly likely regardless of this formal evidence.

Nottingham
February, 1997

Abbreviations

AB	*Analecta Bollandiana*
ACO	*Bibliothèque des Écoles françaises d'Athènes et de Rome*
ByZ	*Byzantinishe Zeitschrift*
CC	*Corpus Christianorum. Series Latina*
CSEL	*Corpus scriptorum ecclesiasticorum latinorum*
DACL	*Dictionnaire d'archéologie chrétienne et de liturgie*
DDC	*Dictionnaire du droit canonique*
DHGE	*Dictionnaire d'histoire et de géographie ecclésiastiques*
DOP	*Dumbarton Oaks papers*
Ep, Epp.	*Epistola[e]*
FR	*Felix Ravenna*
HE	*Historia ecclesiastica*
HF	*see: Gregory of Tours, under Sources.*
HL	*see: Paul the Deacon, under Sources*
JECS	*Journal of early Christian studies*
JEH	*Journal of ecclesiastical history*
JRS	*Journal of Roman studies*
JTS	*Journal of theological studies*
LP	*Liber pontificalis*
LRE	*see:* Jones, A.H.M., under Secondary works referred to
LThK	*Lexikon für Theologie und Kirche*
MAH	*Mélanges d'archéologie et d'histoire*
MGH	*Monumenta Historica Germaniae*
AA	*Auctores antiquissimi*
Epp.	*Epistolae*
SSRL	*Scriptores rerum langobardicorum*
Chron. min.	*Chronica minora,* ed. T. Mommsen
PG	*Patrologia graeca,* ed. J.-P. Migne
PL	*Patrologia latina,* ed. J.-P. Migne

PLRE	*Prosopography of the Later Roman Empire*, vol 3, ed. J.R. Martindale, (Cambridge, 1992)
RAC	*Realenzyklopädie für Antike und Christentum*
RBen	*Revue Bénédictine*
RE	*Realenzyklopädie der Altertumswissenschaften*, ed. Pauly-Wissowa
REByz	*Revue des études byzantines*
RechSR	*Recherches de science religieuse*
RHE	*Revue d'histoire ecclésiastique*
SC	*Sources Chrétiennes*
SCH	*Studies in Church history*
SEAug	*Studia ephemeridis "Augustinianum"*
Settimane	*Settimane di studio del Centro italiano di studi sull'alto medioevo (Spoleto)*
StMon	*Studia monastica*
StPatr	*Studia patristica*
StT	*Studi e testi*
TRE	*Theologische Realenzyklopädie*
TRHS	*Transactions of the Royal Historical Society*
TU	*Texte und Untersuchungen*
ZKG	*Zeitschrift für katholische Theologie*
ZRG Kan. Abt	*Zeitschrift für Rechtsgeschichte*, Kanonistische Abteilung

Maps

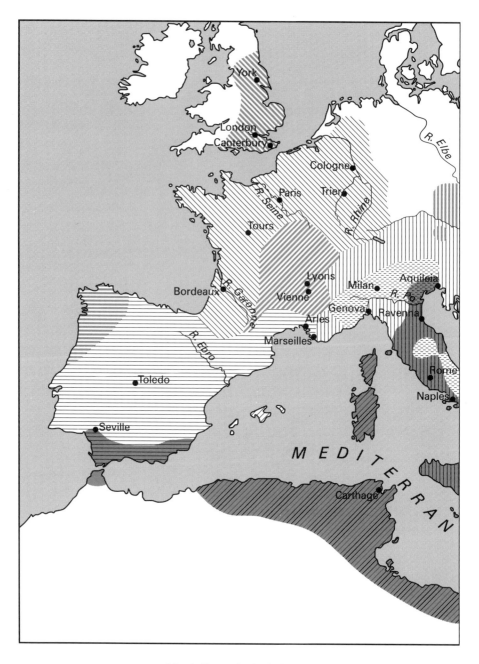

Map 1 Europe in the sixth century

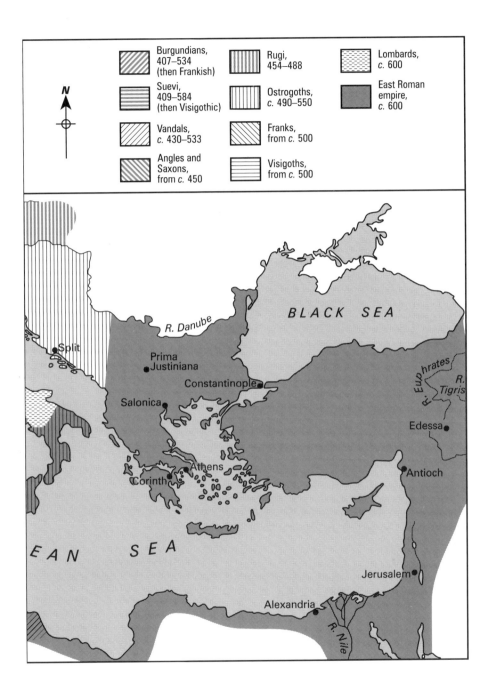

N

Burgundians, 407–534 (then Frankish)	Rugi, 454–488	Lombards, c. 600
Suevi, 409–584 (then Visigothic)	Ostrogoths, c. 490–550	East Roman empire, c. 600
Vandals, c. 430–533	Franks, from c. 500	
Angles and Saxons, from c. 450	Visigoths, from c. 500	

BLACK SEA

R. Danube

Split

Prima Justiniana

Constantinople

R. Euphrates

R. Tigris

Salonica

Edessa

Athens

Antioch

Corinth

EAN SEA

Jerusalem

Alexandria

R. Nile

Map 2 Distribution of Gregory's correspondence

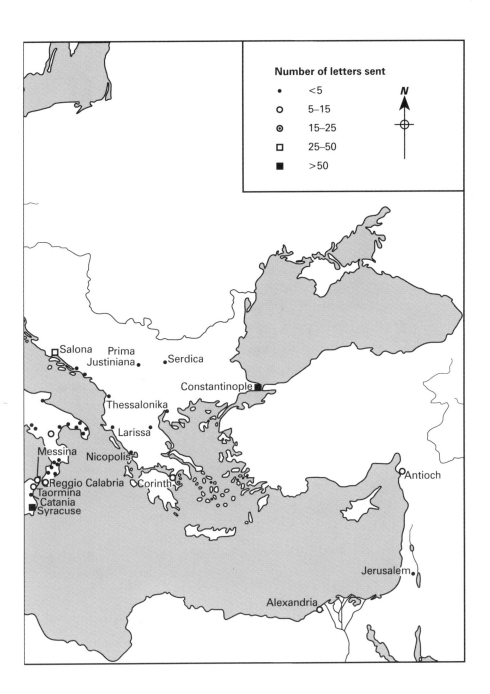

Map 3 Ecclesiastical jurisdiction (based on map VII in A.H.M. Jones,
The Later Roman Empire (Oford, 1964)

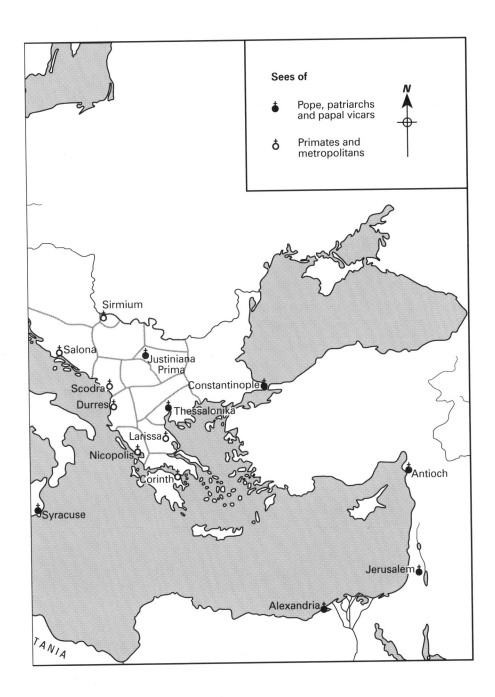

CHAPTER I

Introduction: a contemplative in a troubled world

THE SOURCES

Although Gregory left us no autobiography, he is known to us almost entirely through his own writings. For the last thirteen and a half years of his life, the period of his pontificate (September 590 to March 604), over 850 surviving letters (see below, pp. 14–15) give us a fairly full picture of his work. His writings also contain occasional hints about his earlier life. A handful of other sources add little more than scraps of information. One of the earliest of these is the entry in the *Liber pontificalis*. Since the early sixth century various materials had been combined into a collection of papal biographies, known as the *Liber pontificalis*.[1] By Gregory's time it had taken its shape as a collection of brief biographies, a new entry being added soon after each pope's death, by papal clerks with access to the papal archives. At this period, however, they are short and uninformative. The entry for Gregory adds to what we know from his own writings only the little he did in the way of adorning, furnishing and reconstructing the interiors of some Roman churches. Its mention of some liturgical innovations hardly merit description as 'reforms': they do not go beyond what would have been regarded as the normal role of the president of the liturgical assembly.[2]

Within months of his becoming bishop of Rome, his contemporary, Gregory of Tours, included in his *History of the Franks* (x.1) a report of Gregory's accession and its circumstances, brought back by one of his deacons just returned from Rome. It was to be much used by later writers. Gregory did not lack later biographers; but these are the only independent sources, apart from scraps of references in early writers such as Isidore of Seville.[3] The earliest biography is that composed by an unknown

---

[1] See Duchesne, *LP*, 1, i–clxiii, and Davis, *The Book of Pontiffs*, ii–vii.

[2] Chavasse, 'Le calendrier', especially at 245.

[3] On the biographies, see Stuhlfath, *Gregor I*, 63–89. The Greek *Life* known to Photius (*Bibl.* 252) contributes no reliable independent information: Delehaye, 'S. Grégoire'. See Hemmerdinger, 'Le "Codex" 252'.

monk of Whitby around AD 700. Much of his material is legend – mostly originating in England and designed to delight English readers. It was used by some later biographers, including an interpolator of a *Life* written by the Lombard historian, Paul the deacon, at the end of the eighth century. A biographical sketch is given by Bede in his *Ecclesiastical history* (II.1), based on Gregory's own writings and the *Liber pontificalis*. The fullest of the later *Lives* was written by John, a deacon in the Roman Church in the time of pope John VIII (872–82). He made use of the previous biographical accounts as well as of Gregory's own works, and of some documentary sources. He was given access to the material in the papal archives, including the papyrus volumes of Gregory's *Register* which, though already crumbling, were still preserved there at the time.[4] Although he made use of very few sources which are not still available to us, as a biographer, John has rightly been described as a giant standing on the shoulders of giants.[5] He read his documents with care and sympathy, and succeeded in producing one of the finest of early medieval biographies. The Gregorian letters he used are all contained in one or other of the collections made before his time, or cited by an earlier writer and known to us independently. John Moschus, a monastic traveller and collector of edifying anecdotes, has a story about Gregory, which was known, in a recent translation, to John the deacon.[6] Apart from a few scraps, we are thus driven back to Gregory's letters and a handful of autobiographical references elsewhere in his writings. His letters cover only some fifteen years of his life; a truly biographical treatment, following the development of mind and personality, is not possible in Gregory's case.

For his pontificate we have a rich quarry of his letters at our disposal.[7] Though some of the correspondence has been lost, what survives is richer than what there is for any earlier pope, and indeed has no parallel for several centuries to come. Some care, however, is needed in using the correspondence. By Gregory's time the papal *scrinium* had a sophisticated body of clerks, and had developed its own procedures and formularies. Papal letters dictated to notaries and subsequently copied passed through its machinery. Much of its output consists of routine administrative documents. Some of the material in later collections of formulae seems to have

---

[4] John Diac., *Vita*, Praef. & IV.71, where John notes the two-volume selection made in the time of Pope Hadrian. Ildefonsus of Toledo mentions a Register in twelve books: *De vir. ill.* 1 (*PL* 96. 199). On the Register, see below, pp. 14–15, 206–9.

[5] See on all aspects of the work, Berschin, *Biographie*, 3. The description quoted is on p. 382. On John's use of *polyptycha*, see below, chapter 8, p. 112.

[6] *Vita* IV.63; *Pratum*, 151. See Chadwick, 'John Moschus', esp. 45 and 58.

[7] On them, see the section on *Gregory's writings*, below.

its origin in the practice of the *scrinium* in Gregory's time, and some of Gregory's practice has its roots in the practice of his predecessors. In the papal correspondence as it has come down to us we have to take care to distinguish what is personal to the pope, and what reflects administrative routine.

GREGORY'S ITALY

Gregory was born around 540, into a world in which peace and stability could not be taken for granted. 'In the midst of the unsteady flow of time [the man of God] knows how to keep steady the steps of his mind', he said in a discourse.[8] He would need to remember this admonition. The fifty years before he became bishop of Rome was a period of insecurity unparalleled in Roman history, certainly since the 'crisis of the third century'. For well over a century, much of the Western part of the Empire had been under the control of Germanic rulers. Britain, Gaul and most of the Iberian peninsula remained so, and were in effect autonomous kingdoms in Gregory's time. In 533 the emperor Justinian (527–65) launched his ambitious plan of reconquering the Western provinces which had been lost to Germanic settlers over the previous century. The reconquest began with a campaign in Africa, where the Vandals were quickly defeated; in Gregory's day North Africa was again in imperial hands, though incursions of local African tribesmen prevented the return of security. The somewhat later attempt to reconquer the Iberian peninsula had established only a small and precarious foothold under Byzantine control in the province of Baetica on the Mediterranean coast. Slavic settlers in the Balkans did not create a new kingdom, but their enclaves inserted dangerous gaps into the imperial order.

Italy had had nearly half a century of peace and security under the régime of the Ostrogothic kings. The great Theodoric (king 493–526) had striven, with the aid of his Roman advisers and administrators, to secure *civilitas*, the orderly rule of law embracing his Roman subjects and the Gothic occupation forces. Latent tensions were never wholly overcome, but it was only in his last years that the stability of the order he had brought to Italy was seriously disturbed. From the 530s until well after Gregory's death Italy was never again at peace for more than short spells. The wars of reconquest failed to secure quick and complete victory. Fighting continued until about 550, and even then, after the defeat of the main Gothic

8 *Mor.* XXXI.28.55.

power, peace was not fully restored. Around 560 pope Pelagius I referred
to the 'devastation which more than twenty-five years of continuous warfare, still now by no means abating, inflicted on regions of Italy'.[9] Rome
had been several times under siege, either by Gothic or by imperial forces.
Blockades, destruction, depopulation and, especially, famine – and family
talk of them – must have been among Gregory's earliest memories. The
wars were officially declared ended in 554 with the return to normality
decreed by Justinian in his *Pragmatica sanctio*. But neither Gregory nor his
fellow-Italians can have enjoyed much of the 'former happiness' which
Narses, Justinian's victorious general, was credited with having brought
back to Italy.[10] Gothic resistance continued in parts of Italy, especially
in the North, where imperial troops remained engaged in mopping-up
operations of the remnants of Gothic and other Germanic forces almost
until the eve of a new Germanic invasion, by the Lombards, in 568. The
wars against the Lombards and their impact, will occupy us later (see
below, chapter 7). But war was not the only, or the gravest, of the calamities
suffered by Italy.

From 542 plague swept through the provinces of the Empire, including
Italy. It broke out repeatedly at intervals throughout the rest of the century.
It seems that in its first, most virulent, outbreak it carried away on average
something like a third of the population in the areas affected.[11] Its impact
on morale and spirituality cannot be estimated. It was significant enough
to cause the transfer in 543 of the festival of the Presentation from
October to 2 February. In Rome, on his accession to the see in 590,
Gregory held solemn processions of intercession and thanksgiving after
'the manifold and unceasing calamities' – the plague and its sequels: flood-
ing of the Tiber, famine, disease – 'with which we have been visited for our
sins and faults, and in which heavenly mercy has come to our help and
brought us remedy'.[12] Eighty people died during the procession; dragons
and water-snakes swam down the Tiber.[13] Evagrius, the Greek Church
historian writing during Gregory's pontificate, had himself survived an
attack of the plague while a school-boy, and lost his wife, several of his
children, many of his kin and his servants in subsequent recurrences.

---

[9] *Ep.* 85.
[10] *Auctarii Havniensis extrema*, 3: *totiusque Italiae populos expulsis Gothis ad pristinum reducit gaudium.*
[11] For a summary and literature, see Allen, 'The "Justinianic" plague'. Cf also Rouche, 'Grégoire le
    Grand'. On the plague and its effects, 43–4.
[12] *Registrum*, App. IV; cf. IX. The relation between the repeated call to a *septiformis laetania* (App. IX) and
    the events referred to by Paul the Deacon, *HL* III.24 and Gregory of Tours, *HF* x.1 is not clear. The
    arguments of Chadwick, 'Gregory of Tours' against the authenticity of the sermon attributed to
    Gregory by Gregory of Tours have not been universally accepted.
[13] Gregory of Tours, *HF* x.1.

Perhaps it was from despair that he turned to writing history; but his matter-of-fact account, written almost with detachment, shows no evidence of deep spiritual crisis directly attributable to the plague,[14] any more than does the work of his Western contemporary, Gregory of Tours.[15] If there was such a crisis – and it is hard to imagine that there was not – its nature eludes all but the most desperate attempt to read between the lines of our sources. A more agitated account by John of Ephesus, the monophysite historian, has survived; it comes closer to furnishing some insight into the survivors' minds: 'the hearts of people were numb and therefore there was no more weeping or funeral laments, but people were stunned as if giddy with wine. They were smitten in their hearts and had become numb.'[16] In some places, as in Amida on the Empire's eastern frontier, social cohesion came close to breaking point.[17] For Gregory mortality in the plague served as a spur to conversion: In September 591 – the plague was still raging in the first year of his pontificate – he urged the bishop of Narni to use the opportunity to admonish and exhort both Lombards and Romans living in the place, and especially to urge the barbarian heretics to convert to the true faith.[18] The closer the last judgement, the more we must fear the strict Judge.[19]

Of the spiritual impact of the plague we can only get the merest glimpse. Its visible consequences, however, were far-reaching. Apart from the immediate effects, famine and inflation, panic and sometimes rioting, the plague contributed to the drastic shifts, demographic, economic and social, which transformed Italy in the second half of the sixth century.[20] War, plague and insecurity combined to produce both urban and rural decay. While there was not much large-scale destruction, towns and their defences were often left in a crumbling state. More serious was the loss of populations, in town and country alike. The fragile prosperity of the earlier sixth century was shattered, and rural depopulation played its part.[21] Shortage of manpower, the incidence of taxation and low productivity

---

[14] Evagrius, *HE* IV.29; on it see Allen, *Evagrius Scholasticus*, 178, 190–94. How far experience of the plague contributed to Gregory's apocalyptic mood (on which see below, chapter 4, pp. 51–3) we can only guess.

[15] On the plague, see his *HF* IV.5, X.1.

[16] *The book of the plague*, 4 (Witakowski, 92–3).

[17] Harvey, *Asceticism*, 63–5.

[18] *Ep.* II.2. On the plague in Gregory's time see Paul the Deacon, *HL* IV.2; 4; 14. On another severe outbreak in 599, see *Ep.* IX.232; X.20.

[19] *Ep.* IX.232.

[20] On the transformation of Italian society, see Brown, *Gentlemen*. For a finely balanced judgement on the economy, see Rouche, 'Grégoire le Grand'.

[21] On population, see Rouche, 'Grégoire le Grand', 43–4.

all kept agricultural production at a low level and the economy stagnant. All these things combined to disrupt the fabric of Italian society. Many of the old aristocracy had fled from Italy, to Constantinople and elsewhere. Some returned after 550, but many did not; and in any case, the continuity of these families was now threatened, and their social position eroded by developments in government and administration. There was no longer a leisured class to carry on the tradition of literary culture. Gregory's description[22] of Roman desolation was not far off the mark. The city was 'in bad shape' and depopulated; this was no time for building.[23] Building activity revived only in the more settled conditions of the seventh century. Trade had revived only to a moderate extent since the Gothic wars, and was largely confined to the more flourishing coastal cities.

The effect of war and its semi-pacified sequel was a catastrophic upheaval in the administration and social structure of Italy. The eclipse of the civil administration and the predominance of the military authorities over civilians was a natural corollary of these conditions. Civil and military spheres were never self-contained and separate, but always, in practice, overlapped. Military personnel now came to exercise many of the functions proper to the civil bureaucracy; and with the military take-over, civilian functionaries slowly and haphazardly lost their importance or faded away. A supreme military commander with the rank of *patricius* was established, both in Italy and in Africa. They were the local representatives of full imperial authority. By the 580s they were known as Exarchs. Both Exarchs had large official establishments at their headquarters, in Ravenna and in Carthage respectively. With the break-up of many of the old senatorial estates, military personnel were well-placed – along with churchmen – to acquire land; and many did so, building up local power-bases. The old ruling class, the senatorial aristocracy, was gradually replaced by the new powers in society: ecclesiastical and military. Centralized bureaucratic civil administration was eclipsed by localised concentrations of power. Where civilian aristocrats and administrators had once been in control and exercised influence and patronage, wealth and power came more and more to be monopolised by local military and ecclesiastical élites. Municipal authority was often concentrated in the hands of the bishop. Often it was extended, with the help of his clergy, officials and monastic communities, over the territory beyond his

---

[22] See below, chapter 4, pp. 51–3.
[23] 'in bad shape': Krautheimer, *Rome*, 62; and generally, 59–87. On Gregory's building activities, see *LP*, 66, and below, chapter 8, note 77.

see. In the new world of narrower horizons bishops and clergy – along with soldiers – came to represent increasingly localised, sometimes intense local interests. Clerical and military officials inherited the prestige of the old civil aristocracy. Clergy found themselves drawn irresistibly into a variety of secular activities and responsibilities. The traditional Roman administrative system was undermined, and imperceptibly but permanently superseded. Lombards occupied much of the plain of the Po and, further South, large areas of central Italy, creating a hiatus in the machinery of government and in the stability of the traditional Roman order of society.

Horizons in Italy – and elsewhere, for that matter – were contracting. Effective power was coming to be concentrated in local or regional 'parish-pump' societies; for most people, action and imagination were limited by narrow frontiers.[24] While the boundaries of their world were shrinking, the distances that separated these little worlds grew. Gregory still lived in a world much wider than that of the majority of his contemporaries, not only by virtue of the wider family traditions he inherited, nor only through the friendships and contacts established during his stay in Constantinople and kept up, but, above all, by virtue of his office. Even he, however, felt remote from his scattered friends. 'Separated from you by great stretches of land and sea', he wrote to the bishops of Antioch and Alexandria, 'yet I am bound to you in my heart'.[25] The range of Gregory's correspondence, its distribution and delivery, can give some impression of both the ease and the difficulty of regular communications, so widely different in different areas.[26] It is striking, if not unexpected, that Gregory should have had no difficulty in keeping up a steady stream of correspondence within the southern half of the Italian peninsula and Sicily, especially with his own agents in charge of the Roman Church's lands, through whose hands much of his correspondence with clergy and others in their areas passed. His contacts with the North, excepting the clergy of Milan in exile in Genoa, and Ravenna, the seat of government, were much more tenuous. Constantinople, Carthage and its hinterland, Dalmatia (the latter reached *via* Ravenna) and Mediterranean Gaul were within fairly easy reach of regular communication. Further North, Gaul, Spain and Britain were far more difficult. The despatch of a special messenger after

---

[24] See e. g. Guillou, *Régionalisme*; Cracco Ruggini, 'Universalità'; and, for North Africa, Markus, 'Country bishops'. For Italy, see also Rouche, 'Grégoire le Grand', 46, who suggests that Gregory's administration of the patrimonies may even have accentuated the process.

[25] *Ep.* V.41. Cf. *Ep.* VIII.2 (Antioch): *nobis Orientis paene et Occidentis spatium interiacet.* Cf. *Ep.* VI.63 (Carthage).

[26] See Appendix on the destinations of Gregory's correspondence.

a missionary on his way through Gaul to Britain is startlingly exceptional in the correspondence.[27] The network of regular routes thinned out drastically beyond the orbit of the Empire.

GREGORY AND HIS FAMILY

Gregory was born not into 'one of the foremost senatorial families', as Gregory of Tours would have it;[28] but it was a wealthy family with extensive properties in and around Rome and in Sicily. Like many others, it might have had some distant link with the *gens Anicia*.[29] For a hundred years the family had been prominent in Rome. It had a reputation for piety, and was prominent in ecclesiastical and secular society. Felix III (pope 483–92) was Gregory's great-great-grandfather; and another pope, Agapetus (535–6), may have been a relative. Three of Gregory's aunts had entered the religious life. One of them 'rose to the heights of holiness by her continuous prayer, the dignity of her living and her outstanding self-denial';[30] another, however, the youngest of the three, 'oblivious of the fear of God, of shame and respect, and of her consecration', flouting senatorial conventions, married the steward of her possessions.[31] Another aunt, widowed, was one of the many pensioners assisted by the Roman Church.[32] Gregory's father, Gordianus, had been an official of the Roman Church.[33] Along with his mother, Silvia, the family group was depicted in a fresco on the walls of an oratory in the grounds of their property on the Coelian Hill, where it was still to be seen when John the deacon described it in the 870s.[34] There is no record of members of the family bearing secular office until Gregory himself, who was Prefect of the City in 573.[35] He may have had a brother (who would have been called Germanus) who followed him in that office;[36] a brother, Palatinus, a *vir gloriosus* and *patricius*

[27] On this, see chapter 11, pp. 183–4.
[28] *HF* x.1.
[29] On the ubiquity of Anician relatives, see Seeck in *RE*, 'Anicius n. 22'. For a stemma of Gregory's family, see *PLRE* 3, 1545.
[30] Gregory, *Dial.* IV.17.1.
[31] Gregory, *HEv* II.38.15.
[32] Gregory, *Ep.* I.37. The other women referred to may also have been relatives.
[33] John Diac., *Vita* I.1; IV.83 calls him *regionarius*; the term appears to have been applied retrospectively; Gordianus is likeliest to have been one of the Roman Church's *defensores*.
[34] *Vita*, IV.83. There is, of course, no means of determining when the fresco was painted. The name of Silvia appears for the first time in the Whitby *Life*, 1, whose author must have received it from a Roman source.
[35] This is now generally agreed, despite the reading *praeturam* in some MSS of *Ep.* IV.2 and Gregory of Tours (*HF* x.1), from which John the Deacon's statement in *Vita* I.4 must derive. Gregory may have held a minor office before the prefecture, though there is no evidence for it.
[36] See *PLRE* 3, 'Germanus 7'.

with whom Gregory kept in touch as pope, especially in public matters concerning Sicily, is better attested.[37]

The office of urban Prefect (of Rome) had in previous centuries been the prized monopoly of the Roman aristocracy. In the fourth and the fifth centuries it involved control of law and order in the City and parts of the surrounding area, the exercise of judicial authority over members of the senatorial order and some Roman guilds; and so long as the Senate survived, the Prefect presided over its meetings.[38] The members of the senatorial order were now dispersed or liquidated; the Senate as a corporate body had long been in decline and ceased to function. Gregory lamented its disappearance in some famous apocalyptic lines;[39] and of the prefecture there is no trace after 599, though both 'Senate' and 'Prefect' reappeared in the eighth century as antiquarian titles for new offices.[40] Too much must not be made of the fact that Gregory's only documented act as Prefect of the City was to witness an ecclesiastical deal.[41]

Gregory took his secular responsibilities seriously enough to cause him anxiety. What troubled him most, however, appears to have been that very anxiety: his deep personal involvement in wordly affairs. 'While my mind obliged me to serve this present world in outward action (*quasi specie*), its cares began to threaten me so that I was in danger of being engulfed in it not only in outward action, but, what is more serious, in my mind'.[42] Looking back, as pope, on his earlier life, Gregory saw himself torn, even while he was deeply engaged in worldly affairs, between secular and spiritual claims on him. In later life, as we shall see, the tension between worldly action and the life of contemplation was to continue to preoccupy him. The 'love of eternity' had long been rooted in him, but, he wrote, the chains of habit kept him in the secular state, until – very soon after 573 – he resolved no longer to put off his 'conversion', and escaping shipwreck among 'the things of the world' gained the safe haven of monastic life. Here, described in the traditional language and imagery of ascetic conversion, Gregory found the resolution of a tension which was widely shared

---

[37] *Epp.* IX.44; XI.4, and *PLRE* 3, 'Palatinus'.
[38] See Jones, *LRE*, 523–62.
[39] *HEz* II.6.22. Its last recorded corporate act was the sending of two embassies to Constantinople in 578 and 580: see Brown, *Gentlemen*, 21–2.
[40] On their fate, Brown, *Gentlemen*, 21–37.
[41] See below, page 134.
[42] *Mor.*, Dedicatory letter to Leander (*MGH Epp.* I, *Ep.* v.53a.1). This letter is the principal source of information on Gregory's life before his pontificate. As it is not included among the Appendixes to Norberg's edition of the *Registrum*, I shall henceforth refer to it as *Ad Leandr.* Unless specific reference is given to other sources, the present account is based entirely on this letter. The quotations in the sequel are taken from it. On the active and contemplative lives, see below, chapter 2.

among Christian aristocrats and had evidently also been present in his own family history. Gregory was now free to dispose of family properties he inherited. One of them was on the Coelian Hill in Rome, not far from the historic centre of the City, facing the Palatine Hill. It was next to the library which was intended to be the focus of the Christian University that Cassiodorus had hoped to establish there in collaboration with Gregory's predecessor and relative, pope Agapetus. An inscription recorded that later he composed his *Dialogues* in what had probably been Agapetus's library.[43] Here Gregory established the monastery dedicated to St Andrew, which he now entered, under 'my abbot, the most reverend Valentio', predecessor, apparently, of Maximian, who was later 'father' of the monastery.[44] Another six monastic communities were established on family properties in Sicily.[45]

Gregory's withdrawal into monastic life was not destined to be permanent. The ascetically inclined ex-prefect was too useful to be left in his monastic retirement. Soon after this pope Benedict I (575–8) or his successor, Pelagius II (578–90) enlisted him in the service of the Roman Church as a deacon. Gregory thus found himself plucked from the quiet of his monastic retreat and once again 'plunged into the sea of secular affairs'. 'Unwilling and resisting', Gregory accepted office, with 'the burden of pastoral care' it brought him. What his duties were we can only conjecture; but very soon Pelagius sent him to Constantinople as his representative (*apocrisiarius*, or *responsalis*) there. To share his forced return to 'life in an earthly palace', Gregory took with him 'many of his brothers from his monastery', including abbot Maximian, later to be bishop of Syracuse. Their company provided a safe haven amid the turmoil of the worldly affairs he was required to attend to. Their religious observance included daily readings. This was the setting of Gregory's talks on the Book of Job which, in the completed and revised form we know as the *Moralia*, were dedicated to Leander. Leander, bishop of Seville, had come to know Gregory at Constantinople. He was in the capital at the same time, on diplomatic business of the Visigothic kingdom.[46] The tensions between the active life and

---

[43] Cassiodorus, *Inst.* Praef. On the site and its history, see Marrou, 'Autour de la bibliothèque'.

[44] Valentio: *Dial.* IV.22.1; Maximian: III.36.1; IV.33.1. There is nothing to suggest that Gregory ever took on the office of abbot. At the time of the gift made in 587 (*MGH Epp.* 2, App. 1) Maximian was abbot; presumably until his departure for Sicily when he became bishop of Syracuse, in 591 when Gregory was already pope: *Registrum* (*CC* 140 A) App. 11. Cf. Stuhlfath, *Gregor I*, 32–4; 52–4.

[45] Gregory of Tours, *HF* x.1, from which Paul the Deacon's (*Vita* 3) and John the Deacon's (*Vita* 1.5–6) derive.

[46] *Ad Leandr.* 1. On its date, see Meyvaert, 'The date', 199 n. 18. For the sending of *Moralia*, *Epp.* I.41; V.53. On Visigothic affairs, see below, chapter 11.

the contemplative form one of the central threads of Gregory's discourses; for reasons not hard to understand. The only evidence concerning Gregory's work while acting as the pope's ambassador at the imperial court is a letter sent to him by the pope in 584, seeking imperial help in Italy among 'so great calamities and tribulations which the perfidy of the Lombards have inflicted upon us'; but we may safely assume that questions concerning the schism in the Italian Church and imperial policy concerning it took a large share of his attention.[47] During his stay in the capital Gregory found himself involved in a controversy with the patriarch, Eutychius, concerning the resurrection of the body. This had been the subject of debate in Constantinople since the time of Justinian, and Eutychius had written a book about it. Gregory rallied to the defence of the full corporeal reality of the risen body. Although his argument shows wide reading in Western patristic sources, the debate is also eloquent testimony to the cut-and-thrust of intellectual life which distinguished the capital from Western theological circles.[48] Gregory's report oversimplifies 'the long debate', resolved only by the intervention of the emperor Tiberius II (d. 582) who upheld Gregory's view and condemned Eutychius's book to be consigned to the flames. Both contestants, however, emerged gravely ill from their encounter. Eutychius died soon afterwards, uttering words which Gregory took to mean a belated conversion.[49]

His official duties brought Gregory into contact with the imperial family. A network of acquaintances and friendships, at court and elsewhere, came into being which was to provide Gregory with intermediaries and persons in whom he could repose confidences. In addition to his companions and Leander, there were other Westerners, among them the deacon Constantius whom Gregory was later to manoeuvre into the see of Milan.[50] In courtly and aristocratic circles Gregory was valued as a spiritual guide. His circle of friends included the Anician exile from Rome, Rusticiana; her daughter Eusebia and Eusebia's husband, Apion; two noble ladies at the court, Dominica and Gregoria;[51] and no doubt others. He evidently knew the two emperors with whose reigns his term of office in Constantinople overlapped, Tiberius and Maurice, and he was close to

---

[47] Pelagius II *Ep.* 1 (*MGH Epp.* 2, App. 11). On the schism, see below, chapter 9.
[48] For an illuminating commentary, see Duval, 'La discussion', who speaks of 'un bouillonnement intellectuel' at Constantinople (359). For reservations about the Byzantine intellectual milieu, see Cameron, 'The language', esp. 15–16.
[49] *Mor.* XIV.56.74 (*in longa contentione perducti*); for the whole account see *Mor.* XIV.56.72–4.
[50] See below, pp. 134–5, 140–2.
[51] Rusticiana: *Epp.* II.24; IV.44; VIII.22; XI.26; XIII.24. Dom(i)nica: *Epp.* I.6; III.63; VII.27; Eusebia: *Epp.* II.24; IV.44; VIII.22; XIII.33. Cf *PLRE* 3, Stemma 9. Gregoria: VII.22. Kate Cooper has suggested that she may be the dedicatee of the *Liber ad Gregoriam* attributed to Arnobius the Younger.

the latter's family. He acted as god-father to the emperor Maurice's eldest son. In court circles Gregory made a number of friends with whom he continued to correspond from Rome: Theoctista, Maurice's sister; the empress Constantina; Theoctistus, a relative of the emperor's; the court physician, Theodore and another doctor, Theotimus (Gregory was often ill)[52]; Narses, a *comes* and later *religiosus*, evidently a trusted intermediary of Gregory's at Constantinople; Philippicus and Priscus, both *patricii* and *comites excubitorum*; Aristobulus, ex-prefect and translator from Latin into Greek; Andrew, a *vir illustris* whom Gregory urged to go into monastic retirement rather than imperial service; John, quaestor of the imperial palace, whose patronage seems to have prompted the emperor to confirm Gregory's election to the see of Rome.[53] Gregory also made important friends among the higher clergy: despite later friction, he was clearly close to the patriarch John the Faster, a scholarly man of ascetic disposition, who had dedicated a book on baptism to Leander;[54] Gregory shared interests with the strongly Chalcedonian Domitian, nephew of the emperor, the metropolitan of Melitene, and probably his close friend, the *vir gloriosus* Leontius with whom he was to have dealings later; and he may have met other eastern bishops in the capital.[55] His friendship with Anastasius, the ex-patriarch of Antioch (see below, chap. 6, pp. 89) had begun during his stay in Constantinople. His relations with many of these friends remained close, and they were often asked for their assistance with business at court. With some, notably Theoctista, Gregoria and especially Rusticiana, he continued in his role as spiritual adviser.

Recalled to Rome in 585/6, Gregory returned to his monastery, devoting himself mainly to reading, contemplation and exposition of the scriptures. It was the happiest time of his life.[56] Recollecting it as pope, Gregory does not mention that he maintained his contacts with the Roman Church

[52] As he himself remarked: *Dial.* IV.57.8. For a list, see Meyvaert, 'The date', 200, n. 21; Caspar, *Geschichte*, 2, 344 n. 1.

[53] Theoctista: *Epp.* I.5; XI.27; Constantina: *Epp.* IV.30; v.38, 39; Theoctistus: *Ep.* VI.17; Theodore: *Epp.* III.64; v.46; VII.25; Theotimus: *Ep.* III.65; Narses: *Epp.* I.6; III.63; VI.14; VII.27; Philippicus: *Ep.* I.31; Priscus *Ep.* III.51; Aristobulus: *Ep.* I.28; Andrew: *Ep.* I.29; John: *Ep.* I.30.

[54] Gregory's friendship for John is attested by his *Ep.* I.4; The dedicatory letter to *RP* (*MGH Epp.* 1, *Ep.* I.24a) could also be cited, if John the Faster were the dedicatee; but this is, I think, unlikely (see below, chapter 10, n. 16). Isidore, *De vir. ill.* 39. On the controversy with John over the title 'ecumenical patriarch', see below, chapter 6.

[55] On Domitianus: see Honigmann, 'Two metropolitans', and Paret, 'Dometianus de Mélitène'; Whitby, *The emperor Maurice*, 14–15. On Leontius, *PLRE* 3, 776–7, and below, p. 90. On other Eastern bishops: Anastasius I of Antioch, see Weiss, 'Studia Anastasiana I', 25–7, 34–41; Beck, *Kirche*, 380–81; Gregory of Antioch: Whitby, *Life*, 109–10; Anastasius II: Beck, *Kirche*, 401. On all three and Eulogius of Alexandria, see also Goubert, 'Patriarches'.

[56] *Dial.* I. *Prol.* 3–5.

and continued to assist the pope with advice. But this happy period of reflection and meditating on the scriptures was quickly brought to an end. In February 590 pope Pelagius died of the plague. War with the Lombards had re-started in 587; there had been heavy rains; the Tiber had burst its banks, and floods caused more devastation than anyone could remember. Man-made troubles added to these acts of God: 'we are ceaselessly threatened from outside by the swords of the Lombards, but we stand in graver danger from inside through the treachery of the soldiers',[57] Gregory wrote in September 590.

He had then just become bishop of the City. His labours in the service of the see had made him the natural choice to succeed Pelagius II. It was seven months since his predecessor's death. Gregory had insisted on awaiting the emperor's orders confirming his election (Pelagius II had taken office without obtaining these: perhaps on account of the Lombard crisis). Rumours of prepared hide-outs and intended flight had reached Gregory of Tours, and were built into colourful legends by Gregory's later biographers. Resistance to episcopal consecration was a well-established convention, and not only in literature; but Gregory's aversion was deeply felt. He felt unequal to the responsibilities of his new office; and, more important in his own mind, it plunged him back into the tempestuous sea of worldly affairs from which he had long been seeking to extricate himself. 'Under the colour of the episcopate I have been brought back to the world [*ad saeculum sum reductus*] and here I labour under such great earthly cares as I do not recall having been subjected to even in my life as a layman', he wrote.[58] In his Synodical Letter announcing his accession to the other patriarchs he remarked that 'whoever is called a "pastor" is so heavily involved in exterior business that it is often unclear whether he performs the office of a pastor or that of an earthly potentate.'[59] He had hoped, it seems, that the emperor Maurice would refuse to confirm his election; but imperial confirmation duly arrived, and Gregory accepted the office. 'Our most serene lord the emperor,' he wrote to the emperor's sister, 'has ordered an ape to be turned into a lion.'[60] But the newly metamorphosed lion did not feel fitted for his role. This letter, like others written to personal friends at this time, as well as his Synodical Letter, are

---

[57] Gregory, *Ep.* 1.3. On floods and plague, *Dial.* III.19 and Gregory of Tours, *HF* x.1.

[58] *Ep.* I.5. For a deeper meditation later in his life on the *fuga ministerii*, see *1 Reg.* IV.206–8.

[59] *Ep.* I.24. Cf. the opening of the *Dialogues* (I. *Prol.* 1), where Gregory confesses himself *nimiis quorumdam saecularium tumultibus depressus*.

[60] *Ep.* I.5 (echoing a phrase used by his friend Narses: *Ep.* I.6). For the narrative, see Gregory of Tours, *HF* x.1; cf. *Ep.* VII.5: *ego quoque, qui indignus ad locum regiminis veni, infirmitatis meae conscius secretiora loca petere aliquando decreveram...*: this must refer to his monastic retreat.

heavy with the language of weakness.[61] Gregory's sense of being unequal to the burden placed upon him blended with a reluctance to becoming once again enmeshed in secular affairs. 'I have been hurled from the very heights [of contemplation] by the whirlwind of this trial, I have fallen into fear and dread; for even though I am not afraid for myself, I fear greatly on account of those who have been committed to me.'[62] Regret, a sense of deprivation, of inadequacy and fear, added up to despondency: a Constantinopolitan friend was told that 'I am stricken with such sorrow that I can hardly speak. The shadows of grief darken the eyes of my mind; all I see is dismal, all that is reputed delightful appears to me as lamentable.'[63]

Gregory had experienced the tension between the contemplative life of the ascetic and the active life of service, and it had been part of his family history. Much of his thought during the previous ten years or more had been directed to resolving this conflict. His mind had been well prepared for the office he now took on. Humility and obedience to the call overcame his reluctance. 'We are not to go against the judgement of the Lord who disposes, I have obediently followed what my Lord's merciful hand has allotted to me'.[64] Before long he told a fellow-bishop that since he could not resist God's decree, 'I have recalled my mind to a more cheerful state.'[65] He was no doubt helped to become reconciled to the burdens of his position by the completion, within five months of taking office, of the first major task he had imposed on himself: taking stock and re-thinking his own life. The letters he wrote in the earliest months of his pontificate and, more fully, the *Rule of pastoral care*, also written at this time, struggle with the questions raised by the conflict between the active and contemplative forms of life, and with questions about the nature of the Christian ministry.

GREGORY'S WRITINGS[66]

1. The *Registrum*: by Gregory's time the papal writing office (*scrinium*) had developed a fairly systematic routine. Copies of letters, either dictated by the pope or, for more routine purposes, produced by its staff, were

---

[61] *Epp*. 1.3; 4; 5; 6; 7; 24; 25; 29. On Gregory's 'rhetoric of vulnerability', see Leyser, 'Let me speak'.

[62] *Ep*. 1.5.

[63] *Ep*. 1.6.

[64] *Ep*. 1.26; cf. *Ep*. 1.31; *RP* 1.6; and on this further below, chapter 2, pp. 20–21.

[65] *Ep*. 1.20.

[66] I here give only the barest details. For editions used, see *Sources*. Of the Maurist edition of the works in four volumes (Paris, 1705; reprinted in J.-P. Migne's *Patrologia latina*, 75–9) the *Moralia*, the *Pastoral Care*, *Homilies on the Gospels*, the *Homilies on Ezechiel*, and the *Dialogues* are still usable.

preserved in a 'register' kept in the *scrinium*. Originally there had been fourteen volumes, still to be seen when John the Deacon composed his *Life* of Gregory (see above, n. 4). All that now survives are collections extracted at various times. The most important and largest was made in the time of pope Hadrian I (772–95), known to John the Deacon, containing 686 letters. Two other collections, together with a handful of other sources such as Bede's *Ecclesiastical History* and some collections of canons allow us to supplement these to give a total of over 850 letters. Some letters of the original *Register* have been lost, and some may never have been copied into the *Register*; it is impossible to know how many. It has been suggested that Gregory made his own selection from his correspondence, and that this is the archetype from which the known collections derive. The total size of the original Register can in any case not be reliably estimated.[67]

2. The *Moralia*: based on talks Gregory gave on the Book of Job to his 'brethren' who accompanied him to Constantinople while he held the office of papal *apocrisiarius* there (see above), the work as we have it is the result of Gregory's revision and completion of it soon after his accession to the papal office.[68]

3. The *Liber Regulae pastoralis*: written during the first year of Gregory's pontificate, anticipated in part, often literally, in some of the letters written in the months following his accession (see above).

4. The *Dialogues*: their authenticity, occasionally questioned since the sixteenth century, has been seriously attacked by Francis Clark, most fully in his *The pseudo-Gregorian Dialogues*. It has been – to the present author convincingly – defended by: Robert Godding, 'Les Dialogues ... de Grégoire le Grand. A propos d'un livre récent'; Paul Meyvaert, 'The enigma of Gregory the Great's Dialogues: a response to Francis Clark'; Patrick Verbraken, 'Les Dialogues de saint Grégoire le Grand: sont-ils apocryphes? A propos d'un ouvrage récent'; and Dom Adalbert de

---

[67] On the *Registrum*, Hartmann's Introduction to the edition by Ewald & Hartmann in *MGH Epp.* vol. 2, based on Ewald's pioneering work, is still fundamental. There is a useful short account of Ewald's reconstruction in Hodgkin, *Italy*, 5, 33–43. See now Norberg's Introduction in *CC* 140, and more fully, his *In Registrum Gregorii Magni studia* and 'Style personnel'; Pitz, *Papstreskripte* on procedure. The edition by Norberg follows the principles, and in all but a handful of cases the order, of Ewald and Hartmann's edition. He has, however, omitted letters not contained in the *Registrum*, and revised the order of (and renumbered) a few letters not securely datable. On the possibility – highly unlikely in my view – that Gregory had made his own selection from the Register and that this may be the archetype behind the three surviving collections, see Pitz, *Papstreskripte*, 32–3. Pitz estimates that the papal 'Palast' would have been able to produce some 20,000 letters during Gregory's pontificate; *ibid.*, 252. See my remarks in the Appendix.

[68] *Ad Leandr.* 2. See Gillet, 'Introduction', 7–19. Some fragments have been identified by Meyvaert, 'Uncovering a lost work', as from an earlier version of Gregory's commentary.

Vogüé, 'Grégoire le Grand et ses "Dialogues" d'après deux ouvrages récents', and 'Les Dialogues, oeuvre authentique et publiée par Grégoire lui-même', supplemented by his 'Martyrium in occulto'. (References are given in full in the list of Works referred to). The *Dialogues* are here taken as Gregorian, composed probably in 593–4. Book II is devoted entirely to St Benedict. Some stories told in the *Homilies on the Gospels* are re-used in the *Dialogues*. There has been a great deal of discussion on Gregory's aims in the *Dialogues*, and especially on Gregory's account of St Benedict in Book II. These questions are of subordinate or marginal interest for this book, and are discussed only incidentally in their appropriate place.[69] The Introduction, annotations and Indexes to De Vogüé's edition provide a wealth of information.

5. *Homiliae in Evangelia*: given in Rome, 590–2; some were preached by Gregory in public and taken down by notaries; some read out for him when he did not feel up to preaching; revised for publication.[70] One (1.17) was given to an assembly of bishops and clergy. Some of the stories are duplicated in the *Dialogues*.[71]

6. *Homiliae in Hiezechielem*: preached between 592 and 593; to a mixed audience, comprising lay people, clergy and monks. Revised eight years later, at the request of Gregory's *fratres*.

7 and 8. *Expositio in Canticis Canticorum* and *In librum primum regum expositio*: their authenticity is now generally agreed. The former was perhaps begun before Gregory's pontificate, in his Roman monastic community; intended to be delivered to an audience. The latter dates from the middle years of his pontificate, intended for a mixed audience, to be written down. Revised by abbot Claudius (on whom see chapter 10, pp. 152–4 below) at Gregory's request (598–9); the second finally revised by Gregory himself in the last years of his life.[72] Only a fragment of the first has survived. The remaining discourses mentioned in *Ep.* XII.6 have not survived.

---

[69] On purpose, see chapter 4 pp. 62–7.

[70] Meyvaert, 'The date', gives more weight to the difference between written and spoken homilies than does Banniard, '*Iuxta uniuscuiusque qualitatem*'.

[71] For the MSS, see Étaix, 'Note sur la tradition'.

[72] On all this see, especially, the characteristically thorough investigation by Meyvaert, 'The date', and, independently arriving at similar conclusions (concerning the Commentary on 1 Kings only), de Vogüé, 'Les vues' (= 'The views'); his 'Introduction', 26–30. Meyvaert's conclusions concerning the Commentary on the Song of Songs are (unnecessarily) qualified by Bélanger, 'Introduction'.

CHAPTER 2

Integritas animi: *ministry in the church*

THE CONTEMPLATIVE AND THE ACTIVE LIFE

Questions about the relations between the two lives were almost as old as Christianity itself, and some of them older. Gregory had a venerable tradition of Christian thought to draw upon, and behind that tradition stood a rich quarry of Jewish ideas and of Greek philosophical reflection. How much of this quarry Gregory mined for himself we cannot know.[1] Usually he covers his tracks so well as to expunge all identifiable traces of his sources. Their language and their concepts have soaked into his mind to re-emerge subtly transformed, sometimes scarcely recognisable, but always as his own. In Augustine and Cassian – both of whom he had read in great amounts – he would have found the most important threads that he wove into the fabric of his own, and, as we shall see, very personal, reflection on contemplation and the active life.

Ancient though the dichotomy was between the two forms of life, the 'active' (or 'practical', as it was more often called in the Greek world) and the 'contemplative' (or 'theoretical'), the meaning of the terms and the nature of the tension between the two things they stood for had undergone some profound changes.[2] Origen had been the fountainhead – as for so many things – for the use made by Christian writers of the contrast drawn by ancient Greek philosophers between the two lives. For Origen, the practical was a step on the ladder of perfection: the moral discipline prepared one for the higher stage, contemplation. The two needed to be combined in their proper order in the fullest Christian life. Among later Christian writers the two things Origen had combined were often separated: they stood for different conditions or styles of living adopted by

---

1 On Gregory's sources, see the discussion by Gillet, 'Introduction', 81–109. Gregory mentions the tri-chotomy of the three *ordines: moralis, naturalis,* and *contemplativa, Cant.* 9, adapted for his own purposes from the Stoic three-fold division of philosophy, of which he probably knew through Augustine.
2 In this very condensed summary I follow the somewhat fuller survey given in my *The end,* 183–97. The best summary of earlier thought and of the Greek Christian tradition known to me is Guillaumont, *Evagre le Pontique,* 38–53.

different Christian groups. Towards the end of the fourth century monks, especially – like ancient Greek philosophers – liked to monopolise the contemplative life and to distinguish it from the active life of Christians engaged in the business of the world. Around AD 400 these ideas were hotly debated in Egypt. The notion gained ground that the life of the monk, too, as of Origen's Christian, contained both forms of life as successive stages, sometimes sharply distinguished, in his spiritual development.

John Cassian had experienced these cross-currents in monastic spirituality in the course of his tour of monastic settlements in Egypt at the very time that there was agitated debate on these matters. As was his habit, he learnt from his experience and then went his own way; increasingly his own as he re-thought what he had learnt in Egypt. In successive additions to earlier instalments of his *Conferences* he revised – unobtrusively but unmistakeably – views that he had expressed earlier. Evagrius, the fashionable monastic theorist, had drawn the distinction between the active life and the contemplative very sharply; Cassian set out to blur it. Far from defining two alternative forms of life, or even two sharply separated stages on the ascetic's ladder of perfection, they were telescoped into a unified spiritual ideal. That ideal, moreover, was defined in terms which made it applicable not only to the solitary ascetic contemplative, nor even to the monk living in a community, but also to the life of a monk called to serve the wider Christian community as bishop (as a steadily growing number of monks in Provence and elsewhere were being called). The contemplative life was no longer the height of perfection achieved by the ascetic or the hermit at the end of his *ascesis*. It was the life of the monk, preferably communal, who had equipped himself to read and to understand the scriptures, and to teach them to others when called to do so. For Cassian the discipline of monastic life served to equip the monk to be a preacher, and was sterile unless it did so. In the end Cassian came very close to Augustine's view: the dichotomy of the two forms of life became eclipsed by our common human condition. In the last resort the contemplative life was not one of two alternative modes of living so much as the final reward for our life of labour here, only to be anticipated in an inchoate, fragmentary manner at best. Here our life is Martha's; but Mary's life of contemplation, a life which indeed she does not possess, but to which her life points, is a sign of what we may hope to attain hereafter.

Cassian's monastic ideal had absorbed the features of the ministerial model, in an age when ascetic character was generally valued in bishops. In the spirituality of his *Conferences*, especially of those of the collection written last, the two models of living were conflated. It was a synthesis well adapted for a world in which the qualities expected of a bishop converged with those of the monk. Towards the end of the fifth century an African refugee in Arles, Julianus Pomerius, went a step further. His treatise on *The contemplative life* was in fact written as a handbook for bishops. The serious underlying question that occupied him was how a busy bishop can 'pursue' (but not 'attain': for that, for him as for Augustine and, in the end, Cassian, was not possible in this life) the life of contemplation. He placed the pastoral life on a level with the contemplative, sometimes even hinting that for those chosen to lead it the pastor's was a higher calling. Whoever led the contemplative life was charged with responsibilities to share it with others.

There is so much in Gregory's writing that is reminiscent of Julianus's that it is hard to suppose he had not read it; but there is no conclusive evidence that he had. At any rate, while his own way of resolving the tension between the active life and contemplation has profound similarities with Cassian's and Julianus's, there is also something markedly personal about it. He had access to Augustine's and Cassian's, perhaps also to Julianus's, formulations of the way the contemplative life could be combined with the role of the bishop. But no theoretical statement, even so respected, could ease Gregory's anguish. The conflict between the two forms of life was too deeply rooted in his personal history and in his settled inclinations; and it is on this deeply personal level, rather than in any theological formulation, that we should look for his way of resolving it. In his discourses on Job, Gregory was apt to see himself in the figure of Job: 'Perhaps it was the design of divine providence that stricken I should expound the stricken Job', he wrote to Leander. It was not only in the weakness of his body and in feeling stricken by God that he saw himself mirrored in Job. He wanted to share Job's mind: 'that chastised, I should better perceive the mind of the chastised Job'.[3] The experience behind the *Moralia* is the experience of tension and conflict, and of ardent longing for their resolution.

It was a resolution longed for rather than achieved; or, perhaps, achieved on the personal level of a life experienced and accepted, rather than on the level of a conceptually defined and clarified relationship of the two forms of life. His whole experience before becoming pope pointed towards a way of defining the two lives as alternative forms of living here, in this world. For Gregory the two sorts of life were not identifiable with distinct ecclesial status, the monastic and the secular, or the clerical and the

---

[3] *Ad Leandr.* 5: *ut percussum Iob percussus exponerem.*

lay.[4] Nevertheless, the distinction between the contemplative and the active life was related to the change in his mode of living: of being plucked from the haven of the cloister and tossed into the tempest of the world's affairs. The experience of soul-rending conflict was the result of the change in his ecclesial condition. The overtones of monastic retirement contrasted with involvement in the world bring Gregory's language into a definite, if loose, relation with the change in his 'outward manner of living'.[5] 'I have loved the beauty of the contemplative life like the infertile Rachel', Gregory wrote to the empress Theoctista on his elevation, but he found himself, 'I know not how', joined in the night, like Jacob, to the fertile Leah (Gen. 29).[6] He had already used the traditional image of Rachel and Leah in one of several elaborate treatises he devoted to the theme of the active life and its relation to the contemplative in the *Moralia*.[7] The means for the intellectual resolution of the tension had long been ready to hand; yet the anguish, the sense of loss, of being torn, remained. But now Gregory found a way to resolving it in his experience: it was humility, a ready submission to God's calling like Jeremiah's surrender (Jer. 1:6) that finally reconciled Gregory to his new condition.[8] Pastoral involvement could be integrated into his spiritual goals. This is why one of Gregory's overriding priorities in the first months of his pontificate was the writing of the *Regula pastoralis* (along with the letters in which he gave his correspondents a preview). He had already conceived the idea of writing a treatise which he describes in terms appropriate to Book III of the *Regula pastoralis*; and a fair number of mini-treatises in the *Moralia* anticipate the pastoral advice which Gregory was to go on to elaborate at greater length and more systematically there. Time and again he would dwell on how a pastor should treat his flock, how, especially, he should distinguish the humble from the proud, how to be flexible and to adapt his style in speech[9] and action, his mildness or his

---

[4] This is clear from a survey of the texts, and generally agreed. See especially Frank, 'Actio und contemplatio', and Dagens, *Saint Grégoire*, 135–63.
[5] *Ad Leandr.* 1: *ne exteriorem cultum mutarem.*
[6] *Ep.* 1.5. The letter is full of the themes and allusions present in *Ad Leandr.*, and *Ep.* IX.228, also to Leander.
[7] *Mor.* VI.37.61; see below, n. 24.
[8] *RP* I.6–7. See above, p. 14. There is a striking parallel here with Gregory of Nazianzus's *Apology* (especially 111–14, where Gregory could have read of the calling of the young Jeremiah) summed up thus by Rousseau, (referring to §§ 102f. and 106f.) *Basil of Caesarea*, 87: 'It boiled down in the end to obedience'. On Gregory the Great and his namesake's *Apologia*, see Markus, 'Gregory the Great's *rector*'. On reluctance to take on office, see also *1 Reg.* IV.206–7.
[9] On adapting preaching to audience, see *RP* III; *HEz* I.11.12–7; *1 Reg* V.108; on the background of Gregory's precepts in classical rhetorical theory, see Fontaine, *Isidore de Séville*, 1.278. On its relation to spoken speech and effect on linguistic development, see Banniard, '*Iuxta uniuscuiusque qualitatem*', and *Viva voce*, chapter 3.

severity, to the various differing needs of his people.[10] The constant pre-occupation with this theme indicates the importance it had for Gregory throughout his life. Working on a systematic exposition of it in the *Regula pastoralis* was the therapy that brought about this reconciliation to his office, and became his profession of faith for the new life he now followed.[11]

Much of the *Regula pastoralis* had been foreshadowed in the scarcely penetrable jungle of the *Moralia*. Gregory's paradigm of the Christian life, sketched there, embraced both the active and the contemplative. Christ embodied the two lives in perfection: 'the contemplative life differs greatly from the active; but our Redeemer coming in the flesh and leading both, combined them in Himself'. He worked healing in the city and prayed on the mountain-top; thus He showed His followers that zeal for contemplation must not lead them to neglect caring for neighbours, nor immoderate concern for the neighbours' good to dull their striving for contemplation.[12] Gregory had been tormented by this conflict of action and contemplation almost since the start of his career: in one of his earliest talks on Job, the angels, though 'sent forth to minister to us for our salvation', manage to continue always in the enjoyment of seeing the face of God; but, he lamented, our nature is not like theirs: 'We are circumscribed in space and confined by the blindness of ignorance';[13] in our fractured lives minister-ing to others and contemplating God are constantly liable to fall apart.

By sin, man has lost the ability to perceive spiritually, and is immersed in the flesh:

In paradise the human race had access to the contemplation of its inmost light. But preferring to please itself, in forsaking itself, it lost the light of its Maker and the sight of His face, and hid among the trees of paradise. For after sinning, it came to fear seeing Him whom it had loved ... And then ... it sought again that Face which it had feared in its sin; that it might escape the mists of its blindness and abhor the very fact that it could no longer behold its Creator. Pierced by this desire the holy man [Job] calls out: 'Why dost Thou hide Thy face and count me as Thy enemy?' (Job 13:24)[14]

To see God's face is not given to us in this life. Like Job, Gregory knew that 'the wisdom which is God is hidden from the eyes of the living. For in this

---

[10] Intention of writing *RP*: *Mor.* XXX.3.13. Anticipations and echoes of *RP* III: *Mor.* V.11.17–27; VI.39.64; XV.35.41; XIX.20.30; XX.2.4; 5.14; XXIV.16.40; XXVI.6.6–11; XXX.3.11–16; *HEv* I.17 (preached to bishops); *HEz* 1.3.4; 1.7.4–6; 1.11; 11.9.18–22.

[11] This appears particularly clearly in the dedicatory letter to bishop John (more likely to be John, bishop of Ravenna, than John the Faster, patriarch of Constantinople: cf. below, chapter 10, n. 16)

[12] *Mor.* XXVIII.13.33. This theme is common in Gregory's work; it is dealt with below. pp. 23–6

[13] *Mor.* II.3.3.

[14] *Mor.* XI.43.59.

mortal flesh He could be seen only in finite images and not in the infinite light of eternity'.[15] In passages resonating with the accents of a long Christian tradition, rooted in the language of neo-Platonic thought which had served Augustine so well, Gregory describes the soul's effort in entering into itself, gathering itself from dispersal among the material images of its daily occupation, and rising in inner ascent:

> When a man strives by spectacular exertion to rise hence, it is wonderful if he is brought by his soul to know himself, having cast aside all bodily form; and . . . to prepare for himself a path to reach contemplation of the eternal reality. In this manner [the soul] becomes as it were a ladder for itself whereby to rise from the external into its own inner reality, and from there to its Creator.[16]

Contemplation, however, is a fleeting experience, elusive and fragmentary; the more precarious, the greater the store we lay by it.[17] Whereas the mind can settle itself firmly in the active life, 'it is quickly made listless in the contemplative by the weight of its infirmity'.[18] Moreover, the higher the human mind is raised, the more it is struck by awe of the gulf which divides it from the perfection of the light. 'Dread came upon me and trembling, which made all my bones shake' (Job 4:14): the dread, Gregory comments, 'is the awe of the darkness in contemplation';[19] our sense of security and self-assurance 'liquefies' as we contemplate the abyss; 'my flesh has no words, as my infirmity falls silent before Thee'.[20] The mind's eye soon tires and turns aside; contemplation is never fully achieved, however ardently it is begun; the silence is always broken, assailed by chattering, shrieking voices, the voices of temptation.[21]

  Two reasons must be distinguished for this fragility of contemplative living. Gregory will often blame it simply on the weakness of fallen human nature: the mind's liability to change, our inability to sustain a settled purpose, faltering in our efforts, allowing 'slippery mutability' to divert us.[22] This is part of the unending struggle of flesh and spirit in our sinful state. But Gregory gives even more weight to another kind of reason for

---

[15] *Mor.* XVIII.54.88; the discusssion extends to the end of Book XVIII. Among many passages on similar lines, see *Mor.* V.30.53–36.66; VI.37.56–61; VII.13.15–19.22; X.10.16–19; 15.31–20.38; XXIV.6.11–12; XXX.16.53–54.

[16] *Mor.* V.34.61–2 (*viam sibi usque ad considerandam aeternitatis substantiam paret*); cf. XXV.7.18–8.20; XXVI.44.79–81; XXXI.12.18–20; and Straw, *Gregory the Great*, 213, n. 6.

[17] *Mor.* V.32.57–33.58. Cf. XXIII.21.40–43; XXIV.6.12.

[18] *Mor.* X.15.31 (see the whole section, 15.31–20.38); cf. X.10.16–19.

[19] *Mor.* V.30.53; XVI.28.35; XXVII.17.33–4.

[20] *Mor* V.32.56.

[21] *Mor.* XXX.16.53–54; cf. V.6.9; XIII.41.46; XXIV.11.32. *HEz.* I.5.12.

[22] *Mor.* XI.43.59–44.60; 49.66–50.68; further, see the fine pages of Straw, *Gregory the Great*, 108–9 with references.

the fragmentary and fugitive nature of the contemplative life: the call of external demands which we may not resist but which nevertheless distract us from contemplation. It was, naturally, his own predicament that pushed this hindrance to contemplation to the forefront of his mind. There it remained, and Gregory's concern with the contemplative life was swallowed up in his thought about the Church and his own pastoral ministry within it. But inner conflict, creative acceptance of what he came to see as the duty he was called to, and meditating on his calling, gave his thought new depth. Thus Gregory achieved integration of the active life into the contemplative in what has been called (though not by Gregory) the 'mixed life': they were stages within the life of the pastoral ministry.

THE TWO LIVES OF THE PASTOR

The active life had made heavy claims on Gregory long before he became pope, and as we have seen, he had taken serious note of its claims in his *Moralia*. The thrust of his discussion was the need to accept the inescapable distractions from contemplation in performing the duties laid upon one. Sometimes he spoke as if the two forms of life were successive stages on the way to perfection: 'Those who strive to achieve the height of perfection by wanting to hold the citadel of contemplation should first prove themselves in action on the field of battle.'[23] In line with this image, Gregory went on to treat the active life as a preliminary to the contemplative. Prior in time, it is on a lower rung of perfection: Jacob came to Rachel only after embracing Leah: being first joined to the fruitfulness of the active life he is then rewarded with the repose of contemplation.[24] But even once it is attained, contemplation always remained threatened not only by human weakness, but by the distractions of business, and by the even subtler dangers brought by the urge to carry out good works. The pastor's work necessarily means surrender of contemplative quiet. 'By contemplation we rise to the love of God; by preaching we return to the service of our neighbour.'[25] This notion of the two lives led in succession, the second being on a higher rung of the ladder than the first, implied that

---

[23] *Mor.* VI.37.59. The superiority of contemplation over action is particularly strongly marked in Gregory's comment on the pseudo-Dionysian celestial hierarchy: *HEv* II.34.12–13.

[24] *Mor.* VI.37.60–61. *1 Reg* V.178. See above, n. 7, and Straw, *Gregory the Great*, 189–90; 250; and De Vogüé, 'Les vues', 224–9.

[25] *Mor.* VI.37.56. Sometimes the theme is inverted: the perfect preacher needs contemplation to crown his active life: e. g. *Mor.* XXXI.25.49. See also *HEz* I.3.9: *duae autem sunt sanctorum praedicatorum vitae: activa scilicet et contemplativa; sed activa prior est tempore quam contemplativa, quia ex bono opere tenditur ad contemplationem. Contemplativa autem maior est merito quam activa . . .*

any return from the contemplative life to involvement in the active, however meritorious, constitutes a regression to a lower stage.

It may be that it was to avoid this implication that Gregory often played down this model of a linear ascent from action to contemplation, and stressed, instead, the contemplative's task of communicating the gifts received. 'Inwardly they obey the desires of piety; outward they fulfil the ministry of their office', he wrote of those compelled to take charge of pastoral or ministerial office:

Thus they do not in their intention forsake perfection, nor do they oppose the Creator's will by pride. It is by a wonderful divine benevolence that he who seeks contemplation with a perfect heart, is occupied in serving others; so that his perfected mind may profit others weaker than him, and that he himself may rise to the summit of perfection in humility from the very imperfection he perceives in himself.[26]

Surrendering contemplative withdrawal for ministry will, in its turn, lead to further spiritual progress.[27] The pastor's work is one instance of the citizen of Jerusalem carrying out services for Babylon.[28] Service and contemplation complement each other in the pastoral life. The preacher always needs to return to the 'fire of contemplation' to renew his ardour, if his work of love is not to cool.[29] The life of a faithful minister is a constant returning from action to contemplation and from contemplation to action; like fish, he needs to come up for fresh air from the deep where he serves his fellows.[30] The two lives are dynamically related, they foster and nourish each other in the individual person, as well as in the community. 'From speaking in the public forum, we must return to the court-room of the heart': this is how Gregory pictured the wholeness of the preacher's life in the very last chapter of the *Moralia*;[31] and so long as we are able to trace his reflection, this reciprocity remained at its core. In what is probably the most complete synthesis he offered of his view of the active and the contemplative lives, in one of his Homilies on Ezechiel, the two are most thoroughly intertwined:

We must note that just as the right order of life is to tend from the active to the contemplative; so the soul often reverts profitably from the contemplative to the

[26] *Mor.* v.4.5; *I Reg.* iv.163; *HEz.* ii.6.5: both lives commanded in the Decalogue.
[27] E. g. *HEz* i.9.28. This theme is common in the Homilies on Ezechiel; cf. Fiedrowicz, *Das Kirchenverständnis*, 228, n. 171.
[28] *Mor.* xviii.43.69; the whole section 68–70 is heavily Augustinian in its inspiration.
[29] *Mor.* xxx.2.8.
[30] *Mor.* v.11.19; cf. xxx.2.8; xix.25.42–45. On the pastor and the contemplative and active lives, see Dagens, *Grégoire le Grand*, 145–63.
[31] *Integritatem animi*: *Mor.* xxxv.20.49. Cf. *RP* i.9; and iv.

active, so that the contemplative life having kindled the mind, the active life might be the more perfectly led. For the active life should convey us to the contemplative; but sometimes the contemplative life should send us back to the active life from what the mind turned in on itself beholds. Whence Jacob returned to Leah after Rachel's embrace . . . [32]

This remained the ground-bass. To hand on to others the fruit of contemplation is the preacher's duty, as Gregory reminded a group of his fellow-bishops – in the same breath as warning them against 'carrying the burden of secular cares'.[33] In another homily resonating with autobiographical overtones Gregory went even further. Whereas the active life is a form of the distraction, the mind being dissipated among the objects of its preoccupation, the ministry of preaching is here seen as the return of the pastor's mind from its state of dissipation to its inner self:

When I was living in the monastery, I was able to restrain my tongue from idle talk and to keep my mind almost constantly intent on prayer. But after the burden of pastoral care was placed on the shoulders of my heart, my mind could not recollect itself, being divided among many cares. For I am compelled to deal with the affairs now of churches, now of monasteries; often to judge the lives and actions of individuals. Then, again, to undertake the business of some citizens, to worry about the swords of invading barbarians, to fear the wolves threatening the flock committed to my care. Or to assume responsibilities . . . When the mind, divided and torn, is drawn into so many and such weighty matters, when can it return to itself, so as to recollect itself in preaching and not to withdraw from rendering its ministry of preaching the word?[34]

Gregory's anguish is real, and it is integral to his understanding of his office. It is remarkable that the mind is here said to be recollecting itself, not in contemplation, but in preaching and ministry. It is an index of the depth to which the contemplative ideal has been integrated in Gregory's conception of the pastoral office. In the work which Gregory revised himself, probably in his last years, he sketched his most carefully balanced account of the active and the contemplative lives in the life of the preacher. Martha's example should teach us that

if those of us who serve our brothers cannot sit quietly at our Redeemer's feet, we should nevertheless stand by Him for a little while. We do this well if we glimpse

---

[32] *HEz* II.2.11; the whole treatise extends from 8–15.

[33] *HEv* I.17.5. He accepted that under the compulsion of existing conditions (*barbarici temporis necessitate compulsus* he had laid himself open to this *invitus*) bishops may have to undertake *exteriora negotia*; but it constitutes a grave danger to their ministry, on which they will be judged (*ibid.*, 14–18). Cf. *Ep.* x.19: Gregory vetoes the election of a simple-minded candidate, because nowadays bishops have to look after their flocks' 'external needs' or their cities' defence; cf. *Ep.* xi.6; 29. On the secular cares of bishops, see Hürten, 'Gregor der Große', 32–9.

[34] *HEz* I.11.6. On this see Leyser, 'Let me speak'.

Him as we pass to and fro while serving. And what does it mean to glimpse the Lord in passing, but to direct to Him the intention of our hearts in all our good works? For we pass to and fro as we run around in serving Him, ministering to His members. And passing we glimpse the Lord if in all that we do, we contemplate Him who is present to us when we try to please Him.[35]

This had become the guiding thread of his reflection on the tensions between the two forms of life. The *Regula pastoralis*, hardly surprisingly, is articulated entirely on this ecclesial principle. Pastoral care distracts from contemplation; but contemplation is the pastor's preparation for his work of preaching, and, at the same time, the ever-present goal, which sets his direction and unifies his life, counteracting the dispersal of spirit amid the distracting details of his ministry.[36] This defines the perspective Gregory adopts for his treatise on the pastoral office:

There are some who, though endowed with great gifts, while they burn with the longing for contemplation alone, flee from serving their neighbours by preaching; they love a quiet retreat, they seek a refuge for contemplation. Now strictly judged, such people are without doubt accountable for as many persons as they might have profited by taking public office. How shall we judge the state of mind of someone who might manifestly have become useful to his neighbours, but prefers his own retreat to the service of others, when the Only begotten Son of the supreme Father came forth from the bosom of the Father into our midst, for the benefit of the many?[37]

Anticipated by Julianus Pomerius[38] and others before him, anticipated in his own *Moralia*, this was Gregory's definitive solution of his personal dilemma. Contemplation had to be considered in the context of the pastor's function in the Christian community, and, conversely, the pastoral ministry itself had a radically contemplative direction.

THE RECTOR

The Church is a community of love. In a building 'stone bears stone, because stones are placed on other stones; and that which supports another [stone] is itself supported by another [stone]. It is just the same in the holy

---

[35] *1 Reg.* v.180, and the whole section 177–180. The theme is prominent in the Commentary on I Kings (e. g. IV.100–101; 205) and has received ample comment from De Vogüé, 'Les vues', who stresses the importance of the fact that monks and clergy were both present in Gregory's audience.

[36] *RP* I.4. Compare *1 Reg* I.73, where Gregory speaks of the *immoderata intentio boni operis* which can interfere with the repose needed for the inner sight of contemplation. Compare also *Dial*. Prol. 4. On dispersal of spirit, see above, p. 22.

[37] *RP* I.5; Cf. II.7: *Voluptatem namque censeunt si actionibus deprimuntur, laborem deputant si in terrenis negotiis non laborant.*

[38] See especially *De vita cont.* III.28.1–2.

Church: each member supports another, and is supported by another.'[39] The 'necessity of charity' dictates that we bear one another's burden: those who are filled with spiritual gifts must stoop down [*condescendere*] to [their neighbours' earthly cares] as far as decently they can, to serve them with the 'condescension' of charity.'[40] Whether in speech or in deed, the duty of love lays this 'condescension' on all. What Gregory calls 'condescension' has overtones of Christ's *kenosis* (Philipp. 2:7); by it, the Christian, and the minister pre-eminently, becomes a servant.

Gregory recognised a diversity of gifts in the Church, all of which contribute to its life in different ways.[41] To scale the heights of contemplating God's secrets is given to a few; most of us have to be content with faith.[42] The endowments of individuals differ, and the differences must be reckoned with.

As our creator and guide gives to one what he denies to another, as He denies to one what he bestows on another; so whoever wants to be able to do more than has been given to him wants to exceed the measure set for him . . . He who neglects the measure of his limits risks stepping into the abyss. And recklessly trying to snatch what is beyond him, often he will forfeit even the ability he had.[43]

Sometimes Gregory speaks as if this division of labour assigned contemplation to those in charge, worldly work to their subjects. Thus in an important chapter of the *Regula pastoralis* he likened the superior (*rector*) to the eyes: they discern the road along which to guide the feet, so that 'subjects should carry out the lower tasks, superiors attend to the higher'.[44] Their business is to build the house of the Lord, by preaching and by the example of their holy lives, and, when required, by help.

The distinction between subjects and rulers rested on a classification of the Church's members according to their function. Gregory divided the Church – or something that he was apt not to distinguish from it, Christian society – into three categories or 'orders' of Christians: that of 'rulers', 'preachers' or 'superiors' (*rectores*),[45] the 'continent' or professional religious

---

[39] *HEz* II.1.5.

[40] *Mor.* XIX.25.45. In *Mor.* IX.40.63. Gregory speaks of *ministerium compassionis*. On this subject, see Fiedrowicz, *Das Kirchenverständis*, 205–6.

[41] *Mor.* XXVIII.10.21–24; XXIV.8.19; XIX.25.43; *HEv* I.20.13; *HEz* I.10.32–4; II.1.7. See also chapter 5, pp. 72–3.

[42] *Cant.* 28. On the scale of perfection, 8–9.

[43] *Mor.* XXVIII.10.24.

[44] *RP* II.7.

[45] His term *rector* has been much discussed. I take it to mean 'one in charge', usually, though not necessarily, a bishop or ecclesiastical superior. The term has a suggestion of moral direction. Among terms Gregory uses as equivalent: *magister, pastor, praedicator, praepositus*. To translate *rector* and its Gregorian equivalents I use 'rector', 'one in charge' or 'superior', except when a specific reference (e. g. pastor) is intended.

(*continentes*) and the married or lay people (*coniugati*). Despite some variations in his vocabulary, this is Gregory's regular way of dividing the
Christian people according to their functions. He appears to have
borrowed the idea of the three 'orders' from Augustine.[46] Being interested
in function rather than office, Gregory does not make the application of
his categories at all clear. He conceived them not primarily hierarchically,
but rather as functional groupings in the Church; but hierarchical overtones nevertheless clung to them. Inevitably so in the case of the rector,
who was a hierarchical figure by definition; so much so that Gregory sometimes simply distinguishes the *rectores* from the *auditores*, who are also
described as 'the weaker of the faithful'.[47] Used in reference to bishops or
other ecclesiastical superiors the word *rector* had not been common.[48] It
had a long history since Cicero's *rector rei publicae*. By Gregory's time it was a
word applied to several kinds of official, among them the agents in charge
of Church lands and provincial governors. Used to refer to anything or
anybody that ruled something or somebody else – the mind its body, God
His world, the powers that rule over this present darkness (Ephes. 6:12), it
was not eminently suited to name an office of which 'governing' was not a
definitive or even the most important attribute. As clergy, however, and
especially bishops, came to assume growing powers of initiative and
leadership, especially from the fifth century onwards, the title was less
incongruous, and came to be more often applied to them. It had been used
of bishops, along with the imagery of governing, by several of the writers
known to Gregory, notably by Gregory of Nazianzus in the Latin translation of his *Apologia* (esp. Section 3), which was known to Gregory.

Gregory thus had the support of quite a respectable tradition for using
the '*rector*' as one of his terms for 'bishop' (as well as for other bearers of
office, civil or ecclesiastical). He used a variety of other terms: 'preacher'
(*praedicator*), 'teacher' (*doctor*) and some with more pronounced 'political'
overtones of ruling, controlling, governing: 'superiors' (*praepositi*), 'rulers'
(*regentes*), 'those who are placed in charge' (*in locum regiminis positi, qui
praesunt*). Although his language is fluid and often has wider applicability,

---

[46] The *tres fidelium ordines*: e.g. *HEz* II.4.5–6: *praedicantium, continentium, bonorum coniugum*; cf. 7.3; I.8.10;
Mor. 1.14.20; XXXII.20.36; On the *ordines* see Folliet, 'Les trois catégories'; Dagens, *Saint Grégoire le
Grand*, 312–19; Fiedrowicz, *Das Kirchenverständis*, 188–91.

[47] As in *Mor.* 1.14.20.

[48] Though not as rare as Folliet thought when he noted the unusual sense of *rector* used to designate
'les chefs de l'Église': 'Les trois catégories', 84, n. 1. I have attempted an explanation for Gregory's use
of the term in Markus, 'Gregory the Great's *rector*', on which some of what follows is based. More
precedents than noted by Folliet can now easily be found. Among them particularly noteworthy
are occurrences in Aponius's Commentary on the Song of Songs, known to Gregory: Bélanger,
'Introduction', 35–41.

and sometimes refers to rulers or other bearers of secular authority and was frequently in later ages taken in this sense, Gregory more often has in mind authority in a religious context. It is striking, for instance, that in a chapter altogether rich in political theory where Gregory is discussing the rector's power and authority in general terms, without any specific ecclesiastical reference, he suddenly and dramatically lapses into the first person plural: how 'we' – that is to say bishops – should conduct ourselves towards those over whom we are placed in authority. The rector can in principle be anyone in a position of authority; but bishops and other ecclesiastical superiors are the bearers of authority that came most directly to Gregory's mind. What interested Gregory supremely were not theoretical questions about the foundations of power and authority, or institutional structures through which they were exercised.[49] Invariably what is uppermost in his mind are questions about the rector's conduct.

His structured discussion in the *Regula pastoralis* is devoted to questions about the rector: what sort of a man he should be, what sort of a life he should lead, how he should deal with his subjects. In this work Gregory brought together in an organised shape insights scattered throughout his *Moralia*.[50] Especially, he had to weigh 'what to speak, to whom to speak, when to speak, how to speak, how much to speak'. The rector must be all things to all men: just as the priest had to change his garments on entering and leaving the inner precinct (Ezech. 44:19), so 'nothing is as hard for one in the order of the priesthood as to temper the mind's rigour by compassion, changing attitude according to the persons concerned'.[51] The faithful preacher draws near to his hearers with *condescensio*, a kind of imaginative sympathy, 'as it were receiving each into himself, and turning himself into each, he unites them by compassion . . .'[52] Intellectual compassion and imaginative sympathy require that 'the teacher's language be shaped by the character of his audience; so that it be suitable to each, but never fail in its purpose, the common edification of all'. The audience's minds are like a harp, whose strings the preacher must pluck with subtly varied touch to produce harmonious music. 'So any teacher must touch the hearts of his audience with the same doctrine, but not in the same expressions (*exhortatione*) if he is to build (*aedificet*) all into a single virtue of

---

[49] *RP* II.6. On Gregory's difficulty about conceiving authority in institutional terms, see Markus, 'Gregory the Great on kings'.

[50] See above, pp. 20–21.

[51] *HEz* I.II.28; cf. *ibid.*, 12. On the preacher's responsibility, see the whole section 4–28. See also *HEv* I.17.9.

[52] *Mor.* VI.35.54.

charity'.[53] The details are spelt out in Gregory's *Pastoral Care*. The extraordinary pastoral flexibility we can observe in Gregory's work is linked at a profound level with the serious thought he continued to give to what was demanded of the man who was charged with responsibility for others. In all that the pastor says and does, *prodesse*, to be of use, not *praeesse*, to be in charge, is the supreme imperative.[54] Ruling, at its best – in any context – was synonymous with ministry. And because our endowments are given us by our Creator, 'we must not keep them to ourselves as private use, in proportion to the degree that we realise they were given us by our maker for the common good'.[55] Ministry and the exercise of authority are works of love, and must be carried out with humility:

Our Creator and Disposer so arranges all things that anyone who might become exalted by the gift he has been given is humbled by the virtue he lacks. He so orders things that while He raises one up by the grace He bestows on him, He makes him inferior to another by granting some other gift to another. So each should recognise that someone lower than himself may yet be his better in respect of some other gift. Though he may know that he has the precedence over others, let him place himself beneath others in respect of other respects. All things are so ordered that while all possess different gifts, yet through the mutual requirements of charity, these gifts become shared by all [*interposita quadam caritatis necessitudine fiant omnia singulorum*] ... Hence Paul said 'Serve one another in love' (Gal. 3:13). Love will free us of the yoke of sin when it subjects us to one another through mutual service in love . . .[56]

A hierarchically ordered system of authority, both in the cosmos and in human societies, was deeply embedded in Gregory's world-view, as it was in much of Late Antique imagination. The superior held power over his subjects for their good. Gregory did not question the paternalistic implications. What mattered was that in his actions and attitudes the superior should conform to his model. Augustine had already explained that whereas any Christian is a servant of Christ, a bishop is, further, also a servant of the community of Christ's servants; his distinctive virtue is the virtue of the servant, humility.[57] Gregory, too, saw the exercise of authority as one of the various forms of ministry within the one

---

[53] *Mor.* xxx.3.12. Cf. p. 72.

[54] This doublet, also in Augustine *Ep.* 134.1; *Sermo* 340.1; *De civ. Dei* xix.19 and in the *Rule* of St Benedict *RB* 64.7, is also to be found in Gregory: *Mor.* xxi.15.22–24; xxvi.26.44–6; *RP* ii.6. See also *Mor.* xxiii.11.21: *praeesse magisterio caeterorum*; cf.: xxiv.25.52: Gregory's use of the Augustinian doublet *dominando/consulendo*; and xxiii.13.24: *non dominationem potentiae . . .*; cf. xxvi.26.46; *1 Reg.* iv.3–4. For a comparison with Augustine's conception, see Markus, 'The sacred', 86–7.

[55] *HEz* i.7.21–22. *Privatum* and *commune* (a very Augustinian doublet): see e.g. *Mor.* xxiii.6.13; *HEz* ii.7.17; *HEv* ii.34.14; *RP* iii.21; *Ep.* xi.36.

[56] *Mor.* xxviii.10.22.

[57] *Epp.* 130; 157; 217; cf. *Sermo Guelf.* 32.1, 3, 5; *Sermo* 101.4.

body;[58] and his self-designation as 'servant of God's servants' stood in a long tradition, but one he had thoroughly assimilated. The rector's office is above all a *magisterium humilitatis*.[59] To humility on the ruler's part corresponds reverence for his authority on the side of the ruled. The good or 'elect' ruler who serves the subject's interests has a claim on their obedience, amounting to reverence for God's authority.[60] 'The superior should have humble authority (*humilis auctoritas*) in speaking, the subject should have free humility (*libera humilitas*) [as distinct from fear]'.[61]

THE RECTOR AND THE CHRISTIAN ORDER

In the Church, the rectors' ministry was defined, as implied by their alternative titles, *praedicatores* or *doctores*, in terms of preaching – taken in a very wide sense – or teaching. This is their distinctive work, almost the monopoly of the *ordo rectorum*. Contemplation, by contrast, is not the monopoly of any *ordo*; 'through love, even the simplest may repose in heavenly contemplation, though they are unable to meditate on the mysteries of the holy scriptures'.[62] The grace of contemplation 'is often given to the highest, often to the lowest, often to the ascetic (*remoti*), sometimes even to the married'.[63]

For there are faithful people in the Church who love almighty God in such a way that they are perfected in their works and are also engaged in contemplation . . . Some, although they love almighty God, and have carried out their good works perfectly, are, however, unable to contemplate His greatness with a more subtle understanding. They love, indeed, but cannot investigate the joys of His glory.[64]

The preacher's own life being a mediation between contemplation and action, so, too, his ministry mediates contemplation within the community. His special task in the community – Gregory does not distinguish the work of the preacher from the teacher at all sharply – is preaching and

---

[58] E.g. *Mor.* XIX.14.23.
[59] *RP* I.1; 6 on true humility. Cf. *Mor.* II.49.78. The best account of this theme is Meyvaert, 'Gregory the Great and the theme of authority'.
[60] *1 Reg.* IV.8.
[61] *HEz* I.9.12.
[62] *1 Reg.* II.122; cf. *1 Reg.* II.130. De Vogüé, 'St Gregory the Great on the religious life', 58 says that the *ordo amantium* of II.130 refers to 'the order of monks in the first place, in contrast with the priestly order of "preachers"'. In 'Gregory the Great on Kings', 20–1, I argued that taken in its context, the passage does not make a distinction between the orders, but within the order of 'preachers'. I now think that was mistaken. Gregory's language, however, is very fluid and fluctuating; it is difficult to be sure how he is using his vocabulary. In *1 Reg.* III.170, for instance, he certainly returns to his usual three-fold division in which *contemplationi uacantes* are ranged against the *coniugatorum ordo* and the *electus praedicator*.
[63] *HEz* II.5.19. I have translated *remoti* by 'ascetic'.
[64] *HEz* II.5.1.

expounding the scriptures. That is the job of the *rectores* and *praedicatores*. The aim is to feed contemplation, which is not a monopoly of their class but the spiritual ideal for all. Exposition of the scriptures is the bridge between the 'orders' in the Church; its purpose is to foster contemplative ardour:

those who seek the purity of the contemplative life are to be shown not the ordinary things about the sacred scripture, but rather the higher and more sublime things, so that the more they are delighted by the superior goods they hear about, the more ardently they might raise themselves to the heights by seeing.[65]

There is a very strong hierarchical consciousness at work here, related to the proximity to, or distance from, the height of contemplation. This may have something to do with the nature of the audience addressed by Gregory. The greater part of his preaching was in fact delivered to restricted groups. Many of the homilies were addressed to a 'shifting diversity of listeners in a small group' some of whom were evidently monks, some clergy, some – like Gregory himself – in positions of high ecclesiastical authority, others on the fringes of ecclesiastical office, as assistants, 'helpers' of various kinds.[66] These were the sort of people Gregory would naturally have thought of as *rectores*; if there were monks among them, as there were in Constantinople and often later in Rome, they could come under the order of *continentes*. Only rarely, when he was preaching in public, for which he was often not well enough, and, anyway, probably not inclined to, would he be faced with the ordinary lay people, the *conjugati*. Gregory's only public liturgical preaching is contained in the Homilies on the Gospels; and this is why it is here we find his scriptural exposition at its most direct, least allegorical; with more attention to the literal sense than he would give it when addressing a clerical or spiritual élite.

He was not often addressing 'subjects', but, so to speak, conversing with equals, in a company of his brothers. And one of the principal subjects of these endless conversations was precisely the theme of how 'we', bishops or superiors, should preach to our 'subjects'. Most of Gregory's preaching was analogous to what Augustine was doing in works such as *De doctrina Christiana* or *De catechizandis rudibus*, rather than to what he was doing in his sermons. It was done within and addressed to a restricted circle of an ecclesiastical élite. The people whom Gregory is most often addressing, the class of *rectores* or *praedicatores*, are told how the scriptures are to be expounded to others.

[65] *I Reg.* III.124.
[66] The phrase quoted is from Meyvaert, 'The date', 204–5, referring to the Commentary on I Kings.

Moreover, the *ordo praedicatorum* or *rectorum*, at the summit of the three orders, was itself far from homogeneous. Gregory – greatly impressed with the pseudo-Dionysian image of a celestial hierarchy[67] – sometimes goes to great length to subdivide it, giving the picture of a hierarchy within the hierarchy. 'For there are three degrees of perfection' within the *ordo* of *rectores*: on the lowest level the *pastor*'s perfection consists in his obedience to his superiors (*praelatis*); this pertains to hearing. On the next level, the pastor collaborates with his superiors; this pertains to association. On the highest level, which belongs to preaching, he matches his exalted position (*sublimitatem dignitatis*) by the splendour of his conduct, when endowed with heavenly virtue, that life and that teaching shine upon his subjects which may be seen, but is not to be disputed or judged by them.[68] Hearing (characteristic of obedience), working (characteristic of collaboration), and preaching seem to be the marks which define this hierarchy in Gregory's mind. In another image he takes from the prophecy of Ezechiel, he identifies the *rectores* as the 'front windows' through which the heavenly light enters the Church; the lowly, the insignificant, who yield themselves to the desire for heavenly wisdom are the 'side windows, the windows in the vestibule'.[69]

Gregory's image of the Church is that of a vast community of contemplation, its members ranked according to the level they are able to attain. In this community the work of the preacher expounding the Bible is crucial. To that we now turn.

[67] *HEv* II.34.12–13   [68] *1 Reg.* IV.195.   [69] *HEz* II.5.20.

CHAPTER 3

Sapienter indoctus: *scriptural understanding*

EDUCATION AND LETTERS

Reflecting on one of his stories of holy men, Gregory compared a rather simple-minded saint's 'learned ignorance' (*illius doctam ignorantiam*) with 'our ignorant knowledge' (*nostra indocta scientia*).[1] Since St Paul (1 Cor. 1:18–25) paradoxical expressions such as this were readily used to sum up the Christian ideal of learning in relation to holiness. They tell us no more about their subject than that in the eyes of the narrator he or she met the standard required for holiness; and that the narrator's description is made in a Christian and Pauline, probably an ascetic, perspective. To assess either the extent of the knowledge at any individual's disposal, or the value set upon it, the formula helps very little. Gregory's description of Benedict as 'wisely unlearned' (*sapienter indoctus*) tells us he thought Benedict a saint; it does not tell us what he thought of learning.

By the standards of his time and place, Italy in the late sixth century, Gregory can only be reckoned to have belonged to the best educated élite. We know nothing about his education; nor did Gregory of Tours, who described him as so well educated 'that he was thought second to none in the City'.[2] The golden age of Boethius and Cassiodorus had passed before Gregory was born; the revival of learning in the Visigothic kingdom of which Isidore of Seville is the most eloquent witness had not yet begun. As part of his settlement for Italy Justinian wanted public teaching in the liberal arts to be provided. How far his wish was realised we can only guess. Much of what was available must have been of a quality sufficient to equip the many officials of a literate bureaucracy for their work. A handful of people, such as Gregory himself, Venantius Fortunatus and others, clearly had access to education, public or private, of high quality, at any rate in Rome and Ravenna. There were also private centres with libraries, such as

[1] *Dial.* III.37.20. His well-known description of Benedict as *sapienter indoctus* is in *Dial.* II. Prol.1; cf. Augustine, *Ep.* 130.28. See also Banniard, *Viva voce*, 144–5 and Dagens, *Saint Grégoire le Grand*, 45–50. Gregory's reflections on *sapientes* and *insipientes*: *RP* III.6. Cf. *Mor* XVI.1.1.
[2] *HF* x.1. Still less is John the Deacon's glowing picture (*Vita*, II.13) born out by any evidence.

34

that of the aristocratic Proba, who was able to lend works of Augustine to the abbot Eugippius at Lucullanum near Naples, or the monastic community established by Cassiodorus at Squillace in Southern Italy. The circle of Proba and Eugippius was also something of an intellectual clearing house, which allowed for the exchange of manuscripts, correspondence and ideas between numerous leading intellectuals. There is some evidence that scriptural and theological studies at a high level were kept alive in Provence and in North Africa, even through the darkest times; and there were always monastic and episcopal centres where a basic religious education, and sometimes more, was available. Rome seems not to have had a major institution of religious learning when pope Agapetus and Cassiodorus dreamed of setting up such a Christian school, though it must have been better served by secular schools.[3] The theological learning and expertise still displayed around the middle of the sixth century by African writers such as Facundus of Hermiane and Ferrandus of Carthage were no longer to be found anywhere in the Western Church.[4]

In comparison with his contemporaries in the Western world, Gregory was highly educated in the traditional disciplines of Roman patrician culture. His own writings are testimony to decent grammatical and rhetorical accomplishment, a Latinity remarkably good for its time,[5] and some knowledge of Roman law. His mastery of a simple and forceful Latin style has persuaded some good judges that Gregory belongs to the spiritual and cultural world of Late Antiquity.[6] His acquaintance with patristic literature is hard to estimate; we can be sure that he was widely read in the Latin fathers, Augustine and John Cassian making the deepest imprint on his mind. He certainly knew some Greek patristic literature; mostly in Latin translation.[7] He saw himself as one of their epigoni, especially

---

[3] This is implied by Cassiodorus, *Inst.* Praef. On the plan, see chapter 1, n. 43.

[4] For a survey of the state of education and learning in the sixth century, see Riché, *Éducation*, 140–350. On Gregory, 187–200.

[5] On Gregory's Latin and its relation to the language in use among the Roman ecclesiastical élite on the one hand, among the ordinary people on the other, see Banniard, *Viva voce*, 105–79; on Gregory's scriptural language see Banniard, '*Iuxta uniuscuiusque qualitatem*', and Boesch Gajano, 'Dislivelli'.

[6] See for instance Berschin, *Biographie*, 1, 305–24. Discussing the *Dialogues*, Berschin calls Gregory 'the last great preacher of Late Antiquity' (305). In *Dial.* IV.23 Berschin detects an echo of Virgil (*Aen.* IX.752: *ingenti concussa est pondere tellus*), as an example of Gregory's instinctive speech-patterns falling into classical moulds, rather than as a deliberate borrowing (318–20). Cf. Auerbach, *Literary language*, 96–102, however, stresses the 'naiveté' of the *Dialogues*. On their sophistication, see De Vogüé, 'Introduction', 51–84.

[7] On his sources, see Gillet, 'Introduction', 81–109; also Cracco-Ruggini, 'Gregorio Magno' (Augustine, Theodoret); Paronetto, 'Une présence'; Eisenhofer, 'Augustinus'; Recchia, 'La memoria' (Augustine). Petersen, 'Greek influences' (Origen etc.). Gregory was certainly acquainted with Origen's exposition of the Song of Songs, and had a variety of sources for some of the stories in the *Dialogues*; see Petersen, *The Dialogues, passim*.

Augustine's: if you want nourishing food, he wrote to a Praetorian Prefect in Africa, 'read Augustine's, your compatriot's, works and you will not want my bran in comparison to his fine flour'.[8] The extent of his knowledge of Greek has been much debated; it is unlikely to have been either negligible or sufficient for easy competence.[9]

When it comes to Gregory's own attitude to his learning, we are a little better informed by clues in his own writings. The problem here is to know how to interpret his occasional utterances on the subject of secular culture. The best known of these is the final paragraph of his dedicatory letter of the *Moralia* to Leander. This letter contains Gregory's fullest auto-biographical statement. It is followed by an account of how he has proceeded in commenting on the Book of Job; only after this statement of the exegetical principles he has been following does he say a little about secular letters, and that by way of excusing himself for sending a gift unworthy of its dedicatee: he has been ill, and the faculty of speech is impaired when the mind is weakened by bodily infirmity. He is a musician playing a flawed instrument. So don't look here for flowers of discourse, he begs Leander; but anyway, he has disdained – as, he says, have all other interpreters of the scriptures – obedience to the laws of rhetoric and grammar and has cheerfully perpetrated all the breaches and barbarisms condemned by the 'rules of Donatus': for the authors of the sacred scriptures have themselves not obeyed them. And in so much as it is from these that my discourse originates, it is surely right that the offspring should resemble its parent . . .[10] This self-justification, delivered in a Latin excellent for its day, was a hallowed formula; and Gregory was engaged in an elegant transformation of a formula he borrowed from Cassiodorus. Far from rejecting the rules of discourse, its aim is to bring about a sense of collusion with the reader, sharing a mode of discourse designed to foster conversion of the soul. Far from condemning grammar as such, what Gregory condemns is grammar as a 'means of sterilising the word of God'.[11] There may, however, be a hint of a more specific intention here: Gregory may have known, through his friend Leander, that the latter's brother, Isidore, had a lively interest in classical grammatical theory, and

---

[8] *Ep.* x.16; cf. *HEz* Praef.

[9] The traditional, anti-Greek view is summed up by Riché, *Éducation*, 189–90. Petersen, 'Did Gregory the Great know Greek?' and 'Homo omnino latinus', credits – doubtfully – Gregory with rather more knowledge.

[10] *Ad Leandr.* 5. Gillet, 'Introduction', gives several parallels in a footnote to the passage in *SC* 32, 122, n. 5; also Riché, *Éducation*, 195, n. 108.

[11] See Holtz, 'Le contexte', from which (537) the phrase is quoted; see also Fontaine, 'Augustin, Grégoire et Isidore' on Gregory's highly erudite and cultivated rejection.

may have wanted to warn him off so questionable a pursuit. Moreover, Gregory is here advocating a particularly drastic contempt of the rules of grammar: unlike Cassiodorus, who would have agreed that we should not be worried by 'metacisms' and other breaches of its rules by the scriptural authors, Gregory proclaims his indifference to them in his own prose. His professed contempt of the 'rules of Donatus' betrays a hostility more profound than can be found in either Cassiodorus before him or Isidore soon after. How seriously and literally we should take this profession is another question.[12]

This does not really tell us much about the value Gregory set upon the secular disciplines of rhetoric and grammar. No more is to be got from the other most frequently quoted document, his letter to bishop Desiderius of Vienne. The bishop had been caught teaching grammar. Gregory was distressed to hear the report, for 'the praises of Jove and the praises of Jesus Christ cannot proceed from the same lips'.[13] It has been pointed out that Gregory is here doing no more than reiterating the canonical prohibition of bishops reading or teaching profane texts. It does not tell us what he thought of classical literature any more than the objection he made to a bishop of Naples devoting himself to ship-building tells us his views on the value of ships.[14] To discern Gregory's attitude we need to examine the few passages to be found in his work which touch on the matter.

It is axiomatic for Gregory, as for all the fathers, that salvation is only through Christ, not by philosophy:

There are many pagans who cultivate the disciplines of this world's wisdom, who observe what is reckoned to be right among men, and believe that they will be saved having followed what is right, but do not seek the Mediator of God and men, thinking that it is enough for them to have held to the teaching of the philosophers.[15]

In answer to such people Gregory likes to exploit the Pauline contrast (e.g. 1 Cor. 3:18) of 'the wisdom of this world' with the wisdom of Christ:

[12] Cf. Cassiodorus, *Inst.* ii.i.i. For the comparison with Isidore and Cassiodorus, see Fontaine, *Isidore de Séville*, 1.34–6. Fontaine contrasts Gregory's grudging acceptance of grammar as an unavoidable instrument with Isidore's concern to use it as an entry into a culture: 'un instrument de culture plus qu'une technique' (*ibid.*, 206). Cf. also his comparison of Isidore and Gregory (especially *Mor.* 1.14.18) in their use of Augustine's *De ciu. Dei* xi.31, on the number 7, noting Gregory's more 'embarrassed and suspicious attitude' to the use of secular knowledge (*ibid.* 390).

[13] *Ep.* xi.34. See the comments by Riché, *Éducation*, 196. Avitus, for instance, excused himself from writing secular poetry after his consecration: *MGH AA* 6, 275, referred to by Riché, *Éducation*, 136.

[14] *Ep.* xiii.27. The bishop went daily down to the harbour dressed like a tramp, accompanied by one or two of his clergy, and became an object of derision to the townspeople. I wish to thank Paul Meyvaert for showing me an unpublished paper, 'St Gregory the Great's attitude to secular learning'.

[15] *Mor.* xviii.45.73.

'The wisdom of this world is: concealing the heart with stratagems, veiling meaning with verbiage, proving false to be right and true to be false . . . this perversity of mind is called urbanity . . . while the wisdom of the just is scoffed at, because the virtue of purity is reckoned by the wise of this world to be fatuity'. But Gregory does not leave it at that; he goes on to say 'The Israelites offer to God that which the Egyptians abominate': so the just offer to God the fatuities of the depraved.[16] We are close here to the old image of the spoiling of the Egyptians by the Israelites, used by Origen and Augustine to justify use of secular knowledge in the pursuit of scriptural wisdom. Gregory could give this image a very negative twist;[17] but on other occasions he came closer to Augustine's standpoint. Thus in his comment on Job 9:9 ('He who made the Bear and Orion, the Pleiades and the chambers of the South') he says the scripture here by no means follows the 'vain fables' of Hesiod, Aratus and Callimachus. He concedes that these names of the constellations were indeed invented by 'practitioners of carnal wisdom'; but the biblical authors have made use of the names given them by the 'wise men of the world', so there is no reason, he says, why 'spiritual men' should not make use of the words of the carnal in order to further spiritual understanding.[18]

Gregory's most positive statement concerning the value of secular learning is in the Commentary on the first Book of Kings, the work we may take as his last.[19] Commenting on the verse 'Now there was no smith to be found throughout all the land of Israel; let the Philistines beware, lest the Hebrews make themselves swords or spears' (1 Sam. 13:19), Gregory interprets 'spiritually':

For spiritual warfare we are not armed by secular, but by divine letters. No smith is to be found among the Israelites in so much as the faithful . . . do not fight against evil spirits with the weapons of secular learning . . . Although erudition got from secular books does not by itself suffice for the spiritual battle of the saints, if it is joined to the divine scriptures, we are thereby helped to understand them more deeply. The liberal arts are to be studied only so far as knowledge of them allows the scriptures to be better understood. The malign spirits remove from many hearts the desire of learning, so that they may have neither secular knowledge nor attain to spiritual knowledge. As the text says: 'Let the Philistines beware, lest the Hebrews make themselves swords or spears'. Clearly, the demons know that by

---

[16] *Mor.* x.29.48: *huius mundi sapientia est, cor machinationibus tegere, sensum verbis velare, quae falsa sunt vera ostendere, quae vera sunt fallacia demonstrare* . . . See also *Cant.* 17; *1 Reg.* II.9–10; IV.6; *Mor.* v.41.73; *RP* III.6. On *sapiens stultitia*, see Dagens, *Saint Grégoire le Grand*, 45–50.

[17] In *Mor.* XXXIII.10.19 the *scientia doctrinae saecularis* is destroyed by God.

[18] *Mor.* IX.11.12. See also XXIX.31.67–74.

[19] See above, p. 16.

learning secular letters we are aided in spiritual knowledge ... God has provided this secular culture as a step for our ascent by which we might reach the height of understanding the divine scriptures.[20]

The value of the secular disciplines is upheld, but in unambiguous subordination to scriptural learning, and as a means of deepening it; and only to the extent that they promote scriptural understanding.

Both in asserting their value and in the same breath limiting it in this highly restrictive manner, Gregory stands four-square in a long tradition. His way of representing the relevance of secular learning to a scriptural spirituality had much in common with the sacred pragmatism of Cassiodorus's *Institutes of divine and human learning*, and both Cassiodorus and Gregory could look back to Book II of Augustine's *De doctrina Christiana*. Augustine's programme was a sketch for a Biblical culture. Elements of secular learning entered into it, for secular learning was required for understanding the Bible. But Augustine's formula was ruthlessly exclusive: secular knowledge is admissible only to the extent that it is useful to a Christian in quest of understanding the Bible. Cassiodorus's monks were expected to equip themselves in the disciplines of the liberal arts so that they could pursue spiritual wisdom more effectively. Gregory shared the reserve towards secular culture that both Cassiodorus and Augustine recommended. But for Augustine this culture had been a part of the educated person's normal intellectual equipment; and in the conditions of the Ostrogothic renaissance Cassiodorus could still take much of it for granted. Gregory's disdain is of a different order. In his world the secular learning which had enjoyed their qualified blessing was infinitely more precarious. In distancing himself from the *scientia doctrinae saecularis*[21] Gregory placed himself within an ascetic Christian culture for which the secular world could have little significance against the backdrop of the eschatological drama that – in his view – was about to be played out. A gulf had opened between the religious and the secular culture which Augustine and Cassiodorus could never have envisaged. When, in the following generation, Isidore of Seville undertook the huge task of mapping the knowledge available to him, the two cultures had separated. Its secular components needed to be retrieved from sources which had long since ceased to form part of the inherited and transmitted culture. The task of exploring and codifying its secular content required the adventurous openness of mind of an Isidore. Gregory's

---

[20] *1 Reg.* v.84.
[21] *Mor.* XXXIII.10.19 (cf. n. 17 above).

suspicion and embarrassment about it would have set narrow limits to such an undertaking.[22]

FROM AUGUSTINE TO GREGORY

Gregory's affinity with Cassiodorus and Augustine is not in doubt, but we should not allow ourselves to be misled by it. What makes the difference is the situation in which Christian men of letters, or monks in search of some basic erudition, found themselves in Cassiodorus's time, some 150 years after Augustine; even more in Gregory's, 200 years after Augustine. Augustine thought and wrote in a mixed and varied intellectual culture and he engaged in debate with educated people who did not share his religion or his world view.[23] He read Cicero, Virgil, Plotinus, Ambrose, Cyprian and other ancient writers, Christian and non-Christian. Gregory read Augustine. Augustine, it has been said, 'bequeathed himself . . . to his Western successors . . . For all his foresight, Augustine could not conceive of a Christian thinker being more or less *comfortable* in Christendom.'[24] Gregory was comfortable in his mental world. Its contours were shaped by ideas in great part derived from Augustine. Of course, he, too had read the works of other writers, mainly Latin Christians. John Cassian, especially, seems to have made a deep impression on his spirituality. But in all essentials it was Augustine's conceptual structures that shaped the world of his imagination.

Gregory's world had become a Christian world in a manner Augustine could not have imagined. In Augustine's world the question that haunted Christians was 'what is a Christian?', 'what is it that distinguishes him from his non-Christian fellows?' The society of Augustine's North Africa still contained a complex fabric of intellectual and religious traditions of great diversity. Gregory lived in what was intellectually a far more homogeneous world. Everyone, for practical purposes, was a Christian. There may still be some, Gregory conceded, 'who perhaps do not carry the Christian name'; but if there were such, they were marginal, and he was more interested in those who do bear the name, but are like the *iniqui* who 'deviate from righteousness by the wickedness of their works', who are Christians

---

[22] Fontaine, *Isidore de Séville*, 1.588, speaks of *une ouverture d'esprit* which he compares to that of Clement of Alexandria. For an appraisal of Isidore's achievement, see *ibid.*, 2.796–9; 825–7.

[23] This paragraph and the next are borrowed from my *Signs and meanings*, 45–6. I gratefully acknowledge the permission of the publishers, the Liverpool University Press, for allowing me to draw on that lecture in this chapter. I do not concern myself further here with Cassiodorus's intellectual milieu; on it, see my *End*, 217–22.

[24] Rist, *Augustine* 290; 291 (italics in original).

in name only, from outward conformity.[25] His sermons were intended for a public already well established in the Christian faith.[26] Unlike the infidel, who must be instructed in what to believe, the faithful has to be taught how to behave.[27] Gregory could take Christianity for granted: the framework of understanding, of explanation and discourse was defined by Christianity. His culture was essentially a biblical culture: formulated within scriptural horizons and with scriptural concepts. The question: 'what is a Christian?', 'what is it that distinguishes him from his non-Christian fellows?' had become redundant.

Around AD 400 the great divide would have run between the Church and the un-regenerate world outside it. By around AD 600 the unregenerate world had shrunk to something negligible; the fundamental divide ran between the less and the more perfect within the Church. For Gregory the Church had come to swallow up the world. He could think of *conversio* more easily as something undergone by the Christian soul on its way to perfection, than of a non-Christian to Christianity.[28] The complexity of Augustine's world had collapsed into simplicity. Compared with Augustine, Gregory could take for granted the settled contours of his spiritual landscape. Christianity had come to give definitive shape to a 'totalising discourse'. The boundaries of Gregory's intellectual and imaginative worlds were thus the horizons of the scriptures. How to be a Christian, how to live the fullest Christian life: this was Gregory's central preoccupation in all his preaching; and this was the question into which the anxieties of his age had shaped themselves. Naturally, it helped to give his exegesis a predominantly moral direction.

THE EXEGETICAL PROGRAMME

In all his writings, from the discourses on the Book of Job given to his monks while papal representative in Constantinople, aptly titled *Moralia*, to the Homilies he preached as pope and revised for publication late in his life, what interested Gregory in expounding the scriptures was what they said about the Christian life. The Bible was, of course, the doorway that gave access to this life. It is through Christ that we have access to salvation; but nevertheless, Gregory says, 'we can [also] call the holy scripture our door:

---

[25] *Mor.* XVIII.6.12: *impius namque pro infideli ponitur, id est a pietate religionis alienus; iniquus vero dicitur, qui pravitate operis ab aequitate discordat, vel qui fortasse christianae fidei nomen portat.* Cf. XXVII.18.36–37; XXIX.6.12–7.14; *HEv.* II.29.4; 32.5 on Christians in name only. See also below, chapter 4, n. 40.

[26] E.g. *HEv* II.40.1.

[27] *Mor.* XXIX.31.72.

[28] *HEz* I.10.8–11. See also Straw, *Gregory the Great*, 194–235, and Dagens, *Saint Grégoire*, 247–346.

for it opens for us the understanding of this faith in the Redeemer'.[29] 'In this darkness of our present life, the scriptures are the light of our way . . .'[30]

Light is one of Gregory's favourite images for the scriptures. Nourishment is another. One of his homilies is built systematically on the metaphor of food and drink. Food, unlike drink, Gregory went on to develop the metaphor, has to be chewed up to be swallowed:

Consider and understand: that is to say, first chew then swallow. In our study of the holy scriptures we have to proceed in the right order, so that we should get to know them in order that repenting our iniquity, knowing the evil we have done, we might avoid perpetrating other evils . . . By means of God's words which we have come to understand, we must draw others to [fuller? heavenly?] life.[31]

We should note in passing a feature of this homily which should not now surprise us. Gregory is preaching to a mixed audience which seems to have included clergy, *rectores*, as he would have said.[32] He assumes that their study and their effort to understand the scripture is completed in exhortation, handed on in preaching; and he returns to insist on this in his conclusion.[33] Gregory disclaimed the ability to penetrate the more profound mysteries. Such a disclaimer was a rhetorical cliché; but we may, nevertheless, take him at his word when he disclaimed an arrogant desire to expound things that defeated greater exegetes before him, and insisted that he was given such insight as he achieved for the sake of, and in the company of, his brethren.[34] He was engaged in a truly communal exercise with his equals. Understanding the Bible was an enterprise carried out for the sake of the community, and within the community, drawing on its resources and its traditions of scriptural discourse.

Elaborating the metaphor of eating and drinking, Gregory continued: the harder passages of the Bible have to be chewed and digested; that is to say, expounded and understood. With God's help our weak minds will daily grow in understanding: 'So that to-day we understand more of the sacred text than we did yesterday, and we will understand more to-morrow than we do to-day. So the grace of God's dispensation nourishes us with daily food . . . When our mind receives the food of truth, our inwards are not left empty, but are satiated with the food of life.'[35] The image of

---

[29] *HEz* II.5.3; Cf. II.3.18.
[30] *HEz* I.7.17. For further references see Dagens, *Saint Grégoire*, 55–65.
[31] *HEz* I.10.3–4.
[32] See above, p. 32 on Gregory's audiences.
[33] This is also the theme with which Gregory concludes this section of the Homily in paragraph 12.
[34] See *HEz*. II.2.1 for a fine statement of this.
[35] *HEz* I.10.5–6. The theme of feeding is also fundamental to the *Moralia*: *Mor.* I.20.28–21.29. Cf. *1 Reg.* IV.123.

nourishment allowed Gregory to integrate the central themes of his reflections on Christian living and the scriptures. He quotes the prophecy of
Haggai (1:6): 'You have sown much, and harvested little; you eat, but you
are never sated; you drink and are not inebriated'. He comments:

> He sows much in his heart but harvests little, who knows much about the heavenly
> commandments, whether it be by reading or by hearing, but neglects making them
> bear fruit in his actions. He eats and is not sated who, hearing the words of God,
> desires profit or worldly glory . . . He drinks and is not inebriated who, bending his
> ear to the voice of the preaching, does not change his mind . . . 'If any man would
> follow me, let him deny himself' (Matt. 16:24): he denies himself who begins to be
> what he was not, and ceases to be what he was.[36]

Conversion, culminating in the life of contemplation, is the objective of
understanding the scriptures. Quoting St Paul ('If anyone is in Christ, he is
a new creation; the old has passed away, behold the new has come': 2 Cor.
5:17) Gregory contrasts the 'new man' with the unregenerate 'old man'.[37]
To understand the scriptures is, in the end, to be renewed through their
power.

This is the concern that drives Gregory's exegesis. It would hardly be
disputed that moral interpretation forms its bulk. Other sorts of exposition are hurried over so that 'we might the more quickly come to a larger
exposition of the moral sense'.[38] The avowed aim of the *Moralia* was to
provide the moral exposition requested by Gregory's brothers;[39] and his
exegetical preference, in the *Moralia* and his Homilies, is heavily weighted
towards moral exposition. The *res gesta* generally signified a *gerendum*.[40]
The life of prayer, repentance, self-denial and charity, and, especially, for
those capable of it, contemplation, are the core of the message that the
scriptures should convey to the Christian liberated from servitude to its
letter. As the reader makes progress in the understanding of the scriptures,
'the words of God grow with the reader'.[41] The scriptures contain what
the reader finds in them; and the reader's mind is shaped by his inner
disposition:

> unless the readers' minds extend to the heights, the divine words lie low, as it were,
> uncomprehended . . . It often happens that a scriptural text is felt to be heavenly, if
> one is kindled by the grace of contemplation to rise to heavenly things. And then

---

[36] *HEz* I.10.7.

[37] *HEz* I.10.7–11.

[38] *HEv.* II.40.2; Cf. *ibid.*, 3; *HEz* II.2.1 (*ea itaque doctrinae sermone . . . proferenda quae vitam audientium moresque componunt*); *Mor.* XX.27.56, and, of course, the many places where he does this without saying so.

[39] *Ad Leandr.* 1.

[40] *HEv.* II.21.2; cf. *Mor.* XIX.20.29: *ueraciter factum . . . significaret . . . ueraciter faciendum.*

[41] *HEz* I.7.8: *divina eloquia cum legente crescunt.*

we recognise the wonderful and ineffable power of the sacred text, when the reader's mind is permeated with heavenly love . . . For according to the direction that the reader's spirit takes, so the sacred text rises with him . . .[42]

Reading the scriptures was a moral exercise; understanding depends on faith and love, and, reciprocally, deepens faith and love. Preachers must adapt their preaching to the capacity of their hearers, as Gregory kept on insisting.[43] The scripture feeds the life of the spirit at every level: it accommodates itself to the capacity of the intellect seeking to understand it. 'You have progressed to the active life: it walks with you. You have arrived to an unchanging constancy of spirit: it stands with you. You have come by God's grace to the contemplative life: it flies along with you.'[44] So in his Homilies on the Gospels Gregory could address himself to the general public for whom they were intended. Accordingly, he likes here to dwell on the moral sense; and his treatment is generally less elaborate and more direct than in his commentaries addressed to other, 'professional' audiences.[45] The lesser commandments given by the scriptures for the benefit of the more lowly are not to be despised by those who penetrate the greater of its mysteries, for the lowly progress 'by increments of understanding, as it were by mental footsteps, and come to understanding the greater things'.[46] The scriptures contain riches to exercise the learned and to encourage the weak; they are a river in which the lamb will not be out of his depth and the elephant may swim.[47] Gregory's sense of the inexhaustible riches of the scriptures encouraged him to roam at ease among its meanings. *The* meaning of a text was as much the creation of its reader as it was determined by the text. The exegete's freedom was limited only by the duty to build up the believing community in love:

if one seeks virtue through the words of the Lord, even if they are understood differently than by their author, provided that even in their new meaning they aim to build up charity, the words uttered are the Lord's: for throughout the whole of

[42] *HEz* I.7.8–9. *Ibid.* 9–10 on the reader's growing through the scriptures' historical, moral and 'typical' senses.

[43] *RP* III. Prol., for the image of harp-player. *HEz* II.2.1: *ea itaque doctrinae sermone, largiente Deo, proferenda sunt, quae vitam audientium moresque componunt.* The good preacher will expound some things 'stooping to the level of the simplest [*minimis*], whereas others they will expound contemplating the highest things': *Mor.* V.11.24; XX.2.4; XXX.3.11–14.

[44] *sacra lectio talis invenitur, qualis et sit ipse a quo quaeritur. Ad activam profecisti: ambulat tecum. Ad immobilitatem atque constantiam spiritus profecisti: stat tecum; ad contemplativam vitam per Dei gratiam pervenisti: volat tecum:* *HEz* I.7.16.

[45] See especially *HEv* II.40.1–3, where he hurries over the allegorical sense, to allow him to come more quickly to the historical; but note that here the 'historical' sense has to do with morality. See below, pp. 45–7.

[46] *HEz* I.10.1. See also *HEz* I.3.4.

[47] *Ad Leandr.* 4. Cf. *Mor.* XX.1.1.

the sacred scriptures God speaks to us with this one end, that He may draw us to love of Him and of our neighbour.[48]

Gregory could have found sanction for taking charity as the norm in Augustine's exegetical principles. Charity was decisive. Augustine had also held that no true interpretation could fail to conform to charity, for that was, in the end, what all the scripture was about. But, he was careful to add, a particular exegesis may conform to the law of charity, but may nevertheless be wrong; and though it may not be culpable, it will have arrived at the right destination by the wrong route. And taking the wrong route habitually, Augustine thought, could be dangerous. Such caution is foreign to Gregory. His own homiletic practice illustrates the unlimited freedom from textual restraint to which he felt entitled of his exegesis. He was more interested in the spiritual truth that the text could be made to support than in expounding its meaning.[49]

ALLEGORY AND MYSTERY

The notion that the scriptures should feed the contemplative life was, of course, well established long before Gregory.[50] His preaching began among his 'brethren' in Constantinople, and much of it, as we have seen repeatedly, was addressed to a predominantly clerical audience. In line with a long tradition and especially with Augustine's growing insistence on the primary importance of the literal or historical sense, Gregory affirmed its primacy: 'let anyone who aspires to raise his mind to spiritual understanding not neglect the reverence due to the historical'.[51] But spiritual or allegorical exegesis predominates in his *oeuvre*; in part certainly because this was what his audience needed. The religious élite which, for the greater part, made up his audience was encouraged to penetrate through the outer or carnal sense of the text and to seek the inner or spiritual meaning:

---

[48] *HEz* I.10.14. cf. *ibid.*, 4: *[verba Dei] ad hoc enim intelligenda sunt ut et nobis prosint et intentione spiritali aliis conferantur.*

[49] See my discussion in *Signs and meanings*, 48–62. On Augustine's use of charity as the criterion, see p. 18 and *De doctrina Christiana* 1.36.40–41. Manselli, 'Gregorio Magno e la Bibbia', 89 defends Gregory's exegesis against the charge of being extravagant (*cervellotica*) by appealing to the fact that is is an exposition of the Christian faith; as if that absolved it from extravagance *as exegesis*. The sanest assessment I have come across is Meyvaert's: 'I believe that the most rewarding approach to the material of this sort that [Gregory] has left us is to view it as a grand exercise in the use of the imagination, and not to worry overmuch about the text he is commenting on . . .' ('Gregory the Great and the theme of authority', 5).

[50] I have discussed this in connection with John Cassian's *Conferences*; cf. my *The End*, 184–9.

[51] *Mor.* 1.37.56. Cf. xx.27.56; *HEv* II.40.1.

Those who seek the purity of the contemplative life are to be shown not the ordinary things about the sacred scripture [*non communia de sacro eloquio*], but rather the higher and more sublime things, so that the more they are delighted by the superior goods [*nobiliora*] they hear about, the more ardently they might raise themselves to the heights by seeing.[52]

Preaching to such a select audience, Gregory aims to manifest to them the concealed, inner meaning of the text. 'The sacred scriptures have an outer threshold, the letter; and an inner, allegory. We come through the letter to allegory as it were through the outer threshold to the inner.'[53] Gregory's terminology is untidy, and the meanings he attaches to 'historical', 'allegorical', 'typical', and their relation to 'moral' fluctuate. In the *Moralia* Gregory professed to expound the biblical text in three senses. His brethren had demanded that he should expound 'not only the allegorical sense of the narrative (*verba historiae*)', but – a harder task – that I should attend to the moral bearing of the allegories (*in exercitium moralitatis*);[54] So, Gregory says,

I shall run quickly through some passages with a historical exposition; some I shall examine by means of allegory for their typical sense [*per allegoriam quaedam typica investigatione*]; others again I shall discuss by means of allegory only for their moral bearing [*per sola allegoricae moralitatis instrumenta*]; some, finally, I shall investigate thoroughly in all three ways [*per cuncta simul sollicitius exquirentes tripliciter . . .*]. First I shall establish the historical sense as fundamental; then I shall erect [on this foundation], by means of the typical sense, a mental edifice as a stronghold of faith [*per significationem typicam in arcem fidei fabricam mentis erigens*]; finally, by means of the moral sense [*per moralitatis gratiam*] I shall as it were complete the building by a coat of paint.[55]

Here Gregory seems to have in mind a fundamental distinction between a literal or 'historical' sense, and an allegorical sense, which may be either moral or 'typical'. This, indeed, is his fundamental dichotomy. But little is to be gained by attempting to disentangle the oddly haphazard vocabulary; the moral sense sometimes appears as part of the historical, sometimes as part of the allegorical; his language is fluid.[56] Gregory cared little for neatness of terminology, and was in any case apt to conflate his three

52   *1 Reg.* III.124.
53   *HEz* II.3.18.
54   *Ad Leandr.* 1.
55   *Ad Leandr.* 3.
56   The three-fold scheme is most fully stated in *Ad Leandr.* 3. Some other enumerations: *HEz* I.7.10: historical, typical, 'contemplative understanding'; historical, moral, allegorical; *HEv* II.40.1–2: history (for morality), allegory (for faith); *Ad Leandr.* 1: moral sense as elaboration of allegorical: see n. 54 above.

senses of the scriptures with a dichotomy he thought more fundamental. This is the distinction variously stated between carnal and spiritual, literal and allegorical (or mystical), historical and typical, outer and inner understanding. 'We must seek in the material, or external, words [*verbis corporeis*; *exterioribus*] whatever is within [*interius*] ...[57] By this means they will become for the reader the pulley by which he is lifted up, not crushed by its weight. The letter covers the inner meaning as the husk covers the seed; to understand in the spirit is to penetrate through the husk to the inner meaning.[58] 'Spiritual interpretation' (*expositio spiritualis*) illuminates what is concealed by the letter of the Law.[59] The equation is evident: by allegory the reader is carried from the text's outward or 'corporeal' to its inner, spiritual, sense. Reading is either literal or spiritual.[60] Outer and inner, corporeal and spiritual, literal and allegorical, tend to be interchangeable doublets in Gregory's usage. And it is the second of the contrasting pair that carries the mind to contemplative heights: 'Allegory is a kind of pulley (*machina*) which enables a soul separated from God by a vast distance (*longe a Deo positae*) to be lifted up to God'.[61]

TEXT AND WORLD

A tradition of ascetic reading of the scriptures liberated Gregory's exegesis from the domination of the letter, and at the same time strictly subordinated it to the requirements of the contemplative life. Deep-rooted habits of reading encouraged him, as they encouraged others, to distance himself both from the world of his immediate experience and from the letter which conceals the spirit. Texts would dissolve in the light of the higher

---

[57] *Cant.* 4.

[58] *Cant.* 4.

[59] *Mor.* XVIII.39.60. *HEz* 1.6.12: *in testamenti veteris littera testamentum novum latuit per allegoriam.* Cf. *Mor.* XI.16.25: the Jews understand the Law in the letter, the converted *gentilitas* by the spirit which gives life. It can also mean an inward appropriation, allowing the text to work in the reader's soul:

'Those who do not hear what it says with devotion are not nourished by the word of God ... For the fullness of the word is one thing, the fullness of the book another. Only the elect can receive the fullness of the word, but the fullness of the book can be received by the reprobate too ... He who receives the word of scripture not in love but in knowledge (*non in amore sed in scientia*) receives the fulness of the book, not of the word; a dead thing which cannot give him life. For it is written: 'The letter killeth, the spirit gives life (2 Cor. 3:6)'. This is true of all sacred scripture. For the letter is the body, the spirit is the life of this body ...' (*1 Reg.* IV.123).

[60] *HEz* I.3.4: *aliquando in historia litteram suscipiunt, aliquando vero per significationem litterae spiritum requirunt ...*; Cf. II.1.3; 5: *secundum (iuxta) historiam, spiritaliter*; 1.9.30: *intus ... scriptus ... per allegoriam, foris per historiam.* Cf. II.1.3. *1 Reg.* Prol. 4. For parallels, see Lubac, *Exégèse*, 2, 489–90; comparison with Augustine, *ibid.*, 533–6.

[61] *Cant.* 2; cf. 4; *Ad Leandr.* 2: *per contemplationis ascensum ... HEz* I.3 is largely devoted to this process.

truth that they reveal when read spiritually. Freed from the letter which killeth, the scripture would free the Christian from the material world.[62]

Gregory's attitude to the world of creatures and to the letter of the text were all of a piece. He was not the reflective thinker to develop a theory of signs such as Augustine had worked out in his *De doctrina Christiana* and his *De Trinitate*. The relation between a sign-giver or sign-receiver, the sign, and the signified had become a fundamental structure of Augustine's thought. He had used it not only as the key to understanding language, but also to explain the hermeneutics of interpreting the biblical text, to expound his theology of the sacraments, to formulate his views on the cohesion of human groups sharing symbol-systems, languages and rituals. He had seen human creatures faced with the material world and their Creator on the same model. Gregory followed Augustine's views on all these subjects; but his version lacked the deeply pondered theoretical foundations Augustine had laid for them. Moreover, a number of slight but immensely revealing divergences from Augustine reveal the very different general orientation of Gregory's mind.

Gregory used the Pauline verse 'The letter killeth but the Spirit giveth life' (2 Cor. 3:6) only to justify the exegetical freedom to interpret texts allegorically.[63] Augustine, though he had also understood it in this sense, came in later life to be more reserved both about allegory and the use of the verse to justify it.[64] That reserve is altogether alien to Gregory. Much more than Augustine, Gregory is ready to jump from the letter to its spiritual meaning; and equally he is much more ready to make the leap from the material universe to its Maker. Commenting on the verse 'Who does not know that the hand of the Lord has done this?' (Job 12:9), Gregory wrote:

... all proclaim God to be the creator of all.... This may also be understood literally [*iuxta solam speciem litterae*]: for each creature when looked at gives as it were its own testimony, [by means of] the very form it has [*ipsam quam habet speciem suam*]. Cattle, birds, the earth or fish, if we ask them while we look, reply with one voice that the Lord made everything. While they imprint their form [*species*] on our senses they proclaim that they are not from themselves. By the very fact that they are created, they proclaim by the form they manifest [*per ostensam speciem*] their creator: [this is] as it were the voice of their confession . . .[65]

---

[62] I summarise here the argument of my *Signs and meanings*, chapter 2, where the substance of the remainder of this chapter is more fully developed.

[63] For Gregory's use of the verse: e. g. *Mor.* XI.16.25; XVIII.39.60; *Cant.* 4; *1 Reg.* 1.56; IV.123.

[64] I was mistaken there in what I wrote (*Signs and meanings*, pp. 13–14) about Augustine's use of the Pauline verse 'The letter killeth but the Spirit giveth life' (2 Cor. 3:6): he did not reject his earlier application of the text, though he changed his preference.

[65] *Mor.* XI.4.6.

A famous passage of Augustine's *Confessions* is so like Gregory's that it is hard to imagine that Gregory did not have it at the back of his mind: 'I asked the sea, the deeps, the living creatures that creep, and they responded: "We are not your God, look beyond us" . . . And with a great voice they cried out: "He made us"' (Ps. 99:3). My question was the attention I gave to them, and their response was their *species*.[66] A comparison, however, quickly reveals a characteristic contrast between the two writers. Augustine immediately catches himself: 'Surely this should be self-evident to all who are of sound mind', he asks in the next paragraph; but no, far from it: one has to raise oneself above created things in order to exercise judgement, not to be subjected to them by loving them. Only then will the creatures answer their interrogator:

Moreover, created things do not answer those who question them if power to judge is lost. There is no alteration in the voice which is their beauty (*speciem*). If one person sees while another sees and questions, it is not that they appear one way to the first and another way to the second. It is rather that the created order speaks to all, but is understood by those who hear its outward voice and compare it with the truth within themselves.[67]

This is something that is altogether missing in Gregory. He does not doubt that it will indeed be evident to all that creatures point to the Creator: for him they are transparent without any need to question and to judge the creatures' response.[68]

It has been noted that in comparison with Augustine, Gregory gives far less central a place to the sacraments in his thought about the Church. His references to sacramental rites in the life of the Church are rare, his emphasis very much heavier on preaching, his notion of the Church liable to succumb to a tendency towards 'spiritualisation'.[69] This difference between the two men is surely related, at some obscure but deep level, to their different ways of regarding signs: Augustine's sense of the solidity of signs and the irretrievably sign-bound nature of human living has no equivalent in Gregory; for him the signified was much more directly accessible.

What is absent from Gregory's mind is Augustine's haunting sense of

---

[66] *Conf.* x.6.9.
[67] *Conf.* x.6.10 (trans. Chadwick).
[68] Cf. Straw, *Gregory the Great*, 49–50: 'Gregory's shift of Augustine's position is slight, but significant. Augustine's God plays hide-and-seek with man ... Gregory chooses rather to emphasize God's involvement with creation and the sacramental presence of spiritual truths in the things of this world.'
[69] Fiedrowicz, *Das Kirchenverständis*, 74; 113; 141. This needs to be qualified, however; the pervasive consciousness of sacrifice has strongly eucharistic overtones: De Vogüé, 'De la crise aux résolutions', esp. 310.

the opacity of signs. In our sinful world, for Augustine, signs are radically ambivalent, apt to conceal no less than to reveal. Meaning is not just given, it has often to be striven, even struggled for. We live in a world of signs and communicate with one another through signs, and our communities are formed by shared sign-systems. Yet, in our fallen state, we are constantly liable to fail to communicate: to find, or to make, the signs we use opaque, creating a wall to divide us from our linguistic communities. Even more, we are liable to be imprisoned among the signs with which God communicates with us. The signs are not transparent to us fallen human beings; they are often opaque and intrude themselves between reader (or speaker) and hearer. Gregory's lack of interest in questions as abstract as those about signification, and his habits of ascetic reading of the biblical texts combined to encourage him to make the leap from sign to signified with less effort and less misgiving. Gregorian religion was in every way a religion of detachment: scriptural in its substance, it detached the reader from the letter of the scripture, helping to detach him, at the same time, from the world he was to read in its light.

CHAPTER 4

Appropinquante mundi termino:
the world in its old age

NEARING THE END

Contemplative disposition and deep-rooted habits of ascetic reading encouraged Gregory's detachment from the world of his everyday experience. But this was not all. Preaching on an Advent Sunday, two days after a storm had destroyed houses and churches in Rome, Gregory saw the apocalyptic signs foretold by Jesus (Luke 21:25–33) being realised all round him:

> Of these [predicted] things some we see already accomplished, others we expect with terror to come very soon. For we see nation rising against nation, their distress afflicting the lands – we see this in our time now more than we read about it in books. You know how frequently we have heard reports from other parts of the world of countless cities being destroyed by earthquake. Plagues we suffer without relief; we do not yet clearly see the signs in the sun, the moon, the stars, but we gather from the change in the air that these are not far off . . . As so many of the things foretold have already occurred, there is no doubt that the few that still remain will soon follow: for the experience of what has come to pass gives us certainty about what is to come.[1]

Christians have always known they lived in the 'last age', the time between Christ's first and second comings. Their expectations of its end have varied. Although apocalyptic mood revived from time to time, and North African Christianity under Vandal occupation had been notably fertile ground for flourishing apocalyptic expectations, Augustine's agnosticism about the predictability of the end inhibited speculation about its imminence.[2] Gregory also professed not to know the time of the end,[3] but his sense of its nearness is unequalled since the fading of the early Christians' eschatological expectations. For Gregory this was no generalised theological notion, no mere homiletic device, but firmly embedded in his

---

[1] *HEv* I.1.1; 5. Cf. II.35.1–3.
[2] See Landes, 'Millenarismus absconditus'.
[3] *Mor.* I.Praef.10.21; *HEv* I.13.6. On his eschatology, see Dagens, *Saint Grégoire le Grand*, 352–6, 363–73; and his 'La fin des temps'.

experience, linked closely to perceived threat by Lombard swords, friction
with imperial authority, betrayal of ministerial calling, be it by a patriarch
of Constantinople or by Italian clergy. The coming end cast its shadow –
or rather, light (for the end, for those who love God, is the 'unimaginable,
zero summer' when 'the clouds of our sorrow pass away, and the days of
our life are bright with the light of the eternal Sun'[4]) – on the crumbling
ruins, on the sickness unto death and desolation that Gregory saw all round
him. His daily experience was shaped by his eschatological expectation:

> Towns are depopulated, fortified places destroyed, churches burnt, monasteries
> and nunneries destroyed; fields are deserted by men, and the earth forsaken by the
> ploughman gapes desolate. No farmer dwells here now; wild beasts have taken the
> place of throngs of men. What goes on in other parts of the world, I do not know;
> but here, in the land in which we live, the world no longer announces its coming
> end, but shows it forth.[5]

He pictured the time of the end not only as imminent, but in the most
dramatic of terms: commenting, for example, on Behemoth moving his
tail like a cedar (Job 40:17), he deploys a whole romanesque gallery of
diabolical tortures which the Antichrist will employ to persecute.[6] Moments
of acute crisis were apt to prompt some of the most powerful of Gregory's
apocalyptic expositions of scriptural imagery. Thus at a time of extreme
insecurity in Rome in 593, Gregory was preaching on Ezechiel's allegory
of the boiling pot (24:4–11) in which the bones and the flesh of the rebel-
lious house of Israel are to be boiled down:

> The bones designate the great men of the world [*potentes saeculi*], the flesh the
> people; for as the flesh is carried by the bones, so the weakness of the people is
> ruled by the powerful of the world. But now, the powerful are all removed, the
> bones boiled down; the people perish, the flesh is liquefied. Let it be said: 'Gather
> the bones, that I might burn them with fire; let the flesh be consumed, and let the
> whole mess be boiled and the bones be destroyed.' Where now is the senate? where
> the people? ... The senate is gone, the people perish; pain and fear grow daily for
> the few who are left; a deserted Rome is burning ... we see buildings destroyed,
> ruins daily multiplied ... The pot in which the flesh and the bones were consumed
> is now itself being consumed: for after the people are gone, the walls will fall.
> Where are they who once rejoiced in its glory? Where is their splendour [*pompa*]?
> Where their pride? Where their frequent and unrestrained revelry [*gaudium*]?[7]

Seeing the crumbling away of the fabric of the material world around
him, Gregory was driven to look beyond: even if we had no Gospel to tell

---

[4] *HEv* i.1.3.
[5] *Dial.* iii.38.3. See also *HEz* i.9.9; ii.6.22–24; *HEv* i.17.16; *Ep.* iii.29; x137. In *Ep.* v.37 Gregory widens
the picture to *cuncta in Europae partibus* (see also *HEz* ii.6.24).
[6] *Mor.* xxxii.15.24.
[7] *HEz* ii.6.22. On the crisis in Rome, see chapter 7, pp. 97; 102–4.

us, the world itself proclaims the truth – its ruins are its voice, warning us not to love it;[8] if we still love such a world, 'it is wounds we love, not delights'.[9] Unlike Augustine, Gregory had no hope of his world's regeneration: it was doomed. Augustine used the eagle of the Psalm (103:5) as a symbol of renewal; Gregory found the aged eagle balding from head to foot (Micah 1:16) more suitable as a symbol for Rome – and the world – in its decrepit old age.[10] The afflictions of the earth itself have become 'as it were the pages of a book' which teaches us 'that in the perishing of all things we should account as nothing the things we have loved.'[11] A simple ascetic other-worldliness blends here with his strong sense of the imminent end of the sixth age. Either way, the message is renunciation. Thus the martyrs trampled on a world in its flower: 'life was long, people enjoyed good health, material riches, fecundity in procreation, tranquillity in lasting peace; and yet, even while it was flourishing, in their hearts the world was barren'. But is not so for us:

> Now the world is a barren desert, and yet it flourishes in our hearts. Everywhere there is death, mourning, desolation; we are struck on every side, on every side we are filled with anguish; and yet with blind minds we love the bitterness of the things our flesh desires. We pursue what is fleeting, we cling to what is failing. And because we cannot hold on to what is failing, we fail along with it, as we hold on to it while it crumbles. Once the world held us with its delight; now it is so full of woes, that the world itself calls us to God.[12]

Gregory invariably links such observation of the world's decay with warnings to his audience against too close an attachment to a world already approaching its grave.

His warnings sound a note of peculiar urgency. What he is particularly anxious to discourage is complacency and a sense of security.[13] From a much loved correspondent Gregory withheld the reassurance she had asked for, writing that even if he could, he would refuse to tell her that her sins have been forgiven, for she must not feel secure: 'security tends to be the mother of indolence'.[14] It is not to be looked for in this world; the wicked will finally reap trouble from present security, the good will find

---

[8] *HEv.* I.4.2.
[9] *HEz* II.6.22.
[10] *HEz* II.6.23–4. As far as I know, Gregory does not allude to the image of the eagle of Ps. 103:5 at all. For Augustine, see e.g. *Sermo* 81.8; *Enarr. in Ps.* 38.8.
[11] *Ep.* III.29.
[12] See *HEv* II.28.3 for the finest expression of this. But Samuel in his old age 'flourished as if in youth'; but that was long ago! *I Reg.* IV.39–40.
[13] *HEv* I.1.2. It is the 'eleventh hour': *HEv* I.19.2.
[14] *Ep.* VII.22, to Gregoria (*dulcissima filia*). The same point is made in *Mor.* XXIV.11.27: *conuersio . . . securitatem parit, mater autem neglegentiae solet esse securitas.*

their ultimate security from present trouble; even peace on earth can be misused to boost 'vain security'.[15] Security is the enemy of effort, and effort is what Gregory, for all his other-worldliness, did not spare himself and expected from others. There was much unfinished business – among the many tasks Gregory set himself, the conversion of the English nation[16] – and little time left.[17]

For all his strong leanings towards the contemplative life, for Gregory the remaining time of the world's sixth age was an age for action. He did not think he would himself see the end; he lived in the time just preceding it. In the background of all his thought a sense of the closeness of the end is always present; it is a feature of his preaching as of his pastoral activity.[18] Not only a summons to turn away from material satisfaction or to repent, consciousness of the imminent end could serve to focus attention and give direction to choice. It gave a seriousness to what human laziness would make trivial. Characteristically, for instance, in admonishing a congregation on its duties in electing a suitable bishop, he would remind them to 'consider the coming day of the eternal judge attentively and to prepare for it in penitence'.[19] Whether and how far this eschatological sense was peculiar to him it is, for lack of evidence for comparison, hard to decide. It is notably absent, to take just two examples, in a man of the previous generation such as Cassiodorus, or one of the following generation, Isidore of Seville. Cassiodorus did not translate his evident consciousness of an impending cultural *hiatus* into eschatological terms; Isidore had good reason for sturdy confidence in the future. Gregory's sense of his own time is poised between experience of disaster and a hope born of his awareness of real possibilities. Both were articulated in the language of eschatology.

CHURCH AND WORLD IN THE LAST AGE

From its origin in the Garden of Eden, the river of human history was rushing on its downwards course, towards destruction, where the 'ancient enemy of the human race' was waiting, ready to swallow it.[20] In the secular

---

[15] *Mor.* x.20.37: *sicut enim malis praesens securitas laborem, ita bonis praesens labor perpetuam securitatem parit. HEv* II.35.1: *tranquillitatem quippe humanae pacis ad usum vertimus vanae securitatis . . .*

[16] *Ep.* III.37: *appropinquante . . . mundi termino . . .*, to be seen in the light of the principle expounded to bishops in *HEv* I.17.16. On the English mission, see below, chapter 11.

[17] *HEv* I.4.5: *cum velocitate tempora fugiunt . . .*

[18] Dagens, 'La fin des temps', 275.

[19] *Ep.* III.29. On the election (in Milan) see below, pp. 140–2. For further examples, see Recchia, *Gregorio Magno*, 120–3, and Manselli, 'L'escatologia'.

[20] *HEv* II.26.9; Cf. *Mor.* XXXIII.6.12–13; 9.17: *in hac quippe aquarum abysso. . .*

past Gregory's interest was very limited. He loved to listen to old men's tales,[21] and, although he could speak of fairly recent times with a certain degree of realism, there is a strongly folk-loristic flavour, sometimes bordering on the bizarre, in many of his remarks on events from earlier times.[22] The lack of any inhibiting sense of the unlikely is a sure symptom of the limits of available secular knowledge. Even more, however, it signals a turning away from older conceptions of knowledge. To take the measure of how Gregory saw himself and his own times in relation to the past we need to attend to how he saw the present in relation to the End.

At the heart of his eschatology there was a tension which has been described as between sacred and secular, or between Church and world.[23] While the world lies under the threat of annihilation, the Church seems to be assured of peace and quiet. At the end of days a rising tide of persecution will force the Church to suffer the voices of heresy raised openly against her. For the present, however, the dragon is confined in the depths, his voice is muffled; but then, at the end, he will attack, not only with words, but with the sword.[24] Then, Gregory wrote, the elect will call to mind these present times in which the Church keeps the peace of the faith (*fidei pacem tenet*) and bends the proud necks of heretics – not by force, but by the yoke of reason. They will remember us, 'living as we are in these quiet times of faith' (*qui quieta fidei tempora ducimus*); even though we are exposed to the trials of warfare between peoples, we are not subjected to the extremities foretold for us.[25] When he speaks like this, Gregory seems to allow that imminent end which the world is 'not so much announcing, but already showing forth'[26] to recede to a very distant horizon. It is as if only the world were under imminent threat, while the Church is safely at rest, assured of peace for a long time to come. Like the turtle (Ps. 83:4), the Church 'has made herself a nest which is the utterly peaceful repose of faith [*pacatissimam fidei quietem*] in which to foster her young like fledglings in the warm bosom of her love until they are ready to fly off into the heights [*ad superiora*] . . .'[27]

The cosy imagery could easily be taken to sanction complacency; but – as we have seen – Gregory is on his guard: 'at the cost of so much hardship,

---

[21] *Dial.* I.10.11.

[22] In the *Dialogues* the stories of Basilius (I.4.3) and of Paulinus (III.1; on its sources and parallels, see De Vogüé's notes, and Petersen, *The Dialogues*, 15–18) are obvious examples.

[23] Dagens, 'La fin des temps', 277–80. See also Markus, 'The sacred and the secular', 92–6.

[24] This distinction is also made in *Mor.* XVIII.2.3.

[25] *Mor.* XIX.9.15–16; cf. XIV.21.25–23.27; XX.37.72; XXXIII.20.37.

[26] *Dial.* III.38.3; see above, n. 5.

[27] *Mor.* XIX.27.48; cf. XIX.11.18: the Church guards its *parvulos* in the cradle of its peace: a time of preaching and healing.

the holy Church has come to this stability of faith [*ad fidei statum*] and
desires to remain in this glory of the faith for a long time [*diutius*] in order
to gather many . . .'[28]

Although Gregory excludes any thought of allowing effort to be
relaxed, he saw this present peace for the Church as a time of achievement. The Church's condition of existence underwent vast changes in
the course of its history, as Gregory often recalled. The history of the
Church, like the world's, is analogous to the six ages of human life;[29] but
Gregory tends to reduce this history to the two most dramatically contrasting ages, the age of persecution and the age of the Church's triumph. The
Church has 'different times': times of persecution and times of peace.
Each makes different demands, for laying down our life then, to overcome
earthly desires now.[30] Miracles were needed in the Church's early days;
they are not needed now, or they are of a different type (spiritual rather
than visible), or they serve a different purpose: 'At that time, when the
holy Church was subject to persecution, it needed the help of miracles.
Now, after having tamed the arrogance of infidelity, it no longer needs
miracles [*virtutum signa*] but only the merit of good works – even though it
continues to have frequent miracles to show as and when the occasion
requires.'[31] Now, the age of miracles having passed, 'the words of the holy
scriptures are freely and readily heard in the holy Church'.[32] Gregory
marks the contrast between these two epochs in various ways: God
permits the Church to be troubled in the terrible persecution in the time
of the Antichrist, but not in this time of peace and tranquillity;[33] the
age of martyrdom is over, we cannot now shed our blood for Christ;[34]
this is the time of the Church's glory, when its preachers rejoice in the
honour they have all over the world, when all the heathen have bowed to
their authority; the Church enjoys honour and prestige.[35] The very
rhinoceros (Job 39:9) of earthly power, which had raised itself in pride
against the young Church with dire threats of torture and death and fear
of extinction, has been subdued by God – by means of miracles – to His
service. 'We see this rhinoceros, that is to say, the earthly rulers who
once raged savagely against the Lord, now bending his neck humbly to

---

[28] *Mor.* XIX.27.48.
[29] *Mor.* XIX.12.19; on the six ages of the world, see also *1 Reg.* IV.74 and *HEv* I.19.1.
[30] *HEv* II.32.4–5.
[31] *Mor.* XXXII.18.36; cf. *Mor.* XXX.2.6–7; *HEv* II.29.4; I.4.2–3. For discussion of Gregory's views on
     miracles past and present, see below, pp. 62–3.
[32] *HEz* I.10.37.
[33] *Mor.* XXIX.6.10.
[34] *HEz* II.3.14–15.
[35] *1 Reg.* II.59; 90–91; *Mor.* XXIII.8.15.

His yoke', even assisting the work of preaching His word with their legislation.[36]

Gregory's way of speaking of the Church's triumph, of the honour and glory it enjoyed in the society of his time, is not unlike that of the Christian writers around AD 400 who celebrated the official enforcement of Christian orthodoxy under Theodosius I and his successors. Augustine had, albeit briefly, joined that chorus of jubilant euphoria before turning his back on it.[37] Gregory's remarks, however, have a different historical context, and that gives them a different bearing. There is nothing celebratory about them; they simply describe a situation which has been in existence for some 200 years, not one that has just been brought into being, under his very eyes. Nor could he imagine a reversal of the Church's dominant position. Although he sometimes spoke as if persecution and tranquillity alternated in its experience like night and day,[38] he could not easily envisage real change in its fortunes. Its victory was definitive. Unlike Augustine's generation, for which a mixed society comprising a strong pagan element was still a present reality, Gregory could scarcely have imagined a Roman society which was not radically Christianised (though beyond its limits, of course, there lay another world). We could hardly expect him to have shared Augustine's agnosticism about the future of Christianity in the Roman orbit. In Gregory's historical perspective the Church's position – except for the final persecution by the Antichrist, linked with Christ's second coming and the *eschaton* – was secure, its untroubled supremacy assured. But the euphoria of a Prudentius, even, in passing, of Augustine in the late 390s, is altogether absent from Gregory's language.

On the contrary: he associates the Church's privileged place in his society with the sombre obverse: the conversion of secular rulers now prompts wicked men, who in the past would have attacked openly, to adopt underhand ways. Assuming outward conformity, they subvert the Church by their wickedness:

So the holy Church cannot pass through the time of its pilgrimage without trouble and trial; even if it has no overt external enemies, it must tolerate feigned brothers [*fictos fratres*] within. It is always embattled against vice, it is at war even in the time of peace. Perhaps it endures worse hurt when it is attacked by the morals of its own than by the blows of outsiders.[39]

---

[36] *Mor.* XXXI.2.2; 4.4–5.
[37] See my *Saeculum*, chapter 2.
[38] *Mor.* XIII.41.46–42.47.
[39] *Mor.* XXXI.7.10.

Gregory was as sharply conscious of the ambivalence of official and large-scale christianisation as had been Augustine at his most critical. While very ready to speak of the Church's honour and glory 'in almost all nations', Gregory almost invariably takes care to balance the account with a reminder of the cost in terms of holiness: 'for many even now do not wish to be Christians, but to appear so. To these people God is present in public, not within.'[40] Perhaps inspired by Augustine's ideas on the irretrievably mixed nature of the Church and his imagery of the two Cities, with which he was certainly familiar, Gregory lost few opportunities to insist on the mixed character of the pilgrim Church. 'In the place where the light is to be seen, there the darkness is loved.'[41] The more the world advances in old age the more apt we are to blind ourselves to the growing sinfulness of the present, as 'the vigour of the spirit is relaxed'.[42] Outward conformity and inward betrayal, *tepor* and negligence, attend the Church's progress.

In Gregory's image the Church is dominant in society, or, more accurately, it is a community which has by and large absorbed earthly powers and agencies into its own being. The image reflects the realities of his time. Questions about the value and purpose of the secular order and its institutions and the way they are related to human salvation such as had exercised Augustine no longer had any meaning in Gregory's world.[43] Conflicts can and do still occur between different elements within it; but essentially the conditions of Gregory's world offered no foothold for the distinctions that had still been very real in the fifth century, between 'sacred' and 'secular'. Gregory and his contemporaries defined themselves increasingly in religious terms. When they contemplated their world and its future – such future as it had – it was the fate of the community of Christians, ringed, to be sure, by a penumbra of peoples still to be drawn into it, that they had before their minds.

The eschatological tension between Augustine's two Cities interwoven in all secular societies as well as in the Church in its earthly existence is transformed into another tension in Gregory's mind: that between the inner and the outer, the contemplative and the active, the carnal and the spiritual.[44] The doublets, of course, have their parallels in Augustine; but

---

[40] *Mor.* XIX.13.21. Cf. *HEv* II.32.5; *Mor.* XIII.8.10–9.11; XVIII.6.12; XXV.10.25; XXIX.7.14–17.

[41] *Mor.* XXV.10.25.

[42] *1 Reg.* IV.14. Cf. *Mor.* XX.33.65.

[43] I here summarise parts of my paper 'The sacred and the secular'. On the relations of 'sacred' and 'secular' in the sixth-century Empire and in Gregory's relations with its government, see below, chapter 6.

[44] On these architectonic doublets in Gregory's thought, see Dagens, *Saint Grégoire le Grand*, passim, and Aubin, *Intériorité et extériorité*.

in Gregory's mind they substitute for Augustine's complex and differentiated attitude to the secular world, rooted in his eschatological perspective, something else: a simple call – intellectually simple if spiritually demanding – for holiness. All Gregory's eschatological purple passages[45] serve this end: to proclaim an ascetic Christian morality of renunciation.

HOLINESS NOW

The Apostolic community considered all its members to be called to be 'saints'. With its passing, later generations of Christians found the idea of sainthood fraught wih ambiguity.[46] Were all Christians, at any rate after their death, saints, or only some few of their number? Ritual commemorations of the anniversary of their death (or deposition) did not resolve the ambiguity, for the 'birthdays' of apostles, martyrs, bishops and ordinary Christians all received the appropriate observance. To attach the epithet *sanctus* to a dead bishop's name was often to say no more than 'the late bishop'. It took centuries to tidy up the usage. The 'saint' became the person who received a public cult from the Church. The cult reflected the saint's status as one of the community's representative persons, an exemplar who had embodied in his or her life on earth the virtues valued in the Christian community.[47]

In the early Christian centuries the cult was focussed on the martyr, the Christian who died in witness to his Lord. Apart from the apostles, only martyrs received a public cult. In the age of persecutions, communities of Christians recorded the date and place of their martyrs' death (or 'birthday', as they generally called it) – or their burial, and sometimes preserved narratives of their trial, suffering and execution, a few of which have survived. Seen as an example of heroic courage, of contempt of death, the martyr came, eventually, to represent the possibility of victory, through God's power, conferred on the very weakness of human flesh and blood, with its fear of death and torment.[48] The martyr's victory is the conquest of fear and of the flesh by the spirit. It represents the possibility, through God's grace, of human victory over death, over the frailty of our bodies, the instability of our unruly wills, over weakness of faith and lack of resolve.

---

[45] See especially *Dial.* III.38.3–4, and above, pp. 51–2.

[46] The changes in the notion of sainthood have been particularly emphasised by Pietri, 'L'évolution'.

[47] As sketched by Peter Brown in 'The saint as exemplar'; cf. also my *End*, 25–6. In the sequel I summarise what is more fully dealt with there, with references: on the cult of the martyrs: 92–5; of relics: 142–9; on Christian perfection: 63–83.

[48] On this very important shift, see Rebillard, *In hora mortis* and Dodaro, 'Christus iustus'.

In the century following the end of the age of persecution, the cult of the martyrs came to meet a new need: the need for the tolerated, perhaps comfortable, rich, and prestigious Christians of the post-Constantinian world to identify themselves with the persecuted Church of the martyrs. Fourth-century Christians needed to be assured that their own, triumphant, Church was still identical, across the generations, with the Church of the martyrs. To have the martyrs made present in the community's daily worship kept the past alive in its memory. The cult of the martyrs helped to abolish the distance between the post-Constantinian present and the pre-Constantinian past. Its huge expansion in the Christian calendar in the course of the fourth century testifies to its central importance in meeting this need.

What the cult was not equipped to provide was a model for the Christian life in this new age, for – by definition – the age of the martyrs lay in a past only to be recovered in liturgical, imaginative or historical representation; not in real-life (or, rather, real-death) imitation. The martyrs could not furnish a 'relevant pattern of holiness' in an age which made new and very different demands on Christians who would be perfect (Matt. 19:21). New patterns, however, were emerging and, indeed, in a variety of forms mainly of ascetic and monastic living. Their diffusion beyond the immediate circle of a holy man's disciples was achieved by saints' lives such as the *Life of Antony* and Sulpicius Severus's Martinian writings, to which we should add biographies of bishops such as Paulinus's *Life* of Ambrose and Possidius's of Augustine. The accounts of martyrdom were of only indirect relevance to the new hagiographical genres that came into being.

If the narrative form of martyrs' *Acta* could not give much help in shaping hagiographic narratives, the concept of holiness they embodied was, nevertheless, destined for a long after-life. From early times the category of martyrs was extended beyond its strict boundaries. Would-be martyrs whose worthy intentions were foiled by circumstances such as the sudden outbreak of peace – 'confessors' – were accorded the status of quasi-martyrdom;[49] virgins, too, qualified. Martyrdom became a matter of intention and conscience. The possibility of extending its scope was well established, and was to be widely built on, especially once real, bloody, martyrdom had ceased to be an option. In his sermons on the martyrs Augustine, for instance, liked to use the image of the martyr fighting and

---

[49] E.g. Cyprian, *Ep.* 10.5 for a classic statement: though deprived of the *certamen*, they retain *voluntas integra et conscientia gloriosa*. Cf. *Ad Fortun.* 13, quoted by Augustine in *Sermo* 305.2: *in persecutione militia, in pace conscientia coronatur*.

suffering in the arena to remind his congregation of the daily call to martyrdom. Even ill in bed, resisting the use of magical potions, you are witnessing to the Lord – 'you are in the arena; lying down, you are fighting'; your heart is a narrow theatre: 'God is the spectator of your fight'.[50] The martyr summed up the Christian ideal of perfection; so 'peace, too, has its martyrs'; and around AD 500 Caesarius of Arles thought a Christian's fight with fornication was the hardest of his struggles and entitled him – if victorious – to the title of martyr; one could be a martyr even to sobriety.[51] Thus Gregory, too, unquestioningly represented ascetic self-denial in terms of the tradition of martyrdom: 'there are some who keep nothing to themselves but offer [*immolant*] to the almighty Lord their sense, their speech, their life and all the substance with which they have been endowed. Their offering can be nothing other than the "whole sacrifice" [*holocaustum*]; indeed, they are themselves the holocaust.'[52]

This 'bloodless martyrdom' had both a respectable ancestry and a long future. The martyr had established himself as the prototype of the saint and it proved hard to dislodge him from that position. New patterns of sainthood were interpreted on its analogy. The analogy, however, was based on an underlying theology – the theology suggested by the metaphor of victory in the struggle with the flesh or the devil – not on any narrative similarity, which was absent. Although the martyrological ideal was adaptable, the narrative was not suited to depict new types of sanctity: its focus on a bloody struggle between the saint and the persecutor cut across the grain of the hagiographical stories. But as other forms of holiness came to supersede that of the martyr, the image of the martyr itself also underwent modification. This is most striking in the legends of Roman martyrs which began to circulate in Italy in the fifth and sixth centuries, and had a great future in the Middle Ages. These legends, though worthless as evidence on the martyrs, are invaluable for the light they shed on the religiosity of the time of their composition and diffusion. Catering for the interests of the growing tide of pilgrims to Rome and other readers of romances, their edifying intention is clear in many of the nuances accentuated by their unknown authors: the importance they attach to virginity, to strict orthodoxy and opposition to heresy, especially Arian, to the cult of relics, and so forth.[53] A variety of ideas of holiness came to overlay that of the martyr, and gradually transformed the image

[50] *Sermo* 318.3; 315.7.10. Cf. Markus, *The end*, 93–4.
[51] Caesarius, *Sermo* 41.2; 44.1; 47.2 etc. See Markus, *The end*, 70–1.
[52] *HEz* II.8.16; cf. *HEz* I.12.30; etc. *i Reg.* VI.32. See also below, p. 62.
[53] Characterised by Dufourcq, *Études*, I. 46–66. Cf. the summary, III. 283–4.

of the martyr as pictured in the legends. This process of up-dating made
the martyrological narratives suitable to serve as means for advocating
other, newer, conceptions of holiness.

There was evidently a demand in Rome for hagiographical stories in
some form alternative to the martyrological genre. Not long before
Gregory's time a collection of the sayings of Eastern monastic leaders
had been translated into Latin by two Roman deacons, Pelagius (almost
certainly the later pope Pelagius I, 555/6–60/1) and John (perhaps pope
John III, 560/1–74/5).[54] Their appeal may have seemed too exclusively
ascetic and monastic to serve a more general demand; and, anyway,
Gregory may have thought that this was not what was needed in these
times of affliction. He was aware of collections of martyrs' legends
circulating in Rome, and he may have made some use in his *Dialogues* of
some stories known to us; but on the whole the work owes very little to the
Gesta martyrum.[55] The real significance of his *Dialogues* lies in Gregory's
clear intention to provide an alternative collection of *exempla* of sainthood.[56] Although he thought that you only needed to look round to see
that the world was still full of martyrs,[57] Gregory discarded the mould of
the martyr-story, and thereby liberated the Italian saint of his day, and
saints of succeeding generations, from its tyranny. Hagiography could
celebrate models of sanctity conceived and described as autonomous in
their own terms.

The wish that Gregory placed in the mouth of his interlocutor in the
Dialogues was for modern miracles, worked in Italy: though he knew of
'good men in this land', he professed – echoing Gregory's own old beliefs
in the rarity of miracles in our age – to know of no miracles. Gregory often
thought the age of miracles was past. He had not excluded the possibility
of modern miracles, 'as and when the occasion requires'; but on the whole
he thought (like Augustine, who changed his mind on this question late in
his career[58]) that miracles belonged to the Church's early days. He never

---

[54] Peterson, *The Dialogues*, 152 gives the references. Gregory may also have known Theodoret's *Historia religiosa*: *ibid.*, 181–8, which is sometimes taken as one of his models, e.g. by Cracco Ruggini, 'Grégoire le Grand et le monde byzantin', 87, and her 'Il miracolo'.

[55] Dufourcq, *Études*, III. 292–6; Petersen, *The Dialogues*, 56–89, in whose judgement the parallels are for the most part to be explained by the use of common sources and traditions, or later additions to the *gesta* incorporating Gregorian material. Gregory's knowledge of *gesta martyrum*: *Ep.* VIII.28.

[56] This is the view put forward, very convincingly, by Boesch Gajano, especially in 'La proposta agiografica', 649–64; Cf. also Petersen, *The Dialogues*, 88–9.

[57] *HEv* II.27.4: *totum mundum … aspicite: martyribus plenus est.* On the martyr *in occulto: Dial.* III.26.7–9; 28.2–5. cf. *HEv* I.3.4; II.3; II.32.4–5; 35.7; *HEz* II.8.16 cf. above, n. 52). On Gregory's use of this figure, see De Vogüé, '*Martyrium in occulto*'.

[58] For summary and references, see Markus, *The end*, 149.

came to a clear view on this question. His answer to the deacon Peter, far from being a refutation of scepticism, is Gregory's *retractatio* of his own view.[59] Not a retraction, for he had never denied the occurrence of miracles even in our age, but a necessary revision, filling in the qualifications he thought necessary. The present time, especially the early and mid-590s – with the Lombards closing in on Rome, the emperor averse to Gregory's plans, a patriarch making claims that Gregory thought godless – called for miracles with unprecedented urgency. The *Dialogues* constantly remind us of the deep insecurity of the times: invasions, Lombard savagery, brigandage, hunger, flood, fever and poverty. Among the signs of the nearness of the end,[60] we seek, and find, reassurance. Even now, Italy is full of saints, and indeed of more than might appear; 'even if we undergo great tribulation, we are not entirely deserted by our Maker – so these stupendous miracles that I hear of attest'.[61]

Gregory had been reserved not only about miracles in his own days; he also sometimes suggested that miracles would cease as the end drew near. Among the other signs of the imminent end the drying up of miracles in the Church will herald the coming of the Antichrist: 'for then shall prophecy vanish, the grace of healing shall be taken away; the virtue of great abstinence shall be diminished; the words of teaching shall fall silent and the prodigies of miracles will cease.'[62] The faithful will be put to the test, for the true miracles of God's saints will be overshadowed by the huge power of the adversary:

While the holy Church is, as it were, humbled by the removal of miraculous signs [*subtractis signorum uirtutibus*], the just who venerate her for heavenly hope rather than on account of present signs will have their reward multiplied; and the minds of the wicked who oppose her and refuse to seek the invisible things she promises will be quickly made manifest, when they are no longer compelled by visible signs.[63]

In the light of such statements the *Dialogues* almost read like Gregory's attempt to reassure himself, and his readers, that despite appearances, despite even his own apocalyptic mood, the Antichrist is not yet at work, the end not yet at hand. Italy is rich in saints and their works.

[59] See above, p. 56. On the problem of miracles now, see McCready, *Signs*, 16–22; 59–64; Van Uytfanghe, 'Scepticisme doctrinal'.
[60] *Dial.* III.38.3–4; IV.43.1–2.
[61] *Dial.* III.30.7.
[62] *Mor.* XXXIV.3.7; it is noteworthy that the present age is described as the time of healing and teaching in *Mor.* XIX.23.29. On the Antichrist in the 'dessein profond de Dieu', see Savon, 'L'Antéchrist', esp. 397.
[63] *Mor.* XXXIV.3.7; cf. *Mor.* XXXIII.35.60; and see McCready, *Signs of sanctity*, 79–81; Boglioni, *Miracles*, 100–2.

IN ITALY

Unlike his contemporary, Gregory of Tours, Gregory saw God's presence manifested in the work of living holy men rather than by relics of the great saints of past ages.[64] The spiritual landscape of Italy was more suitably mapped by plotting the great works of recent holy men than the shrines of ancient holiness. Collections of miracle-stories had been made before, including the famous collection made by North African clergy to authenticate the miraculous potency of the relics of St Stephen. Augustine had used it in the last book of his *City of God*, which was certainly known to Gregory. Gregory's was to be a collection with a difference. He stated its aim clearly at the outset: he would tell the stories and comment on them, for the recollection of miracles can provide as much edification as the exposition of the scriptures. 'Just as in exposition we learn how to attain virtue and keep it, in the narration of miracles [*signorum*] we learn how this virtue, once acquired, shows itself.'[65] It has been suggested that the significance of miracles in the *Dialogues* is their occurrence: the record of the events constitutes a *Vita* of God. Whereas the martyrs' *Passiones* were a record of human deeds, this is a record of God's. The work has thus been seen as Gregory's alternative to the established forms of ecclesiastical historiography.[66] However this may be, there can be no doubt that moral teaching was Gregory's direct aim. He treated miracles as on a par with the things signified by the words of the scriptures: 'they show one thing through power, they speak of something else through their mystery';[67] miraculous events have a meaning. The *Dialogues* were to be as didactic in their aim as Gregory's preaching on the scriptures; an aim secured by 'constant alternation of reportage and moral or doctrinal reflection' in the work. Like the rest of his work, they are an expression of his pastoral concern. 'For our mind, when it contemplates the possibility of turning to a better life, seeks out whatever it can discover about the better lives of others, and examines the life now of one, now of another holy person' for imitation; and we duly find 'holy men frequently doing wonderful things, performing many miracles ...'.[68] Here, in a homily

---

[64] Though he also recognised, and sometimes preached about, the power of relics: *Dial.* II.38.2–3; III.15.18; IV.21; *HEv* II.32.6–8. For a comparison, see Berschin, *Biographie*, I. 321–4.

[65] *Dial.* Prol. 9. On this, see Boesch Gajano, 'Narratio e expositio', esp. 636–49. Her description of it (quoted below) as 'caratterizzata da una costante alternanza tra narrazioni e riflessioni morali e dottrinali' appears on p. 1.

[66] Cracco, 'Uomini di Dio', esp. 184–5.

[67] *HEv* I.2.1; *vita et non signa quaerenda sunt*: *Dial.* I.12.6. Cf. McCready, *Signs of sanctity*, 59–60; 87, and Boglioni, 'Miracle et nature', 96.

[68] *HEz* II.5.21–2.

preached during the time the *Dialogues* were taking shape in Gregory's mind, is the programme for them. The function of miracle is to manifest holiness.

Both Gregory's notion of miracle and his miracle stories have received much scholarly attention.[69] His miracles are – as they had been since the time of the evangelists – *signa*, external signs of a hidden reality, or *virtutes*, manifestations of power. But Gregory was more guarded about miracles than much of the fashionable literature of his age. Often, though by no means invariably, their significance is clear: the visible event indicates inner virtue or holiness. But for Gregory miracle remained problematic in relation to what it manifests.[70] There is no clear and invariable relation between miracle and holiness, as he famously reminded Augustine, whom he had sent to preach to the heathen English and who was reported to have busied himself performing miracles.[71] Miracles were an optional extra, to help our unbelief, not necessarily an index of greater holiness;[72] Peter walked on the waters, whereas Paul – no less in merit – was shipwrecked.[73] Gregory thought the virtue of patience – and the same goes for other virtues – greater than signs and miracles.[74] Miracles could as easily conceal devilry as they could reveal holiness; or they could leave open the question as to whether they manifested inner pride or humility, faith or heresy.[75] Evil-doers could perform miracles; hypocrites and 'their head', the Antichrist, deceive the faithful with miracles, counterfeiting holiness.[76] The indicative role of miracles is thus not automatic. Their real meaning appears only in the context of the holy man's life, and the interpretative and explanatory context supplied by the hagiographical narrative. In this respect miracles resemble scriptural signs: to understand the significance of miracles a knowledge of what they pointed to was needed, in something like the way that the figurative meaning of a text required antecedent

---

[69] I would refer especially to Boglioni, 'Miracle et nature', and to McCready, *Signs of sanctity*. The former is the first part of an unpublished doctoral dissertation (Toronto, 1974), and contains the fullest treatment of Gregory's conception of the miraculous I know, with indications of what it owes to Augustine. Apart from Adalbert de Vogüé's Introduction to his edition, my account owes most to the work of Sofia Boesch Gajano (see references). I here summarise only what is demanded by the present context.

[70] On the tradition of the 'problematic' nature of miracles, see Van Uytfanghe, 'La controverse biblique et patristique' (on Gregory, 218–19). For Gregory, see De Vogüé, 'Introduction', 85–90.

[71] *Ep.* XI.36. Cf. *Dial.* I.12.6: *vita et non signa quaerenda sunt.*

[72] *Dial.* II.38.3. For a more positive estimate, see *Mor.* XXVII.11.20.

[73] *Dial.* I.12.5.

[74] *Dial.* I.2.8.

[75] *Ep.* XI.36. Compare *HEv* I.4.3; *Mor.* XX.6.16–14.25 for an extended discussion of miracles performed by heretics.

[76] *Mor.* XXXII.15.22–27; XXXIII.35.59–60; XXXIV.18.33 among many; 'head' of hypocrites: *Mor.* XXV.16.34. Cf. McCready, *Signs of sanctity*, 65–83.

awareness of its spiritual sense.[77] *Narratio* and *expositio* complement each
other. The *Dialogues* are thus neither mere moral exhortation, nor mere
collections of miracle-stories; the two things are integrated in moral and
theological reflection.[78]

Compared with the martyrological literature, Gregory's stories are not
of heroic deeds, nor are their actors heroes.[79] The bulk of the stories are of
the modest acts, in the kitchen garden and the monastic farm – 'delightful
miracles'[80] – of lowly men. Though bishops, clergy, monks and hermits
predominate and few lay people appear among the saints of the *Dialogues* –
no doubt reflecting the reports that Gregory received from his largely
clerical or monastic informants – holiness was not quite a monopoly of the
religious professionals.[81] Even lowly lay people can attain the crown of
martyrdom.[82] A story about the famous abbot Equitius, who went about
the countryside in ragged clothes riding a miserable horse, preaching the
gospel to the rustics of Valeria, gives some clue to the weight Gregory gave
to clerical office in relation to holiness. Officious clerical critics had
denounced Equitius to the then pope, for daring to preach though only an
ignorant layman and not even in possession of a papal licence. He was
duly summoned to Rome to explain himself and to be taught proper
ecclesiastical discipline; but he was miraculously vindicated before the
pope's emissary could conduct him to his master.[83]

But the *Dialogues* do not oppose churchmen to ascetics or monks. On the
contrary, one of their chief aims is to show how the two ideals, that of the
cleric and that of the saint, are complementary.[84] There is no single model
of holiness, lay, monastic, or clerical. The holy men we meet here belong
to all the Church's *ordines*, to a variety of social classes, rich and poor, high
and low.[85] Although no stress is laid on the duality of town and countryside, the city is largely absent from the rural setting of most of the stories.
Rome hovers in the background of the *Dialogues*: not as an urban backdrop
to the action (as it had been in the earlier martyrs' legends), but as the

---

[77] See on the above, chapter 3, especially pp. 45–7.
[78] Boesch Gajano, 'La proposta', 648; 'Narratio', 31. Perhaps Gregory had at the back of his mind
Cassian's warning against miracle-stories to the effect they served to satisfy curiosity rather than
edification. Cf. *Conl.* XVIII.1 and *Inst.* Praef. 7.
[79] '*Für das alte Epos gab Gregor die neue Heroengeschichte der Mönchsväter Italiens*': Berschin, *Biographie*, I, 321.
[80] *iocunda miracula*: *Dial.* III.22.4.
[81] Boesch Gajano, 'Proposta', 626–8 gives a full distribution list.
[82] *Dial.* III.26.9.
[83] *Dial.* I.4.10–18.
[84] This is the argument of Cracco, 'Uomini di Dio', esp. 198–9. Cf. Boesch Gajano, 'Proposta', 631, who
rightly criticises Cracco for minimising the significance of the 'hierarchical'.
[85] Boesch Gajano, 'Proposta', 631; and Cracco, 'Chiesa', 367.

wholly christianised ecclesiastical centre to which the religious life of the Italian countryside needs to be related.[86] The ecclesiastical hierarchy must be animated by holiness in its ministry; conversely, the charismatic holy men, the miracle-worker and the free-lance preacher like abbot Equitius, are to be given their proper place within the official religious structure of the Church. The *Dialogues* reveal an image of the christianisation of the countryside as Gregory knew it and as he wanted to encourage it: carried out by holy men in close touch with rural life, but within the structure of the Church.[87] The *Dialogues* were his answer to the need for a new integration of the elements of Christian living, encompassing the *rectores*, the bearers of ecclesiastical authority on the one hand, and the *viri Dei*, the holy men of the Italian countryside on the other.

---

[86] Boesch Gajano, 'Proposta', 633–6.
[87] Cracco, 'Chiesa e cristianità rurale' and 'Ascesa e ruolo'; see also Pietri, 'Clercs et serviteurs', 117.

CHAPTER 5

The Christian community and its neighbours

Traditionally, the human race was composed of three 'peoples' or 'kinds' (*genera*): in the second and third centuries Christians were seen by their pagan contemporaries as the 'third race'. Jews, long familiar to them, were the second, while they themselves – Romans – were, naturally, the first. This schematisation was turned on its head in the course of the christianisation of the Empire. From the Christian point of view, there were still three 'religions', that of the Christians, of the Jews, and of the 'pagans'. This classification risked creating the illusion that 'paganism' was a religion, like Christianity or Judaism; in fact it was simply the rest, those who were neither Christians nor Jews. The Christian community, as we have seen, was now itself seen as composed of an elite of superiors and ascetics and, below them, the ordinary lay Christians.[1] It was surrounded by Jews and by pagans. At the heart of the Christian community were its spiritual elite: the monks.

MONKS AND MONASTERIES

Of all the holy men in sixth-century Italy, Benedict was the one Gregory most admired. He devoted the whole of the second Book of the *Dialogues* to him. There he remarked that Benedict had composed 'a Rule for monks, outstanding in its discernment' (*discretio*).[2] For Gregory, that true artist in the 'art of arts, the governing of souls'[3], *discretio* was the key to the spiritual life.[4] No higher praise of the *Rule* could have come from his pen. Yet, we should not be surprised that when it comes to monastic 'rules', it is not Benedict's that comes to his mind.[5] The reason is not that he did not know

---

[1] See above, chapter 2, pp. 27–8.
[2] *Dial.* II.36: *regulam discretione praecipuam.*
[3] *RP* I.1: *ars est artium regimen animarum.*
[4] See Straw, *Gregory the Great*, 15–16 and note. Cf. *Dial.* II.2. on *doctores animarum.*
[5] This has been established by Hallinger, 'Papst Gregor der Grosse', who has also shown that the parallels (enumerated on p. 274) between Gregory's prescriptions and those of the *RB* can be accounted for without invoking borrowing by Gregory.

it, as has been suggested;[6] it is rather that like others in the sixth century, he did not think of any single monastic rule as normative. A monastic community was governed by the rule of its abbot, not by any particular written document. It may well be the case that when in the seventh century the notion of a written Rule gained ground – along with Benedict's *Rule* (often associated with others, notably that of Columbanus) – in Gaul and in England, that it was at least in part because of the praise heaped upon it by Gregory in the *Dialogues*.[7]

Considering the amount Gregory wrote on the contemplative and the active forms of the Christian life and on Christian virtue, what he wrote on the pattern and institutional forms of communal monastic life is comparatively little.[8] As for John Cassian, and for Benedict, the monastery was the place where the Christian life could be lived most fully; and that meant, opening into the life of contemplation. Gregory thought of himself as a monk: commenting on the verse 'Whoever of you does not renounce all that he has cannot be my disciple' (Luke 14:33) he said to his mixed group of hearers, composed of monks, clergy, *religiosi*:[9] 'This applies to us too: for we, who have renounced the world and seek the secret of the ascetic life [*remotioris vitae secretum*] are called monks.'

To be a monk, as Gregory explained on this occasion, was to have renounced the world and to have embraced 'the ardent quest for the vision of our Creator'. He had never resolved, as we have seen, the ambiguity inherent in his valuation of the contemplative and the active lives (see chapter 2). They were complementary: like Saul's daughters (1 Sam 14:49), 'they differ but they agree' (*differunt et conveniunt*) in tending towards the one life of love.[10] The difference lies in which of the two predominates. The monastic life was an ascesis directed towards the contemplative life. It was the 'good and straight road' to eternal life, quicker than the twisting roads of the world.[11]

Gregory touched on the specific character of life lived in monastic communities (including nunneries: I do not distinguish them), mainly in his

---

[6] Gregory's knowledge of the *Rule* has been called into question by Hallinger, 'Papst Gregor der Grosse', but it is now generally agreed that he did know it; clinched by allusions to the *Rule* in *I Reg.* (especially to *RB* 58 in IV.70).

[7] Suggested, for instance, by Meyvaert, in his contribution to the discussion of Prinz, 'Das westliche Mönchtum', 135.

[8] As remarked by Gillet, 'Spiritualité', 325, it is mainly concentrated in *I Reg.* On this, see De Vogüé, 'Les vues'; qualifications: 41–2.

[9] *I Reg.* I.61. On the audience, see p. 32.

[10] *I Reg.* v.179.

[11] *I Reg.* v. 41–2. Cf. see De Vogüé, 'Les vues', 60; 224–5. He notes (64) that compared with the *Moralia* and the Homilies, this commentary 'places the accent on the contemplative aspiration of the monastic life' rather than on continence; and stresses obedience (229–31).

Commentary on I Kings. His letters contain some practical advice or regulation for individual cases. Monasteries, 'if they are of the way of God, they have within them the fountain of wisdom through the grace of compunction', and will not need droplets of advice from Gregory's dry well.[12] But many, especially in the ravaged province of Italy, did need Gregory's help. It has been estimated that more than two hundred of his letters are concerned with questions of monastic order and discipline, male and female, in Italy alone.[13] They deal with the internal order of the communities and their arrangements, admission to the novitiate, questions concerning property rights, and, of course the conduct of individuals; with regulating the relations between monastic communities and their local bishops; and those between monks and clergy.

In Italy the lines along which monastic life had developed before Gregory's time had been haphazard.[14] The Council of Chalcedon (451) had laid down some rules, and Dionysius Exiguus added some others, in a collection which was the Roman see's quasi-official collection of canons. Justinian's legislation covered many facets of monastic life, systematising existing practices.[15] Gregory followed the traditional usages as laid down since Chalcedon and incorporated into imperial law.[16] In some cases he preferred the somewhat stricter ecclesiastical usage to what was laid down by law, as, for instance, when he refused to allow marriage to be unilaterally dissolved if only one partner wished to enter the monastic state.[17] He strongly disliked imperial legislation which extended the range of prohibitions on entry into monastic life; but in obedience to the emperor, he accepted it with good grace.[18]

Everywhere Gregory wished to enforce the rules of chastity, poverty, obedience and perseverance in one community which were laid down by Benedict for his monks, but also widely recognised as binding. Local bishops were to have general supervision of monasteries in their areas: over the election of superiors, and breaches of internal discipline. Many instances of the latter arose from transgression of the boundaries that separated the monastery from the secular world or from the Church at large. How the clerical and the monastic lives were to be related was an old question, to which different answers had been given. Jerome, character-

---

[12] *Ep.* VII.27: *si de via Dei sunt . . . per compunctionis gratiam fontem sapientiae intus habent . . .*
[13] Jenal, 'La vie monastique', 148; for summary, 151–2.
[14] On all these themes now Jenal, *Italia ascetica*, gives the fullest accounts.
[15] Jenal, *Italia ascetica*, 811–23.
[16] See the summary by Jenal, *Italia ascetica*, 827–30.
[17] *Ep.* XI.30; cf. *Nov.* 123.40. Cf. *Ep.* VI.49.
[18] See Chapter 6, pp. 87–8; on the conditions, Jenal, *Italia ascetica*, 770–76; 818–20.

istically, had said, dividing the clerical from the monastic profession and in praise, of course, of his own monastic vocation, that 'the monk's business is one thing; the cleric's another; the clergy feed the flock; I am part of the flock being fed';[19] Augustine, by contrast, is the best known of the Latin fathers to have combined the two professions in the monastic community he organised for his own clergy.[20] For Gregory, the distinction between the two professions overlapped the distinction between the contemplative and the active lives. It is not surprising, therefore, to find that his practice should provide examples both of insisting on the separation of the two, and of combining them.[21] It exhibits the same tension and the same integration as does his personal life. Gregory's instincts told him that the clerical and the monastic lives do not mix; and he did not like clerics living in monastic communities, where their presence could lead to trouble.[22] On the other hand, he entrusted special missions – including, famously, the mission he sent to England – to monks and chose monks from his own monastery for episcopal office. He preferred himself to live surrounded by monks, and recommended a form of monastic community as the most suitable form of living for a missionary bishop with his clergy.[23] His decisions on this, as on so many other matters, seem to have been guided by what he considered best to meet the particular pastoral needs of each situation.

The other problem which cropped up frequently involved the relations between bishops and monasteries within their diocese. Gregory insisted on the duty of local bishops to supervise such communities, while at the same time restricting their power to interfere in their internal affairs or their property rights. The privileges accorded to monasteries conformed to the framework of canonical and legal provisions. In one troublesome instance in Ravenna Gregory did darkly threaten the bishop with resorting to other means if his supervision were unjustly to burden local monasteries.[24] That Gregory was thinking of anything like the exemption accorded to Bobbio a quarter of a century after his death by pope Honorius I is unlikely, but possible. It was the Irishman Columbanus, 'a

---

[19] *Ep.* 14.8.

[20] A full sketch of the development in Rudmann, *Mönchtum*, Introduction. I have discussed the 'blurring of the frontiers' in *The end*, 181–98.

[21] Rudmann, chapter 3, ¶2 is actually devoted to Gregory's 'conflicting' decisions, where full details are given.

[22] E. g. *Epp.* v.1; vii.40; viii.17; i.40; iv.11 etc. It is striking that many of Gregory's anxieties on this score were concentrated in Ravenna. Cf. chapter 10, pp. 152–4.

[23] In his reply to Augustine, *Responsum* 1 (Bede, *HE* I.27). On the *Responsa* to Augustine's questions, see below, p. 184.

[24] *Ep.* vii.40; cf. chapter 10, p. 152.

foreigner in a strange land', who gave currency to notions of this kind in the Merovingian kingdom.[25] In Gaul, too, the privileges that Gregory granted conformed with royal provisions.[26] In his monastic practice Gregory remained, as the most meticulously full survey concludes, 'entirely within a traditional framework'.[27]

DIVERSITY WITHIN UNITY

The author of the *Regula pastoralis* is not likely to have forgotten the rules he had laid down for himself along with his fellow bishops at the start of his ministry. That book had been Gregory's personal therapy of reconciliation to a style of life and work he had not sought. Humility made him accept the burden laid upon him; and having accepted it, he had to formulate – for himself, in the first place – the principles that were to guide the pastor's life and work. The work was to build Jerusalem:

> The heavenly Jerusalem is built as a city (Ps. 121:3) insomuch as that vision of its inner peace [Jerusalem = *visio pacis*] is constructed from the congregation of its holy citizens ... In the holy Church each supports his neighbour and is in his turn supported by his neighbour; they support each other so that the building of charity might arise from them.[28]

But the Church is built of living stones; and what the pastor should above all be aware of is the great diversity in the make-up of individual souls.[29] The artist 'building the community' is like a musician:

> The same exhortation is not suitable for all ... Therefore the discourse of teachers should be formed according to the quality of their hearers so that it may meet the needs of each one; but, nevertheless, it should never lose from sight the art of building the community [*a communis aedificationis arte nunquam recedat*]. For what are the attentive minds of hearers, if not as it were the taut strings of a harp, which the artist plucks in diverse ways, so that sounding together they do not produce discordant music? Thus the strings, though plucked with the same plectrum, because not plucked in the same way all at once, will produce a harmonious sound. So in order that he might build all into the one virtue of charity, every teacher must touch the hearts of his hearers with the same teaching, but with a diversity of exhortation.[30]

---

[25] See the fine sketch by Wallace-Hadrill, *The Frankish Church*, 65–70.

[26] The privileges (*Epp.* XIII.9–11) granted to the monastery founded in Autun by queen Brunhild and bishop Syagrius were clearly drawn up at Brunhild's court and submitted to Gregory.

[27] Jenal, *Italia ascetica*, 830: 'durchaus im traditionellen Rahmen'.

[28] *HEz* II.1.5. Cf. chapter 2, n. 39, and *Mor.* XXXIV.12.23.

[29] *Mor.* VI.37.57: *magnopere sciendum est quia valde inter se diversae sunt conspersiones animarum*.

[30] *Mor.* XXX.3.12.

Here, in germ, is the project of the *Regula pastoralis*.[31] As we have seen, Gregory had often thought on these lines. Diversity in unity was the keynote of his conception of the Christian community. It became the guiding thread of the pastoral principles formulated in the *Regula pastoralis*; and this it remained throughout his practice as a bishop.[32]

It is perhaps at this point that we touch one of the vital points at which personality, theology and reflection meet in Gregory's work as a bishop. He liked to think of the Church as the assemblage of a multitude of individual churches each under its own bishop. 'The pillars of heaven tremble' (Job 26:11): the pillars of heaven can be understood, Gregory comments, 'as the churches which in their multiplicity together constitute the one Catholic [Church] spread over the whole world'.[33] Gregory conceived each individual community under its own bishop as a Church in its own right. He took this conception so seriously that he found any expression that seemed to undermine it – even in a formula of customary honorific titulature – deeply offensive.[34] The multiplicity of churches necessarily made the Church a 'concordant diversity of members' (*concors membrorum diversitas*).[35] 'Safeguarding the unity of the sacrament, the Church gathers together the faithful peoples according to the manifold variety of their customs (*mores*) and languages.'[36] The purpose of organisation and hierarchy in the Church was to foster diversity within unity.[37]

Such platitudes of ecclesiology would have been more widely accepted and affirmed than acted upon. For Gregory, however, they constituted guidelines for practical decisions. The best known example of such a decision is his reply to the question addressed to him by Augustine from Canterbury concerning the rite in which the mass should be celebrated there: Augustine knew, Gregory answered, the ritual of the Roman Church, in which he had been brought up and loved; he had found other customs observed in Gaul (and perhaps – though Gregory did not say so and may not have known – in Canterbury by the queen and her Frankish

---

[31] As Gregory actually says in the following paragraph: *ibid.*, 13. Cf. chapter 2, n. 10, where parallels are noted. The image is most fully developed in *RP* III, Prol., where the image of the musician producing harmony recurs.

[32] I borrow the heading of this section from Meyvaert, 'Diversity within unity', a very full account on which it would be hard to improve.

[33] *Mor.* XVII.29.43: *ipsas ecclesias . . . quae multae unam catholicam faciunt toto terrarum orbe diffusam.* Cf. *Mor.* XIX.12.19; *HEz* II.3.12.

[34] On the title of 'ecumenical patriarch', see chapter 6, pp. 91–4.

[35] *Mor.* XXVIII.10.23. Cf. the whole section, 21–4.

[36] *Mor.* XXX.6.22; VI.32.50; XVI.55.68.

[37] See *Ep.* v.59, one of Gregory's most hierarchically conceived letters: *ut, dum reverentiam minores potioribus exhiberent et potiores minoribus dilectionem impenderent, una concordiae fieret ex diversitate contextio et recte officiorum gereretur administratio singulorum.* Cf. chapter 6, p. 86. at n. 14.

chaplain); let him choose from the several churches and collect together whatever was pleasing to God and to the English, new to the faith. For, Gregory wrote memorably, 'things should not be valued on account of their place [of origin], but rather places on account of the good things [they produce].[38] Such sentiments are entirely characteristic of Gregory's mind.[39] He followed the same principles in a number of cases that came to him. He had been accused, for example, of having introduced various new liturgical practices borrowed from the Greeks, in Constantinople or in Jerusalem. No, Gregory replied, taking each case in turn; he had either restored or improved Roman usages. 'Nevertheless, if the [Constantinopolitan] or any other Church has anything good, I am happy that I or my subjects, to whom I forbid anything illicit, should follow it in what is good. It is the height of stupidity to think oneself the first in such a way as to spurn to learn the good things one may come across.'[40] Similarly, when bishop Leander of Seville put to him a query about baptism by triple immersion (as was the usage of the Roman Church) or single immersion (adopted by the Catholics in Spain in contrast with the Arians' triple immersion), Gregory conceded the legitimacy of the existing custom: 'in the Church, because united in one faith, diversity of usages does no harm'.[41] In North Africa Gregory disliked the customary arrangements for the succession in the office of provincial primate. Although he thought them harmful and likely to facilitate heresy, he nevertheless conceded to the Numidian bishops the continuance of their usages which, he wrote, 'appear to have nothing inconsistent with the Catholic faith'.[42] On dating Easter, Irish practice differed from Gallic. Columbanus wrote from Gaul to Gregory expressing surprise why the pope had not long ago 'scraped away' the deviant custom. Gregory had replied through his agent, Candidus, to the effect that 'what has been confirmed by long passage of time cannot be changed'; but this was unacceptable to the Irish monk: 'clearly the error is of long standing; but truth has always stood longer, and is its refutation'.[43] Columbanus persisted; but to three representations he

---

[38] *Resp.* 2 (Bede, *HE* I.27): *non enim pro locis res, sed pro bonis rebus loca amanda sunt.* For commentary, and the textual problem at the end of the passage, see Meyvaert, 'Diversity within unity', 142–5.

[39] As has been shown by Meyvaert, who refers (145) to writers who have founded their rejection of the authenticity of the *Responsa* (or this particular one) on the impossibility of any pope, or Roman, writing such things. Chadwick, Gregory and the Anglo-Saxons', 209 quotes *Ep.* VII.29: *Non enim loca vel ordines creatori nostro nos proximos faciunt, sed ei nos aut merita bona iungunt aut mala distingunt.*

[40] *Ep.* IX.26; for comment, see Meyvaert, 'Diversity within unity', 158–60.

[41] *Ep.* I.41: *quia in una fide nil officit sanctae ecclesiae consuetudo diversa.* On the Spanish Church, see chapter II, pp. 164–8.

[42] *Ep.* I.75; for details, see pp. 194–5.

[43] Columbanus, *Ep.* I.4; 12 (trans. Walker). Cf. *Ep.* 2.5: *multum … nocuit nocetque ecclesiasticae paci morum diversitas et varietas traditionum …*

made to the pope there was no reply:[44] a lack of communication that Columbanus attributed to Satan's preventing his letters reaching the pope.[45]

The disagreement about the date of Easter was less important than the divergence of principle over variety of customs. Columbanus could have claimed the authority of Leo, and older precedent.[46] In a famous letter Pope Innocent I (401–17) had written to bishop Decentius of Gubbio:

> If bishops wanted to keep the ecclesiastical institutions as they were handed down by the apostles in their integrity, there would be no diversity, no variety in the rituals of orders and consecration. But because each one thinks he should observe not what has been handed down but what seems good to himself, different views and different observances are seen in the various churches . . . Who does not know or realise that everyone should observe that which has been handed down by Peter the prince of the apostles to the Roman Church which guards it still; or that noone should introduce or add anything which has no authority, or to receive anything from another source? . . . They should follow what the Roman Church has kept, from which they [the other churches] have without doubt originated . . .[47]

The contrast between Gregory's and Innocent's views has often been noted. Gregory's attitude may be unexpected, and it is anomalous if Innocent's – or some later views, such as Gregory VII's prohibition of the use of Slavonic in the liturgy in Bohemia; or his insistence on the Roman rite in Spain – are taken as representing a papal norm. Gregory (I) nevertheless has a good claim to a place in a respectable tradition. Boethius had spoken in much the same way of the Catholic Church *per orbem diffusa* being bound by the authority of the scriptures, by universal tradition, and by its own customs; but, he went on to qualify this, 'it is bound by this tradition, as it is by the universal tradition of the fathers, but each [individual Church] exists and is governed by its own constitution and its own customs according to the diversity of places and the judgement of each'.[48] Boethius did not think he was making any outrageous or even remarkable statement: he was echoing Augustine, and probably a widely current view.[49]

---

[44] *Ep.* 2.5.

[45] *Ep.* 3.2.

[46] Leo I *Ep.* 96 had written to the bishop of Arles on the same matter: *Ad praecipuam religionis nostrae pertinet sacramentum ut in festivitate paschali nulla sit toto orbe diversitas . . .*

[47] *Ep.* 25.1–2 (*PL* 20, 551–2). On Innocent I, see below, chapter 12, pp. 201–2.

[48] *De fide catholica*, 257–65.

[49] *Epp.* 36.9.22; 54.1.1–2.2. Cf. John the deacon (perhaps the later pope John I, and sometimes suspected of being the author of Boethius's tractate), *Ep. ad Senarium*, 13 (*PL* 59, 406).

CHRISTIANS AND JEWS

Writing to a bishop of Naples, a city which, like so many others in the
Mediterranean world, contained a fair sized Jewish community, Gregory
recommended him to seek to convert them by reason, 'demonstrating to
them what we say from their own books'.[50] Jews and Christians shared a
Bible and a history. This was the framework both for their debates and for
their self-definition in relation to each other. In the Christian view, as
Gregory put it, the Jews had 'the letter of the law'; they do not have 'the
state of illumination but the affliction of blindness'.[51] 'They are blind, in
that although they hear of the signs which blazed forth to announce the
Redeemer to their fathers, they nevertheless do not believe the reality
[signified by the signs] to have come about. Thus they are blind not by failing to see what has been promised, but by not believing in its realisation.'[52]
Over the centuries, the *topos* of Jewish blindness has made its sinister contribution to the ominous stereotyping of the Jews in the Christian
imagination.[53] For Gregory, as for Christian writers before him, it was in
the first place the basis for a Christian hermeneutic of the Old
Testament.[54] It was such a re-interpretation of their own scripture that
Gregory recommended the bishop of Naples to undertake with the Jews
of his city. Biblical hermeneutics, polemic and proselytism could thus
converge in the actual relations of a Christian and a Jewish community in
a late Roman city. On rare occasions we can see something like this taking
place: in a debate, for instance, between a Frankish king and a Jew
reported (and joined) by Gregory of Tours.[55]

Jews and Christians shared much of their past and their scriptures; but
within Christendom the Jews were a foreign body: 'a society within a
society, a pearl for ever irritating the oyster'.[56] Their place in Roman
society was defined, with growing severity, by imperial legislation.[57] Jews
and Christians could live together in relative amity, mixing freely in
Roman towns, even frequenting each other's places of worship. There

---

[50] *Ep.* XIII.13.
[51] *1 Reg.* III.5: *non habet statum luminis sed lapsum caecitatis*. The theme is too common in Gregory, as in
patristic literature in general, to illustrate. Cf. Blumenkranz, *Juifs*, 239–78.
[52] *Ibid.*, II.49.
[53] Cf. Cracco Ruggini, 'Pagani, ebrei', 98–9 on polemic leading to conflict.
[54] I discuss this theme in my *Signs and meanings*, 1–70. For a particularly perceptive study of this theme, see
Fredriksen, 'Excaecati', esp. 320–2.
[55] *HF* VI.5.
[56] Wallace-Hadrill, *The Frankish Church*, 53.
[57] The legislation is gathered, in English translation, with useful notes and bibliographies, in Linder, *The
Jews*.

were occasions of friction, as Gregory's correspondence testifies. Some arose from proselytism – Jewish or Christian; most had their roots in offence being taken at obtrusive celebration of Jewish festivals, at the location of Jewish places of worship, or the ownership of Christian slaves by Jewish masters. All these matters were regulated by law.

It was to the law that Gregory appealed as the sanction of his own decisions: 'Just as Jews in their communities are not to be allowed to breach the limits which the law lays down for them, so in those things which are permitted to them their rights are not to be violated.'[58] This principle is laid down in the preamble to a letter in which Gregory deals with the complaints – apparently against some act of expropriation for the purpose of establishing a church – of some Jews from Palermo. He tells the bishop to look into their complaints, and in case of disagreement, to arrange for each side to appoint arbitrators to decide the question as may be fair (*quae aequitate conveniunt*), referring the matter to him in case of continued dispute, in the meanwhile suspending the intended consecration. As the bishop, however, had gone on to consecrate a church on the occupied land, Gregory ordered the Jews to be compensated both for the land and for the books and equipment that were removed; 'so that they are in no way oppressed or allowed to suffer any injustice'.[59] Debts to Jewish lenders are to be conscientiously repaid, and their IOUs returned to them when they repay theirs;[60] they are not to be deprived of their synagogues;[61] they are not to be prevented from celebrating their festivals;[62] if noisy synagogue celebrations interfere with worship in the nearby church, the Jewish community is to be found, as the law provided, alternative accommodation.[63] It seems that Gregory often went further to safeguard Jewish interests than Justinian's legislation laid down; perhaps following older customs sanctioned by previous legislation.[64]

If Jewish communities and individuals were to be given their rights as defined by law, to be protected against expropriation, against official or episcopal harassment or other injustice, Gregory was no less determined that they should be made to abide by the legal restrictions imposed on

---

[58] *Ep.* VIII.25: *sicut Iudaeis non debet esse licentia quicquam in synagogis suis ultra quam permissum est lege praesumere, ita in his quae eis concessa sunt nullum debent praeiudicium sustinere.* The principle is often repeated: *Epp.* IX.38; II.45.

[59] *Ep.* IX.38.

[60] *Ep.* IX.40; I.42.

[61] *Ep.* I.34 (cf. *Ep.* II.45 for the sequel); IX.196 on a synagogue invaded by a Jewish convert to Christianity.

[62] *Ep.* XIII.13.

[63] *Ep.* II.45.

[64] Katz, 'Pope Gregory'; cf. *CJ* I.9.13, to be compared with the milder *CTh* XVI.20. Sometimes, however, Gregory's decisions were harsher: e. g. the case in *Ep.* II.6: cf. Blumenkranz, *Juifs*, 312.

them. Aside from minor irregularities,[65] the principal cause of his concern were contraventions of the rules controlling the ownership of Christian slaves by Jews. Justinian's legislation here tightened earlier practice. It sought altogether to outlaw Jewish ownership of non-Jewish slaves, and laid down heavy punishments for any infringement.[66] The bishops and the churches' *defensores* were to be responsible for the execution of these laws along with the imperial functionaries.[67] Gregory generally followed the provisions of this legislation: '[The Jews] are not permitted to have Christian slaves.'[68] The authorities and the bishops – Gregory included – were evidently motivated mainly by fear of Jewish proselytism and sought to protect slaves, either Christian or potential Christian converts, against pressures of this kind.

In his dealings with rulers outside the imperial frontiers, Gregory also advocated the strict prohibitions of the imperial legislation on Jews owning Christian slaves. In Spain, king Reccared was complimented on having enacted what had been reported to Gregory as 'an excellent constitution against the Jews', despite Jewish attempts to bribe him.[69] The edict enacted at the Council of Toledo in 589 (c. 14) at the initiative of the bishops marks the beginning of the long history of repressive legislation in the Visigothic kingdom and Church, tightly allied. In the Frankish kingdom the absence of a similarly centralised state, and the importance of Jewish communities, especially in the cities of Provence, prevented such drastic action being taken against Jews. Thus in Narbonne, Jews were free to have Christian slaves;[70] and Jewish slave traders were able to acquire Christian slaves in Gaul.[71] Gregory urged the adoption of laws similar to those in force within imperial territories, prohibiting the possession of Christian slaves by Jews.[72]

The only consistent thread in Gregory's policies with regard to the Jews is his adherence to Roman law. In Italy he often softened its rigour, but on the whole he adhered to its prescriptions.[73] Within imperial territory he

---

[65] E. g. *Ep.* I.66: a Jew who had bought church vessels was to be compelled to restore them (and the clergy who had sold them were to be punished).

[66] Linder, *The Jews*, 82–5 gives a useful summary of the history of imperial legislation on this subject. Also Blumenkranz, *Juifs*, 326–41.

[67] *CJ* I.3.54. The legislation applied to Jews, pagans and heretics.

[68] *Ep.* II.45 lays down the general principle. For individual cases see *Epp.* III.37; IV.9; 21; VI.29; 30 (pagan slaves of Samaritans); VII.21; IX.105 (treatment of Christian slaves acquired by Jews before their disposal – cf. also *Ep.* VI.29).

[69] *Ep.* IX.229 (cf chapter 11, p. 167).

[70] *Ep.* VII.21. The rector Candidus was instructed to redeem them.

[71] *Ep.* IX.105 (Christian slaves purchased in Gaul by Jewish merchants in Naples on official instructions).

[72] *Epp.* IX.214; 216.

[73] Cf. Blumenkranz, *Les Juifs*, 205.

wanted the law to be observed; outside its boundaries he wanted to see it adopted. If this produces the impression of harshness, his insistence on the freedoms which Roman law allowed to Jews must weigh on the other side of the balance. In contrast with what was apt to happen in Gaul, as his Jewish informants had complained,[74] Gregory urged that Jews were not to be forcibly baptised. The gradual eclipse of Roman law left Jewish communities more exposed to mob violence and clerical pressure. A famous incident in 576 in Clermont showed what could happen. Clermont was a divided city; the Jews had been involved in the civic conflict not far beneath the surface of urban life. The bishop, Avitus, was a keen proselytiser, though he insisted he 'did not use force to compel [the Jews] to confess the Son of God'; but his preaching must have helped to raise the temperature. Minor local conflicts led to violence, in the course of which a Christian mob destroyed the synagogue. The bishop restored peace by baptising more than five hundred of the Jews. The rest emigrated to Marseille.[75] As Venantius Fortunatus, who celebrated the incident in a poem, was clearly aware, a new, united, cohesive Christian community had come into being. Clermont was a Christian city, cleansed of its Jews.[76] In a society whose boundaries came more and more to be defined by religion, there was less and less room for the anomalous. The Jew had no definable place in the social structure and became an outsider.

Roman law had given the Jews a place in society: they were Roman citizens.[77] In trying consistently to treat them as such, Gregory belonged to a world whose days, in much of Western Europe, were now numbered.[78] He wished Jews to be converted by preaching, not by force: 'those who do not accept the Christian religion should be brought to the unity of the faith', he wrote to a bishop who had harassed the local Jews, 'by kindness and generosity, by admonition and persuasion; otherwise people who might be won over to believing by the sweetness of preaching and the fear of the coming judgement will be repulsed by threats and pressure'.[79] This did not exclude reinforcing preaching with a little extra aid; conversion

---

[74] *Ep.* 1.45. Chilperic was reported to have ordered Jews to be baptised: Gregory of Tours, *HF* vi.5.

[75] Gregory of Tours, *HF* v.11. On it, see Brennan, 'The conversion', who stresses 'the fragile social cohesion' (325) of the city.

[76] *Carmen* v.5: [Avitus] *iunxit ovile sub uno, et grege de niveo gaudia pastor habet* (ll. 135–6). Brennan rightly points out that both accounts, and especially Fortunatus's, 'stress not social tension and disruption but rather the sense of social cohesion' (321).

[77] Cf. Wallace-Hadrill, *The Frankish Church*, 391–2.

[78] In the seventh century the conditions of the Jews deteriorated everywhere: Colorni, 'Gli Ebrei', 243.

[79] *Ep.* 1.34; Cf. *Ep.* xiii.13.

might be made easy, even, perhaps, profitable. If you want to bring outsiders to the Christian religion, Gregory wrote with engaging frankness,
you should do it 'with the aid of a little blandishment rather than with
harshness'.[80] Thus tenants on church lands were a valuable asset; if any
Jewish tenants want to become Christians, let them have some remission of
their rent, if only to encourage others.[81] Preaching, persuasion, induce-
ments: but no force, no pressure, no coercion.

CHRISTIANS AND PAGANS

Pagans were a different matter altogether. They, too, were called to God's
kingdom; they are the *locus* of His mercy.[82] God had sent his chosen
preachers 'to the ends of the earth for the ministry of preaching'.[83]
Preaching to bishops assembled in his cathedral Gregory said 'Behold, the
world is full of priests, and yet workmen in the Lord's harvest are hard to
find, because although we have taken on the priestly office, we do not fulfil
its obligations'.[84] Preaching to believers and to non-believers[85] was – by
definition – the solemn duty laid upon the clergy. Mission and the pastoral
ministry formed an indissoluble unity.[86]

For Gregory and his contemporaries 'paganism' embraced a spectrum
of beliefs and practices. Beyond the imperial frontiers there were peoples,
such as the English (see chapter 11), who had not yet heard the word of
God preached to them and were untouched by the waters of baptism. In
most of the Germanic kingdoms which had in former times been a part of
the Empire, however, rulers had been converted to Catholic Christianity,
and their subjects had for the most part followed the rulers to the font. The
Lombards in Italy as we shall see (chapter 7), were something of an exception: in Gregory's time a mixed nation of non-Christians, Arians and
schismatic Christians, they presented special problems. Everywhere, even
in Gregory's Italy, forms of behaviour and observance embedded in a
traditional culture long remained resistant to innovating pressure by
Christian clergy. Episcopal preoccupations with 'paganism', especially in
remote rural corners of their dioceses, were often anxieties about suspect

---

[80] *Ep.* XIII.13.
[81] *Epp.* II.50; V.7; VIII.23.
[82] *Mor.* XXVII.34.58: *locus autem misericordiae Dei est ipsa gentilitas*. Cf. Benkart, *Die Missionsidee*, 19–29 for this idea and references to many parallels.
[83] *1 Reg.* III.35. Cf. *Mor.* IX.9.10; XXVII.11.19–21; XXVIII.6.15; XXIX.25.50; *HEv* I.4.1; I.19.1; II.29.2. etc.
[84] *HEv* I.17.3.
[85] Kahl, 'Die ersten Jahrhunderte', 48, draws attention to *Mor.* XXIX.31.72, but exaggerates the significance of the distinction Gregory here makes between preaching within and outside the Church.
[86] Cf. chapter 11, n. 102.

customs in communities of baptised Christians which they saw as 'pagan'.[87]

Gregory also knew of paganism still very much alive in Italy and, especially, the islands; it shaded off into magic, witchcraft and customs Gregory thought 'idolatrous'. They were practised by people who had never been baptised, as well as by Christian converts who had relapsed into their former ways or had never abandoned them completely. Gregory did not make any sharp distinction between these different groups, and his vocabulary to describe them is fluid.[88] They were all idolatrous, godless, and to be corrected by bishops, sometimes assisted by the rectors of the Church's patrimonies[89] or coerced by ecclesiastical personnel or the civil authorities or both acting together.[90] In Corsica Christians had apparently relapsed into their old idolatrous ways and were to be corrected by penance to be inflicted by a bishop.[91] There is more evidence for paganism in Sardinia, especially the North of the island. The bishopric of Fausiana was to be revived there to deal with the 'pagans [whom] we know to be remaining there and living in the manner of beasts (*ferino degentes modo*) ignorant of the worship of God'.[92] But it was not only the bishop who was to exert himself in their conversion. Gregory was horrified to learn that local dignitaries were accepting bribes to permit baptised Christians to carry on idolatrous rituals.[93] Landowners were told they had a responsibility for their tenants' (*rustici*) souls and must not permit idolatry on their properties.[94] Peasants on church lands reluctant to 'come to God' must be 'so burdened with rent that the weight of this punitive exaction should make them hasten to righteousness'.[95] Military commanders and civil officials were expected to bring pagans 'to the service of Christ'.[96] Those

---

[87] I have discussed these problems at length in *The end*, especially 1–17; and for the sixth century, in 'From Caesarius to Boniface'.

[88] Thus the distinctions between 'christianisation' and 'de-paganisation', or mission as extra-ecclesial evangelisation as against intra-ecclesial 'after-care' which have been distinguished by modern writers (cf. Kahl, 'Die ersten Jahrhunderte', 40–2, 45–59, who seems to me to attribute far too sharp a distinction to Gregory, esp. 55) are not applicable to Gregory. His usage of terms such as *idolater, gentilis, infidelis, paganus* still needs systematic investigation.

[89] *Ep.* VIII.19 (Terracina: tree-worship); *Ep.* IX.103 (new clergy to be ordained to deal with *infidelitas* and *gentilium cultus*); *Epp.* V.32; VII.41 (both in Sicily).

[90] *Ep.* III.59 (praetor and rector: *idolorum cultores atque Angelliorum dogmatis*); *Ep.* V.7 (the rector: Manichees); *Ep.* XI.33 (the rector: *incantatores atque sortilegos*); *Ep.* XIV.1 (a *scholasticus* is praised for his severity against *maleficos*).

[91] *Ep.* VIII.1: relapsed *neglegentia aut necessitate faciente*.

[92] *Ep.* IV.29.

[93] *Ep.* V.38. On the background to this rural 'paganism', see Boesch-Gajano, 'Teoria e pratica', esp. 185–7.

[94] *Ep.* IV.23. Clients of wealthy people were expected to 'come into the Church': cf. *Ep.* VII.8.

[95] *Ep.* IV.26.

[96] *Ep.* IV.25; cf. XI.12.

who would not mend their ways when admonished by the bishop's preaching must be punished: slaves by beating and torture, freemen by being jailed and subjected to penance.[97] A Sardinian chieftain, duke Hospito, had become a Christian, apparently alone among his tribe while the rest still lived 'like animals, knew not the true God and worshipped sticks and stones'; he was exhorted to bring to Christ all he could of his subjects and have them baptised, and to cooperate with a bishop and a monk Gregory had sent for the purpose.[98]

This was the general pattern of Gregory's missionary strategy. Bishops and ecclesiastical personnel were to work together with rulers and the local authorities – whoever they were – in bringing about the conversion of non-Christians or of baptised Christians whose religious observances were censured as idolatrous. He naturally adopted the same strategy when he sent his monk Augustine to convert the heathen English (see chapter 11). His request to the newly converted king Aethelberht was the same as he had made to duke Hospito in Sardinia: to strive to extend the Christian faith among the people subject to him. The paradigm held up for the king was the emperor Constantine: 'the most religious emperor who converted the Roman state [*rempublicam*] from the false worship of idols and subjected it along with himself to almighty God and our Lord Jesus Christ, turning to Him with all his heart together with the peoples subject to him ...'.[99] The unquestioned model behind Gregory's missionary enterprise was the long-established pattern of the coercive regime of the Christian Roman Empire. Force was acceptable, even a normal means, for the propagation of the faith.[100] It was only when the realities of the situation among the English became known to him, and when their significance sank into his mind, that he abandoned the strategy that he had instinctively adopted, along with the Roman imperial heritage.[101] The lesson was not lost on the missionaries at work in the borderlands of the Frankish kingdom in the following generations.[102]

---

[97] *Ep.* IX.205 (*idolorum cultores vel aruspicum atque sortilegorum*).
[98] *Ep.* IV.27.
[99] *Ep.* XI.37. Further, see pp. 181–2.
[100] Cf. *Ep.* I.73, quoted in chapter 6, n.13.
[101] I have dealt with this in more detail in 'Gregory the Great and a papal missionary strategy', and in 'Gregory the Great's Europe'.
[102] See Fritze, '*Universalis gentium confessio*'.

CHAPTER 6

Christiana respublica:
within the confines of the Empire

THE CHURCH IN THE EMPIRE AFTER JUSTINIAN

Before Gregory's time Christianity had spread beyond the confines of the
Empire, both in East and West. From the river Indus to the Irish Sea
and beyond, outposts of Christianity could be found in organised communities, often under bishops, though not always in full conformity
with the standard pattern current within the Empire. Missionaries had
penetrated to remoter areas of China and India. The core of the Christian
Church, however, was and remained within the *imperium Christianum*.
Ancient habits of thought encouraged the identification of the Empire
as the natural setting of Christianity and its divinely sanctioned
vehicle. Since Constantine the emperors – the short-lived Julian excepted
– had identified themselves as Christian; increasingly, since the time of
the Theodosian dynasty, the religion of the emperors had become the
religion of the Empire. The Germanic kingdoms of Western Europe,
established on what had been imperial territory, though they could still
be seen in an imperial perspective (see below, pp. 95–6), in fact now
curtailed the reach of imperial authority. We have become accustomed
to see Gregory's pontificate in terms of two spheres of action which had
thus taken distinctive shape in the course of the preceding century and
a half: within the Empire, and beyond its boundaries.[1] The diversity of
the political conditions in which he had to act inevitably imposes such a
distinction.

Within the Empire, Gregory's Church was the imperial Church shaped
by Justinian's legislation, rounding off the work of his Christian predecessors.[2] This was both the major sphere of his activities, and the permanent
backdrop to his awareness of his world. Under Justinian the Church had

[1] For a magisterial account of Gregory's pontificate in such terms, see Caspar, *Geschichte*, 2, 306–514.
[2] Gregory's knowledge of Justinian's legislation seems to have been established by Damizia, *Lineamenti*,
who has traced over 100 instances of parallels in Gregory's correspondence.

become a public institution of the first importance, and had thereby necessarily become exposed to an unprecedented extent to the interest of imperial authority and the intervention of its agencies. In Justinian's legislation civil law and canon law overlapped; the enforcement of canon law became the responsibility of government officials as much as of the bishops. Conversely, the privileges of clergy were enhanced, their judicial rights extended, their duties of supervising the civil administration in their cities and regions enlarged. In this 'imperial Church' – a phrase which renders the radical integration of Church and Empire less effectively than does the German '*Reichskirche*' – it was much harder to drive a wedge between the 'sacred authority of the bishops' and the power of the secular rulers than it had been a century before Gregory, when pope Gelasius had made this distinction[3] in an attempt to set limits to the exercise of imperial authority in the Church. The two were more closely intertwined, and the 'sacred' character of the Christian Empire and its emperor's status at its head were now more deeply embedded in the Christian imagination.

Gregory was no political theorist;[4] to diagnose his attitudes we need to consider the political attitudes as revealed in his actions, and the stock representations of the Empire and the emperor that flowed instinctively from his pen. His language reveals the hold on his mind of the established clichés of Roman imperial ideology. The empire or the state are, quite simply, 'the Christian empire' or the 'pious', the 'Christian', or even 'the holy commonwealth';[5] the emperor labours under the burdens of defending 'the Christian state'.[6] His 'most Christian reign' will be secured against the attack of enemies by the prayer of his priests,[7] and Gregory will invoke heavenly grace to guard the imperial family and 'to bend the necks of the nations into subjection to the Christian Empire'.[8]

If we are to proclaim freely the right faith and to arrange everything in peaceful concord, we should pray unceasingly for the lives of our most serene lord and his

---

[3] *Ep.* 12.2: *auctoritas sacrata pontificum* and *regalis potestas*.

[4] Cf. Straw, 'Gregory's politics' and Markus, 'The Latin fathers', 116–22.

[5] E.g. *Epp.* v.38; ix.68 (where *christiana res publica* refers to the Empire: see Markus, 'Gregory the Great's Europe', 34, n. 39; on the treaty referred to, see chapter 7, n. 55). In *Epp.* 1.73, 11.47, Gregory refers to the Empire as *sancta res publica*; as did the Istrian bishops in (*Ep.* 1.16a: *MGH Epp.* 1.18). I use 'commonwealth' or 'state' to translate *res publica*.

[6] *Ep.* vi.64: *pro christianae reipublicae regimine* . . .

[7] *Ep.* v.37: *Quae enim, serenissime domine, uirtus humana, quod carnei robur brachii contra uestri christianissimi culmen imperii irreligiosas praesumeret manus erigere, si studeret concors sacerdotum mens redemptorem suum lingua pro uobis atque, ut oportebat, meritis exorare?*

[8] *Ep.* vii.7: . . . *oremus, ut eorum uitam protegens gratia superna custodiat et christiano imperio gentium colla substernat.*

offspring, that almighty God might subject the barbarian nations under their feet, and grant them long and fortunate times, so that faith in Christ might reign throughout the Christian Empire.[9]

Following a well-established tradition, Gregory took Constantine and Helena as his pattern for Christian rulers. The English king Aethelberht was bidden to imitate (see below, pp. 181–2) 'the most pious emperor Constantine, [who] converting the Roman state (*rempublicam*) from the false worship of idols subjected it, along with himself, to almighty God and our Lord Jesus Christ, and turned to Him with all his heart and mind together with the peoples subject to him.'[10] The marriage of Christian orthodoxy and imperial authority in the fourth century is the model Gregory instinctively adopted, and, along with the model, the implication that the rulers' duties included the defence and enforcement of Catholic orthodoxy.[11]

Gregory spoke the language of a Christian version of Roman imperial ideology and used its political imagery. This is most obtrusive in letters he wrote to Phocas, the bloodthirsty soldier who had come to the throne in 602 after the murder of the emperor Maurice and members of his family and supporters. Greeting the tyrant as a liberator, Gregory here deploys the fossilised cliché according to which the emperor is a lord of free men, whereas the kings of the barbarians rule slaves.[12] On the same lines, he did not hesitate to praise an Exarch of Africa – though scarcely a man to be coupled with Phocas – for his 'warlike acts' crowned with success by divine favour through prayer. For he had fought 'not from a desire to shed blood, but to further the cause of the state in which we see God being worshipped, in order that the name of Christ might become familiar throughout the conquered peoples through the preaching of the faith'.[13] This may seem to reflect – as does his usual way of addressing the emperor as 'his most serene', 'most pious' or 'most Christian' lord – only habits of deference inculcated by the conventions of formal correspondence; but it

---

[9] *Ep.* VII.5: . . .*ut nobis liceat rectam fidem libere fateri et cuncta quae agenda sunt concorditer in pace disponere, pro serenissimorum dominorum uita, pro pia quoque subole incessanter orandum est, ut omnipotens deus eorum pedibus barbaras nationes subiciat, longa eis et felicia tempora concedat, quatenus per christianum imperium ea quae in christo est fides regnet.*

[10] *Ep.* XI.37. On this tradition, see my 'Gregory the Great's Europe', 25, esp. n. 14. For Helena, see *Epp.* XI.35 (to queen Bertha) and XIII.40 (to the empress Leontia).

[11] E. g. *Ep.* XI.28, IX.136. The responsibilities of rulers of the barbarian nations were modelled on those of the emperor: see below, chapter 11.

[12] *Ep.* XIII.32. The same is said to Leontius in *Ep.* XI.4. The report in *LP* 68 (on Boniface III, 606–607) that Phocas had issued a decree in favour of the Roman see's primacy may be a garbled reference to some pro–Roman pronouncement; if so, this might help to explain, though hardly to justify, Gregory's attitude to him.

[13] *Ep.* I.73.

is too deeply embedded in Gregory's hierarchical understanding of the political and the world order to be no more than that. Writing, for instance, to the bishops of Gaul (to justify the institution of a papal vicar over them), Gregory sketched the over-arching world-picture:[14]

The provisions of divine providence have laid down that degrees and various ranks should be distinguished, so that the lesser showing reverence towards the greater and the greater treating the lesser with love, diversity might bring about the unity of concord and that each office might function rightly. For the universe could not exist except by being subject to a great diversified order like this. Creatures cannot be governed, or even live, in a single undifferentiated equality; for as the example of the celestial host teaches us, there are angels and archangels who are not equal but differ in power and in rank . . .

The pope who found the pseudo-Dionysian treatise on the *Celestial hierarchy* touching chords deep in his mind also found it natural to ground the traditional ideology of the Empire in such an image of the cosmic hierarchy. The Empire, as well as the Church, belonged to the order of things established in the world by divine decree. It was therefore the duty of the bishops and clergy to pray for the success and welfare of the emperors, for they are 'very necessary to the world'.[15]

Conversely, the emperor must help to enforce the piety and purity of the clergy, repress heretics, and serve the heavenly kingdom; for 'earthly rule cannot be carried out rightly without adverting to its heavenly implications, and the peace of the commonwealth depends on that of the Church'.[16] The 'ruler' stood, almost by definition, at the head of this hierarchy. Gregory was not interested in questions which were to preoccupy so many of his medieval successors as to the precise relation of secular rulers to the 'rulers' of the Church. Both could indifferently be referred to by the same title, 'rector', also born by the personnel in charge of the Church's estates (*rectores*), so much so that in many texts it is not at all clear what 'ruler' he has in mind. The *Regula pastoralis* can be, and has been, taken to be addressed to kings no less than to bishops; when king Alfred sent copies of his English translation of the 'Shepherd's book' to his bishops, he clearly thought it would help them in the discharge of their office; but he would also have found something in it for himself. In this he would have been very close to Gregory's intention.[17] The two functions, the secular

---

[14] *Ep.* v.59. Cf. chapter 5, n. 37.

[15] *Ep.* vii.24. Cf. Straw, 'Gregory's politics'.

[16] *Ep.* v.37: *neminem recte posse terrena regere nisi noverat divina tractare, pacemque reipublicae ex universalis ecclesiae pace pendere . . .*; cf. vii.5, 6, 7; ix.136; xi.28.

[17] Markus, 'Gregory the Great's rector'.

and the spiritual ruler's, were complementary. 'Those endowed with the wisdom to deal with external things determine secular matters (*terrenas causas*); those endowed with spiritual gifts should not be involved in secular business, so that while they are not forced to take charge of lesser goods, they may be enabled to care for higher goods.'[18] Secular matters are clearly subordinate to spiritual; and in respect of spiritual matters, those who care for secular affairs are to be subject to the authority of those who minister to spiritual things. Conversely, ministers of the spiritual good are to subject themselves to the authority of secular rulers. The rhinoceros of earthly power (Job 39:9–11) is to be bound and serve heavenly purposes: then 'he bears the yoke of faith through the love of God'.[19] All authority, secular or spiritual, is to be service: it should serve the subject's, not the ruler's, good;[20] power (*potestas culminis*) is fraught with danger;[21] its exercise requires humility.[22] If all this is moral admonition rather than political theory, it is nevertheless the body of moral commonplaces which underlies Gregory's dealing with the secular authorities in general and with the emperor in particular.

HARMONY AND CONFLICT

This reciprocity of service, however, was not one between Church and State; it was between persons who bore office of one kind or another and wielded power in a Christian society. There were, of course, occasions when pope and emperor found themselves at odds, and when Gregory felt called upon to protest against some particular exercise of imperial power or policy. He could, and on one occasion, did, refer to hierarchical rank and precedence in a conflict between a bishop and a high civil servant in terms of official status; but this was exceptional in Gregory's practice.[23] More characteristically, he kept his grievances to a personal level, carefully refraining from raising them to institutional conflict. A revealing case is that of the objection he raised to an imperial law extending previous legislation, issued by Maurice to restrict the entry into the ranks of the clergy or monastic communities of persons engaged in or having recently

---

[18] *Mor.* XIX.25.42.

[19] *Mor.* XXXI.2.2–7.10; quotation from 4.5. Cf. *RP* I.1: a significant parallel.

[20] *Mor.* XXI.15.22–4; cf. *RP* II.6. On the relation to Augustine, cf. Markus, 'The sacred', 86. Cf. also *Mor.* XXIV.25.52–4; XXVI.26.44–6.

[21] *RP* I.9.

[22] Gregory, *passim*. On the pastoral ministry, see above, chapter 2.

[23] *Ep.* II.38; see below, p. 131, at n. 22. I deal with other cases of conflict with the emperor and the government in their appropriate places. Fischer, 'Gregor der Große und Byzanz', deals with the whole range of problems between the pope and the emperor. .

left civil administrative or military office. To a friend at the court Gregory wrote of the law the emperor had issued – 'for my sins' – 'which made any-one who loved him honestly weep bitterly'.[24] He began a passionate and immensely personal remonstration to the emperor: 'One would be guilty before almighty God if one were not entirely frank (*purus*) in all one does and says to my most serene lord [the emperor]. I, your unworthy servant, am not speaking in this submission either as a bishop or as a servant of the state, but in my private capacity . . .' But the law would prevent the salvation of many; so Gregory, though he was 'only dust and a worm' addressing the emperor his lord, yet, 'because I feel this law to be offensive to God the author of all, I cannot remain silent. For power over all men has been granted by heaven to my pious lord the emperor in order that those who desire the good may be assisted, that heavenly ways may be made more manifest, that the earthly kingdom may serve the heavenly . . .'[25] Gregory was dismayed and critical; but he loyally promulgated the law among the metropolitan bishops of the Roman patriarchate:[26] 'Being sub-ject to the emperor's command [*iussio*] I have transmitted it to the various regions, and, because the law does not at all conform with almighty God, I have notified my most serene lord [the emperor] by means of this letter. I have thus done my duty to both, in obedience to the emperor and to God, by not concealing what I think.'[27] The emperor's power was based on his authority.[28] But it should not be used with scorn for clergy, Gregory wrote on a painful occasion complaining about a lack of trust when he was trying to arrange a truce with the Lombards, but rather 'with special considera-tion for the sake of Him whose servants they are; ruling them, the emperor should render them the respect due to them': and this was on the very secular matter of war and peace in Italy![29] Mutual respect rather than formal boundaries should define the relations between priest and ruler. A sharper contrast with Gelasius's protest to the emperor Anastasius, or Ambrose's to Theodosius, it would be hard to imagine.[30] As for himself,

---

[24] *Ep.* iii.64.

[25] *Ep.* iii.61. Note the closeness to his views on the relations of secular and spiritual authority (above); and compare the very similar attitudes (personal protest combined with duty to God and obedience to the emperor) Gregory expressed in his protest against the use of the title of 'ecumenical patriarch' in *Ep.* v.37 (see below, pp. 91–5).

[26] *Ep.* viii.10; cf. x.9. The law had evidently been slightly modified, presumably in reponse to Gregory's protest, or 'interpreted' by Gregory.

[27] *Ep.* iii.61.

[28] *Ep.* vii.24 (*CC* 140.479, lines 25–9).

[29] *Ep.* v.36: *excellenti consideratione propter eum cuius servi sunt eis ita dominetur, ut etiam debitam reverentiam impen-dat.* On the question at issue, see chapter 7, 104–6.

[30] See Caspar, *Geschichte*, 2, 467. Caspar draws attention to the echo Gregory's letter (iii.61) contains to Augustine, *De civ. Dei* V.24: *Geschichte*, 2, 469, n.3.

Gregory had laid down the norms for the conduct of subjects and their superiors: 'that the former obey humbly, the latter take charge with moderation'; subjects, when they rightly criticise what is wrong, must 'judge privately [*apud semetipsos*] while, constrained by the fear of God, must not withhold their respectful obedience' (*ferre sub eis iugum reverentiae non recusent*).[31]

In much the same way, Gregory refused to treat the deposition of the patriarch of Antioch, Anastasius, by the previous emperor, Justin II, as a constitutional issue. Judging it inadvisable to begin his pontificate by raising the matter with the emperor,[32] he was content to include Anastasius in his correspondence among the other patriarchs, and invited him to join him at Rome, in honourable exile.[33] Whatever protest Gregory may have intended to make to the emperor was pre-empted by the emperor's reinstatement of Anastasius to his see when it became vacant. Gregory probably regarded the deposition as 'done by an act of [naked] authority, not according to law',[34] but neither questioned the emperor's right to depose a bishop, provided the deposition was not unjust and uncanonical,[35] nor disputed the incumbent's title. Tact, friendship, and concern for justice combined in Gregory's conduct in such affairs with willingness to accept the role assigned to the emperor in the Justinianic dispensation.

The clearest statement perhaps of the principles on which Gregory liked to proceed in situations of this kind is contained in a letter to an imperial official stationed in Dalmatia. He had been involved in a long-drawn out conflict in the metropolitan see of the province, Salona.[36] The province belonged to the sphere of the Roman patriarchate, and was thus subject to papal jurisdiction; but its geographical position and natural links had loosened the pope's control, and exposed its Church to the interference of local officials and the intervention of the court. Local pressure groups, clergy and officials gave Gregory trouble and anxiety: 'If civil officials are to observe the right order and their traditional discipline, it is intolerable that they should throw ecclesiastical orders into confusion by rash presumption. . .' To the official's plea to the effect that the court was

---

[31] *RP* III.4.
[32] *Epp.* 1.6; 27.
[33] *Ep.* 1.7; 25; in his synodical letter to all the patriarchs (*Ep.* 1.24), including Gregory, the present patriarch, Anastasius is addressed as *ex-patriarcha*.
[34] *non iure sed auctoritate*, as Gregory wrote concerning another uncanonical deposition: *Ep.* III.8.
[35] As in the case of the emperor wishing to depose a bishop who suffered from 'illness in the head': *Ep.* XI.29.
[36] For details, see below, chapter 10, pp. 157–9.

opposed to severe action, the pope replied that 'this cannot hold us back from concern for justice nor undermine our intention to seek out the truth'.[37] Proper respect for established rules, for truth and for justice are Gregory's overriding consideration. Their neglect, he says, will quickly harm the Church at large. Rehearsing the case in a letter to the empress, Gregory mentioned that he had deferred to the emperor's orders, and he appealed against new orders which would require him to honour the culprit and prevent him imposing the right canonical discipline.[38] Instinctively deferential to the emperor, ready to appeal to him – as required by the law – over the conduct of local officials, Gregory nevertheless set himself firm limits. As he wrote to his representative at the court: 'You know what I am ready to put up with; [but] I would rather die than allow the Church of St Peter to be corrupted [*degenerari*] in my days. You know my way: I am long suffering; but once I have decided to tolerate no more, I am ready to face any danger cheerfully.'[39] Patience, flexibility, tact and adroit diplomacy, however, helped Gregory to avoid crises in the conflicts with imperial authorities in which he found himself involved.

The same qualities can be seen in action in Gregory's relations with high civil functionaries. When the honorary consul Leontius was sent by the emperor to investigate the administration of recent officials in Sicily and Italy, Gregory cooperated and treated their enquiries with respect; but he protested vigorously against a punishment of Libertinus, ex-praetor of Sicily, on a charge whose validity Gregory professed himself unable to judge, as inhuman and excessive.[40] Gregory's own statement of his principles is characteristically restrained and dignified: 'Your magnificence should remember that you have never received any letter of recommendation from me on behalf of anybody, except to ask for your protection within the bounds of justice.' If he suspected injustice, Gregory would protest: in the first instance to Leontius himself, then, if necessary, appealing to the emperor. But as Gregory does not know the facts of the case, he will not do either. He went on to urge Leontius not to act intemperately in the heat of anger. Let him act on reflection, with fairness and humanity.[41] Justice, decency and legality were the substance of what Gregory wanted

---

[37] *Ep.* v.29.
[38] *Ep.* v.39.
[39] *Ep.* v.6.
[40] On the inspection by Leontius and his team and Gregory's dealings with the affair, see *Epp.* viii.33; 34; ix.4; 16; 32; 34; 50; 54–57; 62; 63; 78; 107; 131; 183; x.12; xi.4. For a detailed discussion, see Arnaldi, 'Gregorio Magno', 85–104.
[41] *Ep.* xi.4. On the details of the case, see Dudden, *Gregory the Great*, 243–6; Brown, *Gentlemen*, 152–3 and *PLRE* 3.776–7.

from civil officials. In interceding for petitioners, protesting and appealing to higher authorities, Gregory was carrying out the duty that Justinian's legislation laid upon him.[42]

THE ECUMENICAL PATRIARCH

Gregory's patience was more seriously tested by the conflict over the use of the title of 'ecumenical patriarch' (*patriarches oikoumenikos*; *patriarcha universalis*) with the patriarch of Constantinople.[43] The title was almost 100 years old, originating in the Acacian schism; bishops of Constantinople had been using it at any rate since early in the sixth century. By this time it had become the patriarch's customary official style. But it had become highly objectionable at Rome. According to Gregory, writing in June 595, Pelagius II had quashed the *Acta* of a synod held in Constantinople in 587 on account of this 'unspeakable word of pride', and had forbidden his representative in the city to communicate with the patriarch, John the Faster.[44] On succeeding Pelagius, Gregory protested verbally, not in writing.[45] He had been friendly with the patriarch, and wishing to avoid a clash, he had delayed in taking the matter up; but he had done so eventually, and was rebuked by the emperor for his intransigence.[46] Gregory's protest was evidently one of an unbroken series. The conflict came to a head in June and July 595, in the course of an exchange of letters with the patriarch over a case that had come up two years before.[47]

The patriarch's report on the case, for which Gregory had long been pressing him, arrived at last; and 'almost every paragraph', as Gregory complained, bristled with the offensive title.[48] This was evidently too much for the pope. 'I suffer innumerable griefs', he wrote to a friend, 'but I thank God that I am afflicted less than I deserve'.[49] His patience was fully stretched already: the emperor's much-resented reprimand for his intransi-

---

[42] On other cases of protection against officials, see Dudden, *ibid.*, 246–8. Justinian's legislation: *CJ* 1.4 contains several examples.

[43] For a survey, see Vailhé, S., 'Le titre', and 'Saint Grégoire le Grand'; on its significance, see Tuilier, 'Le sens', and my 'Gregory the Great's Europe', 30–33.

[44] Pelagius II's letter is referred to in *Epp.* v.39; 41; 44.

[45] *Ep.* v.44. It may be that the plural *de causa . . . fratrum nostrorum* in *Ep.* I.6 refers to John the Faster, as well as to the status of Anastasius of Antioch.

[46] *Epp.* v.37; 39; 45; VII.24, 30.

[47] *Ep.* v.41; for the original appeal, see *Ep.* III.52. I argued in 'Gregory the Great's Europe', 31–32 and n. 32, that Gregory's protests formed an unbroken series, and reached a climax in June and July 595. I borrow here the conclusion, p. 32.

[48] *Ep.* v.45.

[49] *Ep.* v.46.

gence, which seemed to him so unjust;[50] the pressing danger from Lombard
swords;[51] the breakdown of his plans for peace with the Lombards[52]
through the Exarch's malice towards him, which surpassed even 'the
swords of the Lombards';[53] the rapaciousness of officials, their tolerance
of pagans and their oppression of the poor;[54] and imperial connivance at a
scandalously uncanonical episcopal election;[55] all this, along with 'taking
care of bishops and clergy, of monasteries and the people, to watch against
the plots of the enemy, to be always on guard against the deceit of the
[Lombard] dukes – what labour and what pain all this brings …';[56]
Gregory had no leisure even for reading the scriptures.[57] All this, and on
top of it all his illness:[58] this was clearly no time to play down the apocalyptic conflict with evil, for compromise with wickedness. Under the scourge
of the accumulated troubles of the summer of 595 Gregory's patience
snapped, and the old conflict flared into crisis. It is unnecessary to invoke
his maturing plans for a mission to the English, or an alleged desire to
extricate 'the Church of God from the Church of the State', to account for
the conflict over the title.[59] It was not part of a plan to emancipate the
Church from a Byzantine captivity, or of a design for a new orbit in
Western Europe for the unhindered exercise of papal authority.

There was, of course, a principle at stake, but it was a pastoral and
ecclesiological one. What distressed Gregory was the pride embodied in
the title and in the patriarch's insistence on it. His very first letter on the
subject highlights the heart of the matter at stake. Prefacing his protest
with a statement on the interdependence of the spiritual and the secular
welfare of the Empire (see above, pp. 84–5) he commends the emperor's
concern for both; but dissent among the clergy has let the emperor down:
'no human power would dare to raise its godless strength against
the majesty of your most Christian Empire if the concordant minds of
the clergy were raised in prayer to the Redeemer for you, both with
their voices and, as they ought to, by their merits! And the swords

---

[50] *Epp.* v.37; 39; 45.
[51] *Ep.* v.36; 39; 44.
[52] *Ep.* v.36.
[53] *Ep.* v.40.
[54] *Ep.* v.38.
[55] *Ep.* v.39: on this, see below, pp. 157–8.
[56] *Ep.* v.40; cf. v.42. On the crisis in the relations between the pope and the emperor Maurice, see also chapter 7, pp. 104–6.
[57] *Ep.* v.46.
[58] *Epp.* v.42; 43.
[59] I have dealt with this in detail in 'Gregory the Great's Europe'. The phrase quoted is from Bognetti, *L'età longobarda*, 2, 230, one of several statements of such a case.

of a most savage people [the Lombards] would not thrive on such cruel
slaughter among the faithful, unless our lives – ours, who are called priests
but are not – were weighed down by the deeds of the utmost wickedness!'
Blaming clerical depravity, and writing in the first person plural, Gregory
laments the breach of harmony, brought about by dissent and arrogance
among the clergy. He professes himself ready to obey the emperor's order
to be conciliatory, but, as 'it is not my own cause, but God's, and because it
is not I alone but the whole Church that is troubled', he implores the
emperor to use his august authority to cut clean the wound – 'the invention
of a certain proud and pompous phrase': the offending title.[60] Gregory
presents the conflict in an apocalyptic context and in apocalyptic terms:
the vanity and profanity of the usurped title gives power to the Empire's
enemies (Gregory sent a separate letter, v.36, concerning the Lombard
menace) who have 'subjugated all parts of Europe, laid waste cities' and
emptied the land;[61] and while they are reducing Italy to ruin, 'priests, who
should be weeping prostrated in ashes, are claiming titles of vanity and
taking pride in profane words!' – and so the title suddenly becomes the
'name of blasphemy', the name borne by the apocalyptic Beast (Rev. 13:1).[62]
The apocalyptic dimension of this episode is more than 'flamboyant
rhetoric'; it belongs to 'the fundamental categories in which Gregory
perceives and transfigures the event'.[63]

   Gregory saw the patriarch's use of the title as the act of an individual
bishop's anti-Christian pride, threatening a breach of the Church's peace
and holiness. It was not an issue between Church and State, nor even a
conflict over the status of the two sees, Rome and Constantinople. The
grounds of Gregory's protest, fully stated in his remonstrance to the
emperor, are further clarified in his correspondence with two eastern
patriarchs, with both of whom he was on terms of friendship, the bishops
of Antioch and of Alexandria. He asked them both for support: never to
call anyone 'universal' in their letters, for that would be to deprive others
of their due by giving undue honour to another.[64] Anastasius, the patriarch of Antioch, had evidently thought the matter trivial, and urged the
pope – as had the emperor – to let it drop.[65] Eulogius, the patriarch of
Alexandria, at first failed to reply – in embarrassment? – to Gregory's

[60] *Ep.* v.37: *superbi atque pompatici cuiusdam sermonis inuentione* . . . ; cf. *Ep.* v.41.
[61] *Ep.* v.37; on the apocalyptic imagery, see above, chapter 4, pp. 51–2.
[62] *Ep.* v.37, line 74. For the apocalyptic perspective, see also *Ep.* v.44.
[63] Savon, 'L'Antéchrist', 398–9.
[64] *Ep.* v.41. For a general (and very Augustinian) commentary on pride as isolating 'singularity', see *Mor.*
   XXIII.6.13: *nec enim prava condemnatio est, ex eo bono quod communiter datur private gloriari* . . .
[65] *Ep.* VII.24.

request;[66] when he did reply, clearly assuming that the squabble was over a mere formality and raised only an issue of rank or precedence, he applied the title to Gregory, thus betraying a total misunderstanding of Gregory's protest. He has given up, he wrote, the use of the 'proud title' when writing to the patriarch of Constantinople, as Gregory had 'ordered'. Objecting, in passing, to Eulogius considering his request as an order, for he would never give orders to his brother, Gregory explained, once more, the point he had stressed, which Eulogius 'had not perfectly grasped':

> For I said that neither to me nor to anyone else must you write in such terms; and see, in the preface to your letter to me, who have forbidden this, you have thought fit to include the title of pride, calling me 'universal pope'. Please, I implore your holiness not to do this again; for what is bestowed on one beyond what is reasonable, is taken from yourself . . . I am rightly honoured when each is not denied the honour due to him. For if you call me 'universal pope', you deny that you are what you call me [a bishop] universally.[67]

To use the title 'universal', whichever bishop it was bestowed on, was to undercut the legitimate standing of each and every bishop in his own church: if any particular bishop was 'universal', no bishop anywhere else could be in possession of full episcopal status.

In this controversy Gregory was frustrated. His protests had no effect on the patriarch John or his successor, Cyriacus, or at the courts of Maurice or his successor Phocas, and were treated as without serious significance by his fellow-patriarchs. After a more or less routine protest made to Cyriacus,[68] and a warning to the Illyrian bishops not to endorse the title,[69] Gregory seems to have accepted its continued use as inevitable, and resumed normal relations with the patriarch. Whether Gregory adopted the style of 'servant of God's servants'[70] in order to contrast his own style with the 'word of pride' he so disliked, or simply continued in an already well-established tradition reaching back to Augustine, his cast of mind is clearly reflected both in his preference and in his dislike. Though he thought a serious theological principle was at stake where others saw only a trivial quarrel over a title, throughout the controversy his objection was to what seemed to him individual acts of arrogance by successive bishops of Constantinople; never does he represent it in terms of an institutional

---

[66] *Ep.* VI.61.
[67] *Ep.* VIII.29.
[68] *Ep.* VII.4; 30; and in 603: XIII.41.
[69] *Ep.* IX.157.
[70] as suggested by John the Deacon, *Vita* II.1. The style appears in the first year of his pontificate, *Ep.* I.41. On the title, see chapter 2, p. 31.

conflict, or a conflict of jurisdictions; and he expected it to be resolved by the exercise of the emperor's authority.

Why Gregory was so ready to endorse the bloody accession of Phocas, and to honour him in the traditional language of Christian exaltation of the imperial office, can only be guessed. He would have had every motive to do so, had he hoped for a solution from him to the problem of the patriarch's title, and the elimination of other causes of friction with his predecessor. Even if Gregory was not, at first, fully informed of the circumstances in which Phocas seized power, it is hard to believe that he was still in ignorance in a later exchange of letters.[71] If his information was fuller than his admirers might wish to be the case, his language would, at any rate, confirm all that we know concerning his attitude towards the institution: even to the extent of allowing his respect for it to obliterate any trace of revulsion from its new incumbent.

That respect for the established imperial system we shall observe in Gregory's work in Italy and in North Africa, provinces where the imperial writ still ran (see below, chapters 7 and 12). Even when he came into sharp conflict with imperial officials, or with the court itself, Gregory never questioned either the ideological foundations or the daily realities of the institutional framework of the Empire and the imperial Church. A very considerable part of Gregory's concerns, however, fell outside the limits of the Empire and the imperial Church: his interest in the churches in the Germanic kingdoms of Western Europe, now in fact firmly independent of the Empire (below, chapter 11). The diplomatic language used in the papal correspondence with their rulers suggests that Gregory saw them within a Byzantine perspective, generally equating them with high Byzantine officials, as they would have been seen by the government in Constantinople.[72] Whatever his practice in his dealings with barbarian kings, he addressed them as if they were – and as the imperial civil service long continued to pretend they were – occupying a place officially assigned to them in the Empire's administrative hierarchy. A world order in which the Roman Empire had its pre-ordained place, in relation to which the shape and organisation of the rest of the world was defined, came naturally to Gregory. He could hardly have conceived of a Europe emancipated

---

[71] *Epp.* XIII.32, 39 and 40: though dated May and July 603 respectively, it is just possible that no news reached Gregory between these two exchanges. John the Deacon (*Vita* IV.23), whose opinion of Maurice as *avarissimus simulque rapacissimus princeps* (III.50) and *Deo aduersus* (II.51) is unduly harsh, explains Gregory's attitude towards Phocas as therapeutic flattery: perhaps rightly.

[72] For the evidence, see my 'Gregory the Great's Europe', 28–9 and n. 24.

from the institutional framework of the Empire. His imagination could not have entertained the *Europa* of which Charlemagne came to be seen as the 'father' 200 years after Gregory's time. That needed more preparation: the slow alienation of Western Europeans from 'the Greeks', as East Romans were becoming spoken of, and the slow growth in the eighth century of an alternative cohesion, under a new Frankish political leadership; the consolidation of a Western, Rome-centred, Latin ecclesiastical culture; and, not least, a reorientation of the papacy's interests. In Gregory's 'ecumenical' imperial perspective the parochialism of the Carolingian age, of a 'Europe' narrowed to the community of Western nations united under the *principatus* of the Roman see, would have been an anachronism. While horizons were contracting in both East and West, the papal perspective remained strikingly ecumenical.[73]

[73] I summarise here my argument in 'Gregory the Great's Europe', esp. 34–6. See below, chapter 11.

CHAPTER 7

Terra mea: *Italy between two worlds*

At a time of crisis in his pontificate, in the summer of 595, Gregory
lamented the 'daily growing oppression of my land (*terrae meae*)'.[1] At that
moment several things, as we have seen in the last chapter, darkened his
horizon. Among his worries the Lombards' activities in Italy were the most
acute; and the friction between Gregory and the emperor and the conflict
with the imperial administration were in large part rooted in the divergence of their views as to how the Lombard threat was to be met.

At the time of their invasion of Italy in 568 the Lombards had long been
in contact with the Empire.[2] They had entered the orbit of Justinian's
foreign policy while settled in Pannonia, with the Gepids as their neighbours. In 568 they moved into Italy, from the North-East. Most of Venetia
and Istria and of the area of the Po plain was easily conquered. 'Dukes'
were left in charge of the conquered cities and regions; dukes were also
established, perhaps through Byzantine agency, further South, at Spoleto
and at Benevento. In the 570s and 580s Byzantine diplomacy sought to
weaken the Lombards, by alliance with Frankish kings whose armies were
abortively mobilised against them, as well as by bribery, and by trying to
subvert royal authority. But by 590 a Lombard kingdom had become
firmly established over the dukes in the North. The areas around Spoleto
and around Benevento survived with more independence from the king,
under their own dukes. Gregory's accession to the Roman see in 590 coincided with the consolidation of the Lombard kingdom under king
Authari (584–590). The chaotic state of Italy was beginning to crystallise
into Lombard-held lands in the Po valley and the southern duchies, while
the Empire controlled the islands, some coastal areas and enclaves in
southern and Central Italy and around Ravenna, where the imperial vice-
roy, the Exarch, and the main body of the imperial army had their headquarters. Tuscany and the territory between Rome and Ravenna were more

[1] *Ep.* v.36. On the context, see chapter 6, pp. 91–2 and below, pp. 104–5.
[2] The best summary of Lombard history is Delogu, 'Il regno longobardo'.

97

precariously protected by small detachments of troops and local militias. Control of this area fluctuated, even during Gregory's pontificate.[3] The defences of Italy had been allowed to run down. In Constantinople Italy's military needs took second place to the defence of the Empire's eastern flank, where the resources of the Empire were stretched by the Persian wars.

In the early stages of the conquest the conditions of the conquered people are obscure. No clear picture emerges from the scanty and confused reports. The Lombards were unkind to upper-class Romans suspected of collaboration with the Empire; many bishops fled, especially during the 570s and early 580s, though most returned to their sees later.[4] Peasants, too, suffered in the warfare.[5] In many areas in northern Italy, however, bishops and clergy could continue to function freely and ecclesiastical organisation survived in unbroken continuity, perhaps aided by the fact that at the time of the invasion the Church in this area was estranged from the Roman see and the Empire (see below, chapter 9). The evidence of burials seems to suggest that ethnic separation between Lombards and Romans was normal, though in places where control had not stabilised and was apt to change hands it seems that they sometimes lived in the same communities.[6] Gregory's pontificate stood on the threshold of a period of more stable coexistence and of gradual mutual assimilation of the two peoples under a consolidated Lombard royal authority.

Gregory had been drawn into the orbit of imperial policy for the defence of Italy even before his pontificate. In 584, as papal *apocrisiarius* in Constantinople, he received notification from pope Pelagius II that 'we have undergone such calamities and so much suffering from the treachery of the Lombards, breaking their sworn obligations, as no report could suffice to express'. Gregory was instructed to make representations to the emperor to move him to come to the aid of the 'whole of Italy' in its grave danger, particularly by sending troops under a *magister militum* and a *dux* to Rome and its region, as the Exarch had professed himself unable to help with the troops at his disposal, which scarcely sufficed for the defence of his own area. The revival of the Lombard kingship under king Authari was evidently seen as a threat to the still unconquered areas of Italy: urgent action was needed before 'the armies of the most unspeakable nation might occupy the places still under imperial control'.[7]

---

[3] E.g. *Ep.* v.15: the Lombards are a barrier to communications.
[4] Bognetti, 'La continuità'.
[5] *Ep.* ix.66: Gregory took it for granted that they would do so in the absence of peace.
[6] This is suggested by Gregory's letters to Italian bishops: *Ep.* i.17 and, for Narni, *Ep.* ii.2.
[7] *nefandissimae gentis exercitus*: Pelagius II, in *MGH Epp.* 2, Appendix ii.

THE PAPACY BETWEEN THE EMPIRE AND THE LOMBARDS

From the beginning of his pontificate the Lombards and the defence of Rome against them were one of Gregory's persistent anxieties. In one of his first letters he complained about Rome being exposed 'ceaselessly' to the threat of Lombard swords from outside, and the sedition of the soldiers within'.[8] This looks like an exaggeration of the military danger; but Rome cannot have felt secure during most of Gregory's pontificate. It was under immediate threat from duke Ariulf of Spoleto in 592, and from king Agilulf the following year.[9] Towns were devastated or depopulated;[10] church treasure, if not removed in advance, was plundered;[11] monks were driven from their monasteries by terror, clergy and people fled from their homes in fear of the Lombards.[12] In 596/7 Crotona in the South of Italy fell to the Lombards and its inhabitants were abducted, families split, and taken into captivity.[13] Apart from short intervals of peace, hostilities continued throughout Gregory's pontificate. In 599, as the truce with the Lombards was about to expire and Gregory could see no hope of Rome being saved by any human power, he wrote of 'disconsolate and forlorn Italy' (*miseram et deiectam*).[14] A few months before his death he complained to the emperor Phocas that no report can express 'how we have been oppressed daily by the swords of the Lombards, and by how many attacks, for thirty-five years now'.[15]

Gregory did not like the Lombards. Like his predecessor Pelagius II,[16] he spoke of them as 'the unspeakable nation of the Lombards', a phrase that became a cliché in his vocabulary of disparagement;[17] in his *Dialogues* they figure only as hostile, sacrilegious, pagans, foils to his holy men.[18] He lamented having become 'for my sins, a bishop not of Romans but of Lombards, whose promises are swords and whose favours are punish-

[8] *Ep.* I.3, of September 590.
[9] *Ep.* II.28; 38; *HEz* II. praef.
[10] *Ep.* I.8; II.13; 38; III.20; VI.9. We should not, however, assume that every decision of Gregory's to combine previously separate bishoprics is evidence of depopulation as a result of enemy action or the fear of it. Bognetti, 'La continuità', 417, suggests that the Lombard occupation was less important in interrupting the continuity of episcopal sees than other factors.
[11] *Ep.* IV.15.
[12] *Ep.* I.38; 39; 57; II.13; IV.15; VI.11; 32; XIII.2; *Dial.* I.4.21.
[13] *Ep.* VII.23.
[14] *Ep.* IX.240.
[15] *Ep.* XIII.39, of July 603.
[16] See above, n. 7.
[17] *nefandissima gens*: *Ep.* V.38; cf. VII.23 and I.17 on *nefandissimus Autharith*. Paronetto, 'I Longobardi', detects a development towards a more favourable view; this seems, however, to relate specifically to Queen Theodelinda and her circle.
[18] Boesch-Gajano, 'Dislivelli culturali', 400–1, notes *Dial.* III.37 as the single exception.

ment';[19] he preferred a dead Lombard, even if reformed and converted, enjoying his reward in heaven, to a living one: an Italian bishop was bidden to exhort the Lombards in his town to convert to the 'Catholic faith, so that, rewarding their conversion, the divine mercy might perhaps come to their aid in this life or, if they should happen to die, as is more desirable, they might pass absolved from their crimes'.[20] On a painful occasion he told his representative at the court that if fear of God did not deter him from taking human life, the Lombards would now have neither king nor dukes, and their nation would be in confusion.[21] The Lombards were the enemy. What Gregory wanted was security, and that was the object he aimed at in the first place.[22]

In the circumstances this meant entering the sphere of military and political affairs, and Gregory shrank from neither. In 592 Ariulf, the duke of Spoleto, was preparing a campaign in Italy. When the news reached Gregory, he lost no time in taking steps to organise defences. He wrote to three of the imperial generals in Italy, the *magistri militum* Velox, Maurice and Vitalian, concerning the stationing of available troops, asking them to consult on matters of strategy, and giving his own directions on the conduct of the defence.[23] Two of them were instructed to satisfy themselves as to the allegiance to the Empire of a small town in Tuscany; they were to take hostages to guarantee its citizens' continued loyalty. If the inhabitants were found to have been disloyal, they were to use their own judgement as to their punishment, 'in such a manner that nothing be done for which we [Gregory] can be blamed by our enemies, nor that anything be neglected – which God forbid! – that the good of the Empire [*rei publicae*] might require'.[24] At Nepi, a little North of Rome, Gregory took it upon himself to appoint a *vir clarissimus* to govern the city – in a capacity not stated (and in the prevailing conditions scarcely relevant) – in this time of public emergency, bidding the citizens to obey him in all things: 'Anyone who may defy his fitting commands should know he is defying our orders; anyone who obeys him in what we have set out, obeys us. If, however anyone should – which we do not believe – after this admonition of ours spurn him, let him know he would certainly be courting his own danger.'[25] Similarly, he sent a

---

[19] *Ep.* 1.30.
[20] *Ep.* II.2.
[21] *Ep.* V.6. There may be an obscure reference here to Byzantine efforts to subvert Lombard royal authority.
[22] Cf. Bertolini, 'I papi e le missioni' especially 334–5.
[23] *Ep.* II.4; 27; 28. If Norberg's dating is right, the last two of these were written in June 592, whereas II.4 belongs to September 591.
[24] *Ep.* II.28.
[25] *Ep.* II.10.

tribunus to Naples and ordered the inhabitants to obey him.[26] Gregory writes in these letters as a man confident of his authority, expecting his orders to be followed. On other occasions he would issue his directions to a local bishop – insisting, for instance, on everybody being required to take part in guarding city walls, nobody being excused.[27]

Gregory, and to a lesser extent his fellow-bishops, were haphazardly assuming secular responsibilities for local defence in much the manner of Severinus in Noricum a hundred years before, when Roman government and defence were being run down in this frontier province; but now, it was in Rome and Italy. The social and administrative developments which were forcing clerical (along with military) authority to the fore (on which see above, chapter 1) were reinforced in Gregory's Italy by the paucity of resources made available by the government for the defence of Italy. The lack of military manpower was well known in Rome.[28] The impoverished public finances in Italy were helped out by loans from and expenditure by the pope. Gregory once described himself as the 'treasurer' (*saccellarius*) who paid for all daily running expenses in Rome just as did the imperial treasurer of the 'first army of Italy' in Ravenna.[29] What the expenditure Gregory had in mind was is not clear; as we shall see (below, chapter 8) the Roman Church's welfare expenditure was considerable. However, there were expenses more directly related to the wars: in the same letter Gregory refers darkly to 'how much we pay daily to the Lombards just to be able to live among them'.[30] Military pay appears to have been payable, though by no means always paid, by officials at Ravenna;[31] although there is no evidence of direct military expenditure by the pope, it is possible that under the circumstances 'unofficial' payments may have been made to make up the shortfall of the official payment in order to retain the loyalty of the troops. It is hard to imagine officers appointed by the pope on his own authority being paid from anything other than the Roman Church's funds.[32] Large funds deposited by the pope in the treasury of the Church of Ravenna had evidently been used by the Exarch for the payment of

---

[26] *Ep.* II.47.

[27] *Ep.* VIII.19. Cf. IX.11. Gregory used his friendship with Maurentius, *magister militum* in Campania, to get a Campanian abbot's responsibility to mount a watch lightened, not cancelled: *Ep.* IX.163. In *Ep.* II.38, however, in Rome it appears to have been the duty of regular troops.

[28] Cf. e.g. above, p. 98.

[29] *Ep.* V.39.

[30] *Ibid.* As Hartmann notes (*MGH Epp.* I.328) in his note *ad loc.*, this need not necessarily refer to tribute, but could be ransom money. On such payments, see *Ep.* II.38.

[31] *Epp.* II.38: the Theodosiaci left in Rome have not been paid by the Exarch and can scarcely be induced to keep the watch on the walls; cf. *Ep.* IX.240. Maurentius, *magister militum* in Campania, had to go to Ravenna to obtain – evidently with difficulty – his and his companions' pay: *Epp.* IX.132; 134.

[32] See above, notes 25–6.

local troops, while arrears were being allowed to accumulate by the government in Constantinople. The troops in Rome were left unpaid. Gregory complained, urging Rome's needs; not only because he who pays the piper should be allowed to call the tune, but also on account of the concern for Rome's good which he was pleased to impute to the emperor.[33] It seems hard to believe, though there is no specific evidence, that no expenditure was undertaken for the defence of Rome.

Gregory was aware of the government's financial plight. His indignation, however, was aroused by what he saw as the government's indifference to the fate of Italy, and of Rome particularly, and the inaction of the Exarch Romanus. Moreover, inaction was compounded by obstruction: '[the Exarch] is stalling over fighting our enemies, and at the same time forbids us to make peace'. It was almost too late now, in the summer of 592, for Lombard dukes had made common cause in preparing for war, and seem to have been asking for exorbitant payment to be bought off; but Gregory had been trying to get a truce agreed. The Exarch frustrated his plan and had snubbed John, the archbishop of Ravenna, in his vain attempts to further Gregory's cause in Ravenna. But Gregory was still counting on bishop John to get the Exarch to agree to his peace initiatives with duke Ariulf.[34] Whether with or without the Exarch's approval, Gregory apparently did procure peace, the expense being met by the Roman Church.[35]

In his concern for the security of Rome, Gregory took no account either of constitutional propriety or of the Empire's strategic interests. This was what set him on a collision course with the Emperor and his officials in Italy. The duke of Spoleto was left in possession of many places in Central Italy, until they were regained in a counter-attack by the Exarch, who had never acknowledged the papally arranged truce. The Exarch had gathered the remnants of soldiers from Rome and took them away, stationing those who survived in Narni and Perugia, 'abandoning Rome so that Perugia might be held'.[36] The Exarch's counter-attack, in turn, provoked the intervention of king Agilulf, 'which caused pope Gregory such terror that he broke off his exposition of the Temple described by Ezechiel'.[37] Retaking the cities conquered by the Exarch, probably in the summer of 593, the king marched on Rome, now denuded even of the few remnants of its troops. Under siege, Gregory ended the last of his Homilies on Ezechiel:

[33] *Ep.* IX.240.
[34] *Ep.* II.38.
[35] *Ep.* V.36: *sine ullo reipublicae dispendio.*
[36] *Ep.* V.36.
[37] Paul Diac. *HL* IV.8, referring to *HEz* II.10.24. Cf. *LP* 66.

Let nobody blame me if I stop after this sermon. For as you all see, our afflictions have grown beyond measure. On all sides we are threatened by the sword, from all sides we face the peril of death. Some [of our people] return with hands cut off, some are captured, others are reported dead. Now I am forced to hold back my tongue from speech, for my soul is weary of my life (Job 10:1). Let nobody ask me about the holy scripture; my harp is turned into mourning, and my organ into the voice of them that weep. (Job 30:31)

Having turned from Ezechiel to the stricken Job, whose words the stricken Gregory had years ago expounded,[38] he now fell into silence: for how can one expound the mystical meaning of scripture when one cannot live?

What is left us, but to give thanks with tears while we suffer the scourge of our iniquity? For He who created us also became our Father through the Spirit of adoption whom He sent. And sometimes He feeds His children with bread, at others he chastises them with the scourge, to teach us by pain as well as by kindness for the sake of our eternal inheritance. Therefore, glory be to the Father . . .[39]

It was truly a moment of crisis, and it would be as such that Gregory would recall it at another time of crisis, in June 595.[40] Gregory had seen with his own eyes his fellow-Romans 'bound with chains by the neck in the manner of dogs', being dragged off to be sold into slavery; those left behind were starving, and Gregory was blamed for the shortage of grain.[41] Gifts of money from the emperor and friends in Constantinople were used to redeem captives, to assist destitute clergy and religious.[42]

How the siege ended is uncertain. There is no evidence of further military action, and Agilulf may have been content with the Roman captives and with his conquests in central Italy. There may be an element of truth in the story, reported by a continuator of the *Chronicle* of Prosper, that he gave up the siege out of respect for the pope.[43] It was not, however, a permanent end to hostilities between the Lombards and the Empire, such as Gregory longed for. Within a few months he was engaged in trying to promote peace-negotiations; not, this time, seeking himself to come to terms with a Lombard leader, but acting as an intermediary between the imperial authorities and the Lombard court. For this purpose Gregory employed his trusted friend Constantius, now bishop of Milan, and the Lombard

---

[38] *Ad Leandr.* 5; cf. chapter 2, p. 19.
[39] *HEz* II.10.24.
[40] See below, and chapter 6, above pp. 91–2.
[41] *Ep.* v.36. On grain supply, see below, p. 122 and n. 76.
[42] *Epp.* v.30; vi.32 (Campania); vii.23; viii.22.
[43] *Auctarii Havniensis extrema* 17, *Chronica minora* i, 339.

Queen Theodelinda.[44] He took advantage of diplomatic negotiations already in progress between the imperial, the Frankish and the Lombard courts, and asked to be kept informed of their progress; and he offered his services to the Lombard king as a guarantor of his good intentions if he should come to an agreement with the Roman government. The negotiations appear still to have been in progress in May 595, when Gregory urged a friend in Ravenna to use his influence with the Exarch in the interests of peace, assuring him of Agilulf's good intentions, despite some minor local friction, which could be settled by arbitration. The pope mentioned his readiness to assist the king if the Exarch were to prove obstructive.[45]

This was the beginning of a crisis: crisis in the peace-negotiations, crisis in the pope's relations with the emperor, and in many ways the severest crisis of Gregory's pontificate. The pope's distress is expressed in a series of letters written to the court, to his friends and his representatives in Constantinople and elsewhere, during June 595. Several things combined to test his patience and to strain his relationships with the emperor Maurice and the government.[46] Among the piled up grievances the collapse of his plans for peace with the Lombards appears to have been the most serious. The story of this breakdown is rehearsed in Gregory's letter of outspoken remonstrance with the emperor.[47]

Gregory had just received a letter from the emperor, containing a sharp rebuke; Maurice had called him 'simple-minded', meaning, as Gregory pointed out, that he was a fool (*fatuus*). Yes, Gregory replied, he was simple as had been Job ('simple and upright': Job 1:1) and as commanded by St Paul and the Lord (Rom. 16:19; Matth. 10:16). But he was accused of being a fool for having allowed himself to be deceived by the Lombards in his report concerning duke Ariulf; others rather than he were believed and he was condemned, in effect, as a liar. 'If the captivity of my land (*terra mea*) were not growing daily, I would hold my peace concerning the contempt and derision in which I am held.' But what he cannot tolerate is that while insulting him, the emperor is doing nothing about the fate of Italy. Let the emperor think what he likes about Gregory, but 'for the good of the Empire [*reipublicae*] and for the sake of the liberation of Italy', let him trust facts rather than reassuring words. Let him show more respect, as did the

---

[44] On Constantius, see pp. 134–5; on Theodelinda see further below, pp. 105–6.

[45] *Ep.* IV.2.

[46] See chapter 6, pp. 91–2 on the other matters. It seems to me highly likely that Gregory's other grievances had remained in the background until he received the emperor's rebuke (*Ep.* v.36). The separate letter concerning the patriarch of Constantinople (v.37) and *Ep.* v.38 to the empress, also one of two, all sent at the same time, may indeed have been written some time before, and have been kept in readiness to be sent off at a suitable moment.

[47] *Ep.* v.36; quotations which follow are from this letter.

emperor Constantine, to bishops, whose profession commits them to the truth. And then Gregory enumerates his grievances, summarising the history of the previous years of peace-negotiations broken off, the defence of Rome neglected, Gregory and his collaborators, the prefect Gregory and the *magister militum* Castus, being blamed.[48] Let the emperor not threaten him (as he had done) with 'the fearful and terrible judgement of almighty God', for we none of us know what we are; and Gregory, a sinner, would rather place his trust in God's mercy than in the emperor's justice. He ends this bitter and painful letter with a prayer for the emperor.

Gregory's life was overshadowed, as he repeatedly complained at this time and was to continue complaining in his remaining years, by 'the swords of the Lombards'.[49] But the Exarch's ill-will towards him was worse than Lombard swords;[50] moreover, the Exarch was supported by public opinion in Ravenna, where Gregory's representative was given a hard time.[51] Negotiations with king Agilulf seem to have reached a critical stage in April 596, when, Gregory hinted, they were being sabotaged by the Exarch.[52] A large thorn was removed from Gregory's side when the Exarch Romanus died at this time, and was succeeded by one rather more amenable, Callinicus. Negotiations were still proceeding in the autumn of 598, and seemed about to succeed, perhaps aided by Gregory's emissary at the Lombard court, the Ravennate abbot Probus.[53] The Lombard king and the Exarch had come to an agreement; but the compliance of the southern dukes was still uncertain. At any rate, before the end of the year Gregory thanked king Agilulf for acceding to the treaty, asking him to prevail over the dukes to fall into line, so that Rome might also come to feel the benefit of the peace concluded with the king;[54] and he requested Queen Theodelinda to use her influence on her husband 'not to go back on the treaty with the Christian Empire'.[55] But this was not the end of Gregory's troubles. Rome remained exposed to Lombard raids, and inadequately defended by unpaid troops;[56] local skirmishing, insecurity, raids, abductions and taking of captives continued.[57] The following year fears of

[48] The wording of the letter suggests that these officers were suspected of complicity in Gregory's peace-initiatives.

[49] *Epp.* v.36; 39; 40; 42; 43; 44; vi.61; vii.23; viii.2; ix.176; xiii.39.

[50] *Ep.* v.40: the Exarch Romanus was a friend of his correspondent, Sebastian, a bishop in Dalmatia.

[51] See p. 154.

[52] *Ep.* vi.33: *aliqui in hoc* [the arrangement of a treaty] *impedire conantur.*

[53] *Ep.* ix.11; 44; 68. He was evidently in touch with Theodore, *curator civitatis* of Ravenna (ix.44).

[54] *Ep.* ix.66.

[55] *Ep.* ix.68: *quatenus Christianae reipublicae societatem non rennuat.*

[56] *Ep.* ix.240.

[57] *Epp.* vi.23; vii.19; 23; viii.19; ix.11; 100; xiii.34. In 598, however, Gregory felt able to minimise the danger in order to attract his Constantinopolitan friend Rusticiana to come to Rome: *Ep.* viii.22.

renewed war were in the air, as the king was rumoured (prematurely; he was to live another fifteen years) to have died;[58] and some Lombard leaders were still treating their obligations lightly.[59] The worst breach of the peace, however, was committed by the Exarch, which led to a resumption of war.[60]

Nevertheless, a more settled era in the history of Lombard Italy began after c. 600. One element in this pacification was the *rapprochement* between the Roman Church and the Lombard court. At the time of their invasion of Italy the Lombards were predominantly pagan in their religion. Christianity, both in its Catholic and its Arian forms, had been established among them; it was king Authari who made a determined attempt to rally his people around Arianism, to strengthen its cohesion and identity among the conquered people. Gregory greeted Authari's death within the first year of his pontificate as a signal for missionary action among the Lombards, among whom Catholic baptism had been prohibited by 'the unspeakable Authari'.[61] But he quickly came to accept Arianism among the Lombards as a fact of life, which he neither mentioned nor tried to remedy.[62] Arianism henceforth was to be the religion of a section among the Lombards, notably at Pavia, where Arian bishops remained established until late in the seventh century, down to at least king Rothari (636–52). Two bishops, a Catholic and an Arian, may also have been in existence in other Lombard cities.[63] Traditionalists among the Lombards tended to rally to Arianism as an opposition under Catholic kings, and Arianism was liable to attract support at times of acute threat to the nation.

Under queen Theodelinda, the Bavarian princess married first by Authari and then by his successor, Agilulf, Catholic Christianity had become firmly established at the court, albeit in a schismatic form. Catholicism in the Lombard kingdom was thus left at arm's length from both papal and imperial control, but amicable contacts were easier to establish and to maintain with the Lombard court, and Gregory was able to exert some political influence through intermediaries such as the bishop of Milan resident in Genoa, or the abbot Probus and the mayor Theodore of Ravenna.[64] Such contacts were to prove their value in the decades after

---

[58] *Ep.* x.16.

[59] *Ep.* xiii.34.

[60] On these events, Paul Diac. *HL* iv.20–28.

[61] *Ep.* i.17, of January 591, addressed to 'all the bishops of Italy', provoked by the prevailing conditions of plague.

[62] The admonition to the bishop of Narni the following year (*Ep.* ii.2, cf. above, n. 20) is the only other occasion on which Gregory touched on the subject.

[63] Paul Diac., *HL* iv.42. Bognetti, 'La continuità', 429.

[64] See above, n. 53.

Gregory's death. The stage was set for a symbiosis of Lombard and Roman in Italy.

GREGORY AND THE CHURCH IN ITALY

Coming to terms with Lombard invaders and settlers was a problem that affected southern as well as northern Italy. A difference more fundamental for ecclesiatical affairs derived from the administrative division between Central and Southern Italy and the North, divided by a line running from near Ancona on the Adriatic coast to the Gulf of Genoa on the Tyrrhenian. Traditionally, in the late Roman civil administrative geography the northern and the southern provinces (*Italia annonaria*; *Italia suburbicaria*) came under different jurisdictions. While the importance of this division was diminishing in the conditions of the sixth century, the administrative geography of the Church normally preserved the outlines of the old civil administrative divisions.[65] The churches of northern Italy came into the orbit of the great metropolitan sees of Milan and Aquileia, and eventually of Ravenna (see Chapter 10 below); the provinces of 'suburbicarian' Italy, including Sicily (which since the reconquest came under the separate administration of a praetor) and the islands (under the Exarch of Africa), were within Roman metropolitan jurisdiction.

Gregory worked within this inherited division, though, as we shall see in the next chapter, the conditions of the Three Chapters schism and of the Lombard kingdom modified the force of traditional boundaries. In exercising his authority in the different areas of jurisdiction he was, however, punctilious in observing the proprieties. Thus, for instance, in April 592, at a time when the insecurity of the Lombard wars made travel in northern Italy hazardous, and his contacts with some bishoprics within the Roman metropolitan sphere (*de episcopis ... ad nos pertinentibus*) were threatened, Gregory asked the bishop of Ravenna to keep an eye on them; graver matters, however, were to be referred to him to be decided by him 'according to the laws and the canons'.[66] Existing canonical provisions were to be safeguarded. Similarly when Gregory extended the exercise of Roman metropolitan authority into the area previously under the metropolitan jurisdiction of the see of Milan,[67] he did so on the legal basis of an adjustment of metropolitan authority made not long before his

---

[65] For a clear summary, see Jones, *LRE* 2, 874–94, and Menis, 'Le giurisdizioni', 277–80.

[66] *Ep.* II.25. The bishoprics were presumably in the province of Flaminia and Picenum, over which the papacy had not formally ceded metropolitan authority to the archbishops of Ravenna (see below, chapter 10).

[67] See below, chapter 9, pp. 136–7.

pontificate.[68] His interventions in the affairs of the Church in Corsica form a special case: though the see of Cagliari enjoyed metropolitan status, Gregory had to take into account its incumbent's serious personal shortcomings.[69]

Much of Gregory's concern (*cura*) for the churches under his authority was of a routine nature. He dealt with a wide variety of problems as they were brought to his notice.[70] Among these one of those that occur most frequently in his correspondence is the supervision of elections to vacant episcopal sees. Generally, in the absence of local difficulties or complications through circumstances, this would involve choosing a 'visitor', usually a neighbouring bishop, whose terms of reference would be laid down in a letter of appointment; to take care of the see, its income, its worship and its clergy during the interregnum, and, most important, to superintend the actual election. Several different types of document were used by the clerks of the papal writing office, depending on the length of time for which the visitor was appointed, and other special circumstances. Sometimes the 'visitor' would be given the right to ordain clergy, or to use the church's finances; in other cases all the affairs of the church would be frozen until the new bishop took up his office. The local clergy, notables (*ordo*) and people, were informed of the appointment of the visitor and given their instructions according to the terms that had been laid down for him. Some of the formulae in use in Gregory's time became incorporated in the collections (which survive from later times) in use in the papal writing office. Finally, the pope as metropolitan would have to confirm or to disallow the election, which would involve further correspondence, and if the candidate chosen failed to meet Gregory's approval – on the grounds usually of moral failings, illiteracy, attempted simony, or marital status – further action.[71]

The normally simple routine followed established forms (*more scrinii nostri*).[72] It could, however, be disrupted, and Gregory's *Register* furnishes many examples of more complicated cases. A vacancy at Naples – a characteristically lively port city – caused by the deposition of the bishop (notified to the clergy, notables and people in September 591)[73] provides an example of the complications which might arise. A visitor, Paul the bishop

[68] See chapter 9, p. 134.
[69] See below, pp. 110–11.
[70] For a more detailed exposition of Gregory's work in this sphere, see Dudden, *Gregory the Great*, 358–401. Pitz, *Papstreskripte* gives a formal classification which, though useful for a study of the work of the papal office, is less so for showing the nature of the range of the pope's activities.
[71] For a general account, see Greenslade, '*Sede vacante* procedure'. See also Pitz, *Papstreskripte*, 117–30.
[72] E.g. *Ep.* ix.167.
[73] *Ep.* ii.3.

of Nepi, a town unusually distant in such cases, had been appointed.[74] Bishop Paul had become so well liked that the Neapolitans wanted him for their bishop; Gregory, urging them to take more time and care over so important a matter, asked them to think again, meanwhile leaving Paul in charge (December 591).[75] At the same time, expecting a more protracted election and a longer vacancy, he gave Paul larger powers.[76] A visitor had to be appointed at bishop Paul's see, Nepi, to celebrate the liturgy, especially over the approaching Easter festivities, during the bishop's absence at Naples (March 592).[77] By February 592, Paul wished to be relieved of his duties; how much the factionalism in Naples that he had mentioned to Gregory contributed to his desire to return home we can only guess.[78] Paul stayed, but the situation got out of hand. He was beaten up on a visit to a local aristocrat's country villa; she had almost certainly been one of his opponents. In September 592 the pope's agents were asked to look into the matter and (with the governor of Campania) to take strong action to punish the culprits.[79] At the same time Gregory wrote to Paul to comfort him.[80] A Roman subdeacon – presumably Gregory's nominee – had been appointed as bishop by December; but for reasons we can easily conjecture, he fled the city, 'tearfully' refusing to be ordained. The provincial governor was now asked to gather the local notables and get them to agree on a person to elect; failing that, to send three 'upright and wise' men to Rome to find, under the pope's eyes, someone acceptable to all (December 592).[81] In May 593 the unhappy Paul was finally allowed to return home to Nepi, suitably rewarded. The Neapolitan clergy were instructed to find representatives to join the lay people already in Rome to elect a bishop; if necessary, the pope's agent was to coerce them with 'ecclesiastical power'.[82] By August a new bishop, the not too aptly named Fortunatus, probably an outsider from Rome, had been appointed. He was well received in Naples and was bidden by the pope to deal firmly with the difficulties there.[83] This was not the end of civic conflict in Naples, nor of

---

[74] The letters of appointment are not in the *Registrum*.

[75] *Ep.* II.8. The sequel strongly suggests that a faction in Naples had tried to hi-jack the election by acting quickly, and that Gregory's caution had been dictated by his awareness of the circumstances.

[76] *Ep.* II.9.

[77] *Ep.* II.23. A *vir clarissimus* Leontius had been sent some weeks before to look after the well being of the townspeople and of the *res publica*: clearly to deal with problems arising from the Lombard troubles (see above, n. 25).

[78] *Ep.* II.14.

[79] *Ep.* III.1.

[80] *Ep.* III.2.

[81] *Ep.* III.15.

[82] *ecclesiasticum in eis vigorem exerce*: *Ep.* III.35.

[83] *Ep.* III.60.

the bishop's involvement in it; but at least after two years Naples had a
bishop: though only for seven years, when Fortunatus's death necessitated
a new election. Gregory did not expect it to go smoothly.[84] The election of
593 at Naples was perhaps the most troublesome Gregory had to supervise; but there were others, and there were those in which he himself took
an active interest. Most, happily, were a routine matter.[85]

In addition to the oversight of episcopal elections, Gregory's *cura*
included decisions on combining, temporarily or permanently, neighbouring churches when the continued existence of both (or even of three)
was no longer feasible, usually as a result of depopulation. Sometimes, for
reasons not wholly clear from the information now available to us,
Gregory would make other arrangements to have the spiritual needs of
remaining inhabitants met by neighbouring clergy. There were also a host
of cases concerning clerical appointments, recruitment, promotions and
precedence, discipline and stipends, cases of complaints of lay people
against clergy, of clergy against bishops, complaints against civil officials,
disputes about property, regulating relations between monasteries and the
local church, approving new monastic and charitable foundations, orato-
ries and the like. Practices here and there that savoured of paganism,
problems concerning Jewish communities and monastic observance called
for his intervention. Protecting the poor, orphans and widows, peasants
against exactions by civil or ecclesiastical officials, were matters of high
priority and occur frequently in the Register. Generally Gregory expected
such matters to be dealt with by bishops in their own dioceses, whom
he was ceaselessly exhorting, and took them up only when their failings
were brought to his attention. Sometimes offenders were summoned to
Rome to appear before the pope; more often directions were issued to
local or neighbouring bishops to look into the matter and correct what
needed correction.

Many of Gregory's interventions in such affairs could be matters of routine, but many must have taken time and effort. Some running sores
 continued over years. Among such were an unsatisfactory bishop Ianuarius
of Cagliari, the metropolitan see of Sardinia, under Roman jurisdiction.
This 'silly, half-witted old man, who shamefully neglected all his duties,
and scandalized every one by his egregiously eccentric conduct'[86] would
make an amusing subject for detailed description. To indicate the style of

[84] *Ep.* x.19.
[85] For an account of some further difficulties, see Dudden, *Gregory the Great* 1, 376–81. The election of
Constantius to the see of Milan is considered in detail in chapter 9, and Ravenna in Chapter 10.
[86] Dudden, *Gregory the Great*, 1. 367.

Gregory's pastoral intervention in such difficult cases, a few of the more colourful incidents which Gregory felt to warrant his intervention must suffice. These interventions were, of course, additional to the many routine matters on which Gregory wrote to him.[87] He was held in open contempt by his clergy; they were oppressed by lay officials against whom the bishop did nothing to protect them; he neglected clerical discipline; his archdeacon was living with women in open defiance of the bishop.[88] Gregory had to send a Roman notary to investigate complaints against him.[89] The same notary and another official were to bring Ianuarius to Rome, along with some of his accusers, that complaints might be investigated.[90] Despite these (and many more) complaints against him, Gregory did not want to undermine his authority as metropolitan,[91] but when news reached him that Ianuarius had hurried out one Sunday before mass to plough up the harvest on a neighbour's field, quickly celebrated mass, and immediately after mass went out to move the boundaries, Gregory discarded his reluctance to rebuke a senior:

Wanting still to spare your white hairs, I admonish you: come to your senses, old man, and refrain from such levity of behaviour and perverse action.[92]

Ianuarius was a hard case. Many were less difficult, but there is no need to follow them in detail. Many cases that were brought to Gregory's notice arrived from areas of the Roman Church's possessions. Here his informants and his agents were usually the administrative personnel in charge of the lands owned by the Roman Church, the 'rectors of the patrimonies', whom Gregory used to make the necessary enquiries and to enforce his decisions. To these we must now turn.

---

[87] The *Registrum* contains twenty-one letters addressed to him, and many more to persons in his milieu and related to his activities.

[88] *Ep* IV.26.

[89] *Ep.* II.41.

[90] *Ep.* III.36. Another colourfully inadequate bishop was similarly to be brought to Rome if the local rector could not get him to reform by his stern and formal admonition: *Ep.* XIII.29.

[91] *Ep.* IV.26; cf. *Ep.* IX.204.

[92] *Ep.* IX.1; cf. IX.2.

CHAPTER 8

Argus luminosissimus: *the pope as landlord*

THE ROMAN CHURCH AND ITS LANDS

His biographer described Gregory as a 'kind of most bright-eyed Argus', who, through his agents in the patrimonies 'let the eyes of his pastoral care roam over the whole wide world'.[1] A major instrument of this Argus-like thoroughness in Gregory's exercise of his pastoral *solicitudo* or *cura* was the machinery set up for the administration of the Roman Church's possessions. Since the time of Constantine churches had built up extensive land holdings. By the end of the sixth century they were the largest landowners in Italy. In Gregory's time the Roman Church must have been by far the richest. It had long had registers (*polyptycha*) of its lands and of the income it derived from them, which were kept up to date.[2] Its possessions were concentrated in Sicily and in Campania; but the 'patrimony (of St Peter)', as these possessions were collectively known, included lands scattered over southern Italy (Bruttium-Lucania and Apulia-Calabria), Tuscany, and elsewhere in Italy, Corsica and Sardinia, Dalmatia, Gaul and North Africa.[3] The job in Sicily seems to have been too demanding for a single administration, and in the summer of 592 Gregory divided it into two, one centred in Palermo for the North-West, the other at Syracuse, in the South-East.[4] The volume of Gregory's correspondence with his agents in these patrimonies, especially in Italy (where it constitutes over a quarter of his correspondence) reveals at a glance the importance that their affairs assumed in his time.[5]

---

[1] John Diac., *Vita* II.55: *...per procuratores ecclesiasticorum patrimoniorum velut Argus quidam luminosissimus per totius mundi latitudinem suae pastoralis sollicitudinis oculos circumtulerit ...*

[2] John Diac., *Vita* II.24. Cf. Gregory, *Ep.* IX.200; II.50. On this subject John the Deacon may have used material not available to us. Cf. above, chapter 1, n. 5.

[3] For details, see Dudden, *Gregory the Great*, I, 299–320.

[4] This appears to be first suggested in *Ep.* II.50.

[5] See Appendix. The correspondence may not reveal the full extent of the possessions; cf. John Diac., *Vita* II.53. Cf. Recchia, *Gregorio Magno*, 11–13. On the subdivisions and organisation, see *ibid.*, 16–24. I have not been able to consult F. Marazzi, *Il patrimonium Sancti Petri dal IV secolo agli inizi del X: prassi amministrativa e strutture gestionali* (Rome, 1988).

They were important enough for Gregory to undertake a systematic reorganisation of their administration early in his pontificate. In some areas, as in Italy during the Gothic wars, their state had become ruinous.[6] His very first letter announces the appointment of a trusted friend, Peter the sub-deacon (his interlocutor in the *Dialogues*; later deacon) to take charge of the Sicilian patrimony,[7] perhaps to replace a *defensor* criticised for dishonesty and injustice to peasants.[8] Peter was warmly commended to the Praetor in charge of the civil administration there.[9] Similarly, the Roman notary Hilarus, appointed before, was sent to Africa, with a commendation to the Exarch and a local general.[10] In Gaul, a Provençal nobleman, the *patricius* Dynamius, *rector Provinciae*, had looked after the Roman Church's possessions in southern Gaul; Gregory, thanked him for his 'faithful' administration,[11] but it was not until 595 that he found one of his own men (*hominem nostrum*), the priest Candidus, to take over; and as winter weather prevented Candidus taking up the post, the 'family of the apostle St Peter' there was temporarily commended to the care of Dynamius's successor, the *patricius* Arigius.[12] In September 595 Candidus was despatched with recommendations to queen Brunhild and king Childebert.[13] In Dalmatia, too, a sub-deacon was appointed to take over the rector's office from the bishop who had been discharging it.[14] Although detail is lacking for other areas, this seems to be the general pattern of Gregory's overhaul of the administration: his own trusted agents took over where previously others – local persons of various rank – had been in charge. He thought clerics should generally be preferred to lay people for this sort of work.[15] During his pontificate everywhere Roman clergy or papal officials are found serving as rectors in all the patrimonies. The staff of *defensores*, and to a lesser extent of the lower rank of *notarii*, provided a pool of dedicated persons on which the pope could draw for carrying out a variety of tasks. They could be sent on special missions, sometimes of a difficult or delicate nature, sometimes with the pope's detailed brief;[16] they

---

[6] Pelagius I, *Ep.* 4.

[7] *Ep.* I.I.

[8] *App.* I (*CC* 140A, 1092–3).

[9] *Ep.* I.2.

[10] *Epp.* I.73; 74. The Exarch Gennadius may have been in charge of the administration of the lands, though the language of *Ep.* I.73 on this is not conclusive. Hilarus had been appointed by Pelagius II: *Ep.* I.75.

[11] *Ep.* III.33. On him, see *PLRE* I, 429–30.

[12] *Ep.* V.31; on Arigius, *PLRE* I, 116.

[13] *Ep.* VI.5; 6. On Candidus, see Grierson, 'The *patrimonium Petri*', 106–7.

[14] *Ep.* II.19; he had taken over by October 592: *Epp.* III.9; 22.

[15] *Ep.* IX.205.

[16] For the mission of the *defensor* John (*Ep.* XIII.46–9) see p. 168.

could serve the pope as his ambassadors;[17] these officials were also often given the charge of papal patrimonies when the rector was not a sub-deacon or a man in higher ecclesiastical orders.[18] Papal agents appear generally to have been given the clerical tonsure on entering the papal service, even the lowliest.[19] The rectors were often assisted by *actionarii*, local laymen whom they could appoint to carry out minor tasks.[20] They may in some cases have had their own representatives in Rome, though it seems likelier that messengers travelled frequently between them and the pope especially in the case of the geographically less remote patrimonies.[21]

The rectors' functions were varied and extensive. Their evolution, if there was one, cannot be reconstructed from the documents at our disposal. Management, responsibilities for legal and financial matters and the like will always have formed the kernel of their work. Pope Pelagius I had described the duties of a *defensor ecclesiae* – from whose ranks rectors were often taken – as concerned with 'legal cases, agreements, acts, public litigation, and whatever is required by ecclesiastical arrangements or the needs of petitioners'.[22] Such duties could be extended not only to legal cases involving clergy, but also to enforcing the pope's directions as to their conduct.[23] The rector was, in effect, the pope's agent in his patrimony: he informed the pope on local affairs, made known the pope's will and ensured it was carried out.[24]

Gregory did not overhaul his rectors' job-description systematically, as he overhauled the personnel of the patrimonial administration. The rectors sometimes received formal instructions, along with the usual letters of recommendation to the local bishop, civil officials and notables. The instructions Gregory gave to his new men were very much in line with what had been customary. He seems even to have made a point of stressing

---

[17] E.g. the *defensor* Boniface, head of the college of *defensores* (*Ep.* VIII.16) was later sent to Constantinople as *apocrisiarius* and ordained a deacon.

[18] Details in Pietri, 'Clercs et serviteurs', who provides a careful analysis. See also Recchia, *Gregorio Magno*, 25–45, who rightly points out (p. 26, n. 2) that the rectorate of a patrimony was a function, not an office. I do not distinguish here between the various ranks of *defensores* and *notarii*: see Recchia, *ibid*, 27–36 and 42–5 and Spearing, *The patrimony*, 32–6.

[19] *Ep.* II.50 (*CC* 140. 144 lines 118–20); IX.22.

[20] E. g. *Ep.* I.42 (*CC* 140, 56, lines 211–12); II.50 (*ibid.*, 144, line 118).

[21] *Ep.* I.42 speaks of a *responsalis* of Peter the sub-deacon; he may, however, have been no more than a messenger. It is hard to imagine a permanent representative acting for a person as close to Gregory as Peter certainly was.

[22] *Ep.* 27 (Gassó and Batlle, 82). He may not, of course, have been a *rector patrimonii*.

[23] E.g. Pelagius I, *Ep.* 91; 41 (the bishop of Tauromenium prohibited from using the pallium); Cf. Recchia, *Gregorio Magno*, 30 for more detail.

[24] Recchia, *Gregorio Magno*, 30. Recchia regards Gregory's practice as 'normalising' what existed already before his time. He rightly remarks (149) in this connection : 'Né è da pensare che Gregorio si lasciasse condizionare dalle istituzioni.'

this in his very first appointment: 'We thought it very necessary, as our pre-decessors have judged, that we should commit everything to a single person, so that where we cannot be present ourselves, our authority should be represented by the person appointed.' So he wrote to the bishops in Sicily when he sent Peter the sub-deacon as his vicar.[25] Peter was to gather the bishops into council once a year,[26] to deal with matters concerning the good of the province and the churches, to succour the oppressed and the poor, to correct all excesses. A wide brief, especially in respect of the large authority it assigned to a lowly cleric over bishops. It seems, however, to have been Gregory's intention that his rectors should act as his vicars, endowed with his own full authority; the terms of reference given to one of Peter's successors at the end of his pontificate were no less inclusive.[27] It may be significant that in the formulae developed by the papal clerks for the appointment of a new rector no mention is made of his duties concerning bishops and clergy, and that the only Gregorian formulae which were taken into the later papal collection were the letters notifying the appointment of a new rector to local farmers and peasants (*coloni, familia*) and to local officials which, naturally, make no mention of his ecclesiastical functions.[28] The lack of settled formulae defining their competence in ecclesiastical matters suggests that rectors were given *ad hoc* instructions for dealing with these.

The ecclesiastical duties assigned to the rectors seem to have constituted the area of greatest variation in Gregory's practice, which, in turn, must have depended to a very large degree on local circumstances and the individuals involved. Thus Peter the sub-deacon received in his very first instructions, as we have seen (above), the duty of convening episcopal councils in Sicily; he was told to enquire into the bishops' faults, and, overriding the customary procedures of election by clergy and people, to send candidates he deemed suitable for appointment to Rome to be approved by Gregory and ordained.[29] Rectors were asked to find candidates suitable to be ordained to the priesthood, to look after the revenues

---

[25] *Ep.* I.I: *vices nostras ... commisimus.*

[26] Cf. *App.* I; and *Ep.* VII.19.

[27] *Ep.* XIII.20. In *Ep.* VIII.16 the duties of *defensores* are said to be *in causis ecclesiae et obsequiis ... pontificum.*

[28] Of the formulaic letters concerning the appointment of rectors in the *Registrum* only *Epp.* IX.29 and 30 are used in the *Liber diurnus* (C 52, 53 Foerster, 207; a fragment of IX.29 in C51). The directive given to Peter the sub-deacon (App. I in Norberg's edition of the *Registrum*) is clearly personal and cannot have been intended to be generally applicable to all rectors; it is in any case not the original document of appointment, but makes reference to one (*capitulare quod dedi*): which may be *Ep.* I.42, which is no less personal in character.

[29] *Ep.* I.18. And to examine their suitability: *Ep.* III.39; for ordination as bishop: *Ep.* VII.38 (the deacon Cyprian in Sicily).

of a church during a vacancy, to consign 'lapsed' priests and deacons to their appropriate penance (also making the necessary financial arrangements for them and their families), to make sure local bishops enforced Gregory's rules for the chastity of their sub-deacons;[30] to transfer relics to an Arian church taken over for Catholic worship;[31] to help to ease friction between bishops, their clergy and people;[32] tactfully to dissuade bishops from over-hasty sentences of excommunication;[33] to bring renegade monks to their senses and meet their obligations, and to prohibit new customs being imposed on monasteries by priests;[34] to depose a sinful abbot and to arrange the ordination of a successor;[35] to look into (with an abbot) the justice of an excommunication;[36] to finish off an enquiry (begun by a bishop) into a charge of witchcraft;[37] to secure the election of Gregory's favoured candidate as bishop, to assist him in his ministry by persuading a neighbouring bishop to transfer a priest to him;[38] to look into complaints of clergy against their bishop's payment of their stipends;[39] to look into the complaints of an aristocrat against his bishop;[40] to stop bishops haunting the law-courts,[41] or living with women;[42] to admonish 'frequently' a bishop to treat his clergy kindly and to arrange a reconciliation between him and them;[43] and, conversely, to carry out severe punishments of clergy where necessary.[44] Gregory's last surviving letter takes up a frequent subject: the correction (here in collaboration with a bishop), 'with the utmost severity', of the custom of monks living perversely and associating with women.[45]

This sample, taken for the most part from Sicily, suffices to indicate the range of ecclesiastical duties Gregory expected the rectors of the Roman Church's patrimonies to perform. They are likely to have caused some

[30] *Ep.*1.42. Cf. *Ep.* IV.34, where the custom is said to have been prohibited by a Roman deacon acting on the authority of Pelagius II.

[31] *Ep.* III.19.

[32] *Ep.* III.34.

[33] *Ep.* II.50; see below, pp. 119–20.

[34] *Ep.* II.26 (to Stephen, a *chartularius*). Cf. *Ep.* I.40 on monks wandering from monastery to monastery. Cf. also *Ep.* IX.145 on a run-away slave trying to become a monk.

[35] *Ep.* III.23.

[36] *Ep.* III.27.

[37] *Ep.* V.32. In *Ep.* XI.33 another Sicilian rector is commended for his zeal in a similar matter.

[38] *Ep.* VI.20.

[39] *Ep.* VIII.7; cf. XI.22.

[40] *Ep.* IX.32.

[41] *Ep.* X.4. In *App.* I the rector's duties include preventing bishops from dabbling in secular business, except in protecting the poor.

[42] *Ep.* IX.111.

[43] *Ep.* XIV.4. Cf. III.34 on helping a bishop to be respected by his people (Campania).

[44] *Ep.* XI.53.

[45] *Ep.* XIV.17. Cf. *Ep.* I.48.

friction between clergy, especially bishops, and the rectors who were in lower orders, deacons and subdeacons, *defensores* or *notarii*. Gregory's correspondence contains many examples of cases in which such friction arose from the overlap of spheres of authority. Some legal cases involving clergy were dealt with by *defensores* when they should in fact have been heard by the bishop; Gregory reprimanded one of his rectors and warned him not to presume thus to encroach on the bishops' rights and defined more carefully the imprecise boundaries between the rector's and the bishops' authority. If the rector failed to defend the 'ecclesiastical order', all would fall into confusion.[46] Difficulties with an unsatisfactory bishop such as Ianuarius of Cagliari (see above, pp. 110–11) placed a particularly heavy burden on the pope's agents, and needed particularly tactful handling. Gregory was anxious that the patronage of the *defensor* should not usurp the bishop's rights.[47] In September 591 Gregory formally appointed bishop Maximian of Syracuse – another close friend – as his vicar in 'all the churches of Sicily',[48] apparently formally superseding Peter the subdeacon's appointment. It will in any case have helped to restrict the rectors' competence in ecclesiastical matters. In North Africa, there is much clearer evidence of resentment among bishops of the authority Gregory gave to his agent. In 592 Gregory intended his representative to call – with the aid of a trusted local bishop – a provincial council;[49] ten years later, the same agent was told to make himself available to come to a council if the bishops thought the cause required his presence.[50] Bitter experience had taught Gregory to scale down unrealistic expectations. There were, as we shall see (Chapter 13), special reasons why the pope's agent might have been unwelcome to participate in the African Church's affairs; but this again illustrates the tension that the intrusion of a papal official could engender in ecclesiastical affairs.

The rector's conduct was expected to conform to Gregory's exacting standards of integrity. He was expected to live up to the title by which he was generally addressed in the pope's correspondence, a 'vigorous man' (*vir strenuus*), loyal and conscientious (*fidelem, sollicitum*); he was to be aware 'of the divine judgement, mindful of our admonition, so as to conduct himself effectively and faithfully, free from the danger of neglect or, which

---

[46] *Ep.* XI.24.
[47] *Epp.* IX.204, 205.
[48] *Ep.* II.5. The function was personal, not attached to his see. The appointment of Maximian as vicar may also be related to the division of the patrimony in Sicily into two parts, each with its own rector: see above, p. 112, n. 4.
[49] *Ep.* II.39.
[50] *Ep.* XII. 8 and 9.

God forbid, fraud'.⁵¹ He had to render annual accounts of income and
expenditure, carry out his duties with energy and exactitude, as well as
tact; and he was sternly forbidden to be high-handed:

If you discover anything that by right belongs to the Church, beware of reclaiming
it by force; especially as I have decreed that under the penalty of anathema no title
[of ownership] shall be placed by our Church on any urban or rural property.
Whatever belongs by reason to the poor [i. e. the Church's patrimony] shall be
claimed for them by reason. Otherwise, in achieving something good by bad
means, we shall be convicted by almighty God of injustice for the way we seek
justice.⁵²

He was to make himself 'loved for his humility, not repugnant through
pride', without, however, compromising his authority in opposing wickedness; his humility should not make him slack, his authority should not be
rigid: 'let justice season your humility, and your humility make your justice
agreeable'.⁵³ Considering the frequency of cases that were likely to bring
the rectors into contact with public authorities, Gregory cultivated, and
expected them to cultivate, good relations with them.⁵⁴ He was also
expected to pay the customary sweeteners or customary bribes to func-
tionaires as required.⁵⁵ There is evidence to indicate that rectors were
sometimes, perhaps often, well liked in their areas: when Cyprian the deacon in charge of the patrimony in the Syracusan region was recalled to
Rome in 598 he left his heart in Sicily.⁵⁶

While Gregory used the rectors of the patrimonies both as an aid in
overseeing and controlling ecclesiastical matters, and as informal channels of information and influence,⁵⁷ their primary function was to act as
his representatives in his capacity as landlord. They represented the pope
to his tenants, peasants and other persons on the Church's estates.
(Gregory's correspondence throws a fair amount of light on their organisation, a subject by-passed here.⁵⁸) In this capacity their functions were still
very wide, including but spreading far beyond controlling tenurial relations, arbitrating in disputes, and taking responsibility for revenue. Broadly,

---

⁵¹ E.g. *Ep.* IX.29.
⁵² *App.* I. Cf. the decree (III) of the Roman synod of 595 (*Ep.* V.57a, *MGH Epp.* I. 52; 364). For examples,
   see *Ep.* 1.63; 71; on a public official affixing a *titulus* on property, *Ep.* 1.38 (*CC* 140. 313).
⁵³ *App.* I: *ut nec humilitas tua remissa sit, nec auctoritas rigida, quatenus et humilitatem rectitudo condiat, et ipsam tuam
   rectitudinem humilitas blandam reddat.*
⁵⁴ *Ep.* IX.239; cf. *App.* I.
⁵⁵ *Ep.* II.50: Gregory advised the rector to arrange for the payment to be channelled through the person
   who would benefit from the request.
⁵⁶ *Ep.* IX.15.
⁵⁷ Their local power is clearly shown by the patronage they could exercise: see e. g. *Ep.* IX.80.
⁵⁸ On it, see Spearing, *The patrimonies*; and especially Recchia, *Gregorio Magno*, 11–114.

their duties, in addition to the mixture of ecclesiastical functions already considered, may be summarised under the following headings: (i) supervision of general (and sometimes not so general) management; (ii) protection of individuals, occasionally small groups, against violence, injustice and exploitation; (iii) giving alms or other assistance; (iv) intervening in various capacities in legal disputes, especially over land; (v) execution of wills and deeds of gift; (vi) securing supplies of various kinds; (vii) collecting, accounting for and forwarding revenue from the estates. It would be neither profitable nor feasible to catalogue and classify examples. A few will suffice to indicate the range of their work.

The most detailed of Gregory's instructions to his rectors were issued to Peter the rector in charge of the Sicilian lands. They show the huge variety of the rectors' work and the extent of the pope's concern. In May 591, to consider by way of example a selection from one of Gregory's longest set of instructions, Gregory wrote to Peter, telling him (among many other things) that the peasants on church lands are to be paid the market price for their corn; there were to be no unwarranted surcharges, no fee for insuring the grain against loss during shipment to Rome. Each peasant was to be given a certificate of the precise payment due, to safeguard his liability after Gregory's death. No false measures to be used: 'If you find any false weights you must break them up and provide new ones.' Peasants are to be lent the money from church funds to pay the land-tax (*burdatio*) due before their crops have been sold, so as to avoid the need to borrow at extortionate interest. They are to be compensated for unjust exactions by farmers (*conductores*). A variety of instructions for payments to individuals, debts owed and alms, executing wills, assisting indigent clergy and others follows.[59] Even more detailed directions were given in another letter, which specifies what cattle, horses and farm-utensils are to be sold and when they are to be disposed of for maximum profit. In the same letter Gregory asks Peter to do what he can to mollify a Sicilian monk: the monk Pretiosus had evidently been given some grave punishment (excommunication?) by bishop Maximian, had appealed to Gregory, who sent him packing back to Maximian, and then regretted his action. He now thought he had treated Pretiosus badly, rebuked him too severely, and he was now bitten by remorse. He had asked bishop Maximian to send Pretiosus back to Rome to allow Gregory to redress the unsympathetic treatment, but his request met with a refusal. What could Gregory do now to get reconciled with the monk, without offending the bishop? Let Peter use his tact, 'if in your diminutive body you have wisdom out of proportion to your size';

---

[59] *Ep.* 1.42: the text takes up over seven pages in the *CC* edition.

and quietly, in private, he should discourage the bishop from pronouncing sentence too hastily. Gregory closes this long letter with a complaint about 'a miserable horse and five good donkeys' that Peter had sent him: he has nothing to ride, the horse being too miserable, the donkeys unsuitable.[60]

The prominence given by Gregory's biographer to his pastoral aims in his use of the administrative machinery of the patrimonies is amply justified.[61] Apart from their work in enforcing discipline among clergy and people (see above, pp. 115–6), and in addition to the use made of them in Gregory's missionary enterprises (see chapter 5), they were constantly required to act as the channels of papal protection and charity. To take examples almost at random from a vast number scattered through the Register: the case of a Cosmas, a Syrian merchant in Sicily, heavily in debt, who has had to hand over his son as surety to his creditors, is to be carefully looked into, and, if found to be as alleged, the rector is to help him from 'the assets of the poor' (that is, from Church funds), furnishing the payment required – and no more! – to secure his son's freedom; and to enter the expense in the accounts as authorised by the pope. The following year Gregory sent a sum to be used for this purpose, the balance left over to be given to Cosmas and his son for their livelihood and the repayment of the remaining debt.[62] A bishop is to be given a 1,000 *modii* of grain, or, if necessary and feasible, up to 2,000, to help to feed his people in a time of shortage.[63] Jewish converts about to be baptised and too poor to provide themselves with baptismal robes are to be given them; nuns of the local monastery to be given what assistance may be needed; the cost to be entered in the accounts.[64] A reconciled schismatic from Istria on his way to Sicily is to be given protection and a stipend, to be entered in the rector's accounts.[65] The complaint of a lady who thinks she is being persecuted by a convert Jew's witchcraft and by his dependants is to be investigated, and the culprit(s) brought to punishment.[66] The orphaned beneficiary of a gift is to be helped to obtain possession of the house he has been given; and the rector is not to excuse his stalling on the matter by pleading inadequate

---

[60] *Ep.* II.50. The episode of the monk invites comparison with the pastoral principles on administering rebuke enunciated in *RP* II.10 and III.17.

[61] See above, n. 1.

[62] *Ep.* III.55; IV.43. In the second letter Gregory refers to the law, probably Justinian's *Nov.* 134.7.

[63] *Ep.* VI.4.

[64] *Ep.* VIII.23; cf. aid to monks, nuns and communities: *Epp.* I.23; 37; 57; III.5; IV.31 (Jewish converts); IX.36; 85 (to repay the cost of redeeming his wife from captivity); 137; 191 (to remit payments due from an impoverished tenant).

[65] *Ep.* VI.38. Cf. *Ep.* VI.47, where a bishop is asked to act thus. On the schism see chapter 9, and on Gregory's aid to reconciled schismatics, p. 132.

[66] *Ep.* VII.41. Cf. IX.39; 194 for other cases of protection.

documentation in his instructions.[67] A slave and his wife are to be given protection against violence by a *vir clarissimus*, who is either to be induced to desist or brought to judgement by arbitrators acting with the rector.[68] The dependants of a nobleman fallen on hard times are to be given clothes.[69] An impoverished *vir gloriosus* is reprimanded for being too shy to ask for money for charitable purposes; the rector is to pay the monastery founded by him in Catania ten *solidi* a year, which he is asked to accept 'without indignation'.[70] Protection against officials, within the limits of justice, was granted to high and low: from 'Augustine the soap-maker' to Libertinus the ex-praetor of Sicily;[71] and the local rectors were usually to act on the pope's behalf to secure it.

ROME: THE COMMON LARDER

The rectors' core function was to be the hub of a sophisticated economic system. The revenues they were responsible for collecting and of which they had to keep records were not intended only for occasional local alms and assistance to the needy. They provided the resources for the Roman Church's running expenses and its large-scale charity. John the deacon, who had access to more documents on the financial administration of the Roman Church than now survive, confirms what one would have expected: the income due from the patrimonies was carefully recorded in the *polyptychon* preserved in the archives and kept up to date. The sums received, accounted for by the regular returns from the rectors, were spent on the salaries of clergy and officials, payments to local cemeteries, monasteries, hospices and welfare-stations (*diaconiis, xenodochiis urbanis vel suburbanis*).[72] In addition, John writes,

To all the poor he [Gregory] distributed the accumulated revenues at the beginning of every month; and at the appropriate times, grain, wine, cheese, vegetables, lard, edible animals, fish or oil, he distributed most carefully [*discretissime*] as the head of the Lord's household [*paterfamilias*] ... so that the universal Church appeared as in fact the universal larder.[73]

He goes on to detail the recipients of the Roman Church's regular alms: 3,000 nuns, who received fifteen pounds of gold for their bedding, and

---

[67] *Ep.* IX.48 and 200.
[68] *Ep.* IX.210.
[69] *Ep.* X.12.
[70] *Ep.* XIII.21.
[71] *saponarii*: *Ep.* IX.114. On Libertinus and protection against high officials, see chapter 6, pp. 90–91 above.
[72] *Vita* II.24–5. Cf. Recchia, *Gregorio Magno*, 29 on accounts.
[73] *Vita* II.26. I have taken the liberty of substituting 'larder' for John's *horrea*.

eighty annually for their living expenses; food and sustenance to the infirm and needy in all quarters of the City, and for those begging at the doors of the papal residence. He mentions a huge volume (*praegrande volumen*) still preserved in the Lateran *scrinium* containing a list of all the regular recipients of papal gifts in Rome, its environs and in places further away, together with the amounts allotted.[74] There were also many occasional payments.[75] Among others the Roman Church's funds had to meet were expenses such as the subsidies to the government, to Lombard leaders (see above, Chapter 7), advancing soldiers' pay, redeeming captives, and purchasing grain for public distribution.[76] The *Liber pontificalis* records some very modest building activity undertaken by Gregory: alterations in St Peter's on the Vatican hill (changes around the *confessio* apparently to facilitate access) and St Paul's outside the walls.[77] The Roman Church's patrimony was used to support such building activities: it had to supply timbers for the churches of St Peter's and St Paul's; occasionally it financed furnishings.[78] All this in addition to the many one-off payments of which we have noted a few examples. As a great historian of the papacy observed, 'the capital had become, especially economically, a papal Rome'.[79]

Such commitments clearly required a highly organised, supervised and efficient administrative system, as well as devoted and motivated staff. We have seen (above, p. 113) how Gregory set about to secure these aims by overhauling the network of his agents in the various patrimonies. The rudiments of a central organisation were already in place; the papal notaries, on whom much of the clerical and accounting work must have rested, but who were also sometimes called to administrative duties of a more exacting sort, were already organised in a college (*schola*). Gregory set up a similar organisation for the Roman *defensores*, defining their rank and their privileges.[80]

---

[74] *Vita* II.27–30: it seems probable that John had consulted this volume.

[75] Examples could be multiplied: e. g. *Ep.* I.54.

[76] Details in Spearing, *Patrimonies*. On the manner in which grain was kept in ecclesiastical granaries (*horrea*) on behalf of the imperial *sitonicum*, see *Ep.* IX.116; V.36; 38; 39 (*CC* 140. 306–7; 313; 316–17). On the overlap between civil and ecclesiastical grain supplies, their storage and the resultant friction, see Hartmann, *Untersuchungen*, 100–2. The Roman Church itself distributed grain in time of need: Peter the sub-deacon was asked to purchase fifty pounds-worth *ab extraneis*, to store it until needed, and to arrange for its shipment to Rome in February 592: *Ep.* I.70. Cf. *Ep.* I.2. For a general account, see Arnaldi, 'L'approvvigionamento'.

[77] *LP* 66. For a summary, see Heitz, 'Les monuments', 37–8 on adaptations at St Peter's and St Paul's.

[78] *Epp.* IX.125–7. This suggests that more substantial restoration work may have been carried out than the work mentioned in the *Liber pontificalis*. Large timbers were also to be supplied for Alexandria: *Ep.* XIII.43. See also *Ep.* IX.17 on a patrimony supplying 24 folding chairs.

[79] Caspar, *Geschichte*, I, 338.

[80] *Ep.* VIII.16. On the development of the papal *scrinium* and its organisation, see McShane, *La Romanitas*, 313–25 and 359–74.

The papal 'household' did not, strictly speaking, form a part of this administrative system. In Gregory's mind, however, it clearly belonged to a set of interrelated institutions, and, along with them, it required reform to meet his clear sense of the hierarchy of functions served by each. He stipulated that the servants of the papal residence (*cubiculi*) should not be lay people, but that the pope should always be surrounded by clergy, or by monks[81] – as he had been while he was his predecessor's *apocrisiarius* in Constantinople. Gregory's purpose was part of a wider reform, also aimed at the traditional dominance of the diaconal college in Rome. Early in his pontificate he deposed the archdeacon appointed by his predecessor, 'for his pride and unspecified misdemeanours';[82] and he undermined the college's prestige by depriving it of its traditional monopoly of singing certain parts of the mass. Deacons were not to be appointed for their fine voices; the singing at mass could well be carried out by sub-deacons or by persons in lower orders, leaving the deacons free for the office of preaching and administration of alms. John the deacon's account of these reforms, with its emphasis on Gregory's love of music, transforms Gregory's evidently pastoral and ascetic intentions into something more resembling the Carolingian kings' patronage of the arts.[83] This was a decisive break with the policies of his predecessors, under whom the Roman clergy, led by the diaconate and the archdeacon, were dominant. Gregory took care to distance himself from these circles.[84] From those who are 'placed at the summit of authority'[85] to all levels in the Church, its pastors are to conform with Gregory's ascetic and ministerial ideals. What was to count now was not official position, but holiness of life.

The machinery for governing the Roman Church's lands was large, complex, well controlled and on the whole both efficient and humane. It secured the revenues needed for meeting the expenses of a considerable ecclesiastical establishment as well as for furnishing the resources needed for a far-reaching programme of charitable assistance of the needy, and of monks and nuns. It provided the pope with an instrument for the oversight of the churches he considered committed to his care; and it enabled him to work with the civil administration in the provinces, to exert pressure on it – by no means always successfully – as and when he thought it necessary.

---

[81] *Ep.* v.57a (*MGH Epp.* 1. 363).
[82] App. III.
[83] *Vita* II.6. On it, the perceptive discussion by Berschin, *Biographie*, 3. 372–87.
[84] On this change, see Caspar, *Geschichte*, II, 403–4, who refers in this connection to the story about abbot Equitius in *Dial.* 1.4 (on which see above, pp. 66–7).
[85] *in culmine praelationis positi: I Reg.* IV.3.

The papal patrimony formed an effective complement to the machinery of civil administration at a time when this was undergoing a major transformation everywhere in the Western provinces (see chapter 1).

CHAPTER 9

Scissum corpus: *the schism of the Three Chapters*

THE SCHISM

Gregory had to face the problems of a Church deeply divided. Even before his pontificate, as a deacon in his predecessor's service, he had to come to grips with the schism which had split the Italian Church since the second Council of Constantinople (553).[1] The roots of the schism reached back into the christological debates settled, though by no means laid to rest, at Chalcedon in 451. The Chalcedonian definition did not find lasting consent everywhere.[2] By the end of the fifth century fierce debate around it had again broken out. In 518 Justin I, a Latin speaker from Illyricum, ascended the imperial throne, to be followed by his nephew, Justinian, in 527. Under them the government became committed to the re-establishment of imperial unity. The old dream of an Empire re-united within its former territories, with a single law and a single faith, became a political programme.[3] Of these, the reform of the law proved, in the event, the only lasting achievement. The establishment of a single orthodox faith accepted throughout the Empire proved elusive. It depended on reconciling Eastern dissidents, 'monophysites', especially in Syria and Egypt, to an interpretation of the Chalcedonian formula which would not alienate Western churchmen. In the century since 451 neo-Chalcedonian theologians had been refining their understanding of the formula adopted at Chalcedon. For many Eastern theologians the primary need was to banish any shadow of association with Nestorianism. Justinian struggled with the theological problems. His attempt to resolve the conflict culminated in the second Council of Constantinople in 553. After a good deal of hesitation

---

[1] The Gregorian authorship of the third letter printed by Hartmann in Appendix III of his edition of the *Registrum*, 449–467, has been established beyond reasonable doubt by Meyvaert, 'A letter'. I shall consider the letter below, p. 128.

[2] See Moeller, 'Le chalcédonisme'. The best general account is still to be found in Duchesne, *L'église*, chapters. 5 and 6. For the theological aspects, the fullest treatment now is Grillmeier, *Christ*, II/2, 411–62.

[3] See on this Markus, 'Justinian'.

and repeated changes of mind, pope Vigilius, abducted from Rome, under intense pressure from the emperor, in the end endorsed the device by which the emperor had hoped to secure unity: upholding Chalcedon, but minimising the offence it caused in the East. The emperor hoped to achieve this by condemning Theodore of Mopsuestia and some controversial writings much in evidence at Chalcedon, by Theodoret of Cyrrhus and Ibas of Edessa, the so-called 'Three Chapters'. To many Western churchmen the condemnation seemed a betrayal of Chalcedon. Resistance was widespread, especially in theologically well-informed circles, such as the North African Church.[4]

One of the leaders of Western resistance in Constantinople had been the Roman deacon Pelagius. On succeeding Vigilius as pope – as the emperor's nominee, strongly opposed in Italy – he had changed his view, and adopted the emperor's. The papacy was now aligned with the court, and it had to make considerable efforts over the next fifty years to explain away its surrender and to allay widespread suspicion about its consistency in upholding the supremacy of Chalcedon. It had few allies in the Western Church. Gregory's predecessors had to work hard, and not always with complete success, to re-establish the reputation of the Roman see in Gaul[5] and elsewhere in the West, deploying diplomacy and equivocation, passing over the embarrassing Fifth Council in silence while re-affirming their firm adherence to Chalcedon.

In Italy the churches in the North, less closely subject to the metropolitan authority of the Roman see than the suburbicarian bishoprics, were in revolt. The bishops of the two great Northern metropolitan sees of Aquileia and Milan broke off communion. Even with the support of the imperial administration and the military authorities, pope Pelagius I (556–561) was unable to obtain the consent of many bishops in Northern Italy; and military considerations inhibited the government from giving its unambiguous backing, adopting toleration of religious dissent in order to secure the political loyalties of the dissidents. In these circumstances Ravenna became the mainstay of imperial orthodoxy in Italy. The city was the residence of the Exarch, the centre of the imperial administration in Italy, and the see of a bishop whose status had inexorably risen, along with the civil importance of his city and with the favour of the court; but even here there were rumblings of dissent.[6]

---

[4] For detail and references, see Markus, 'Reflections'.
[5] Traces of the schism still survived in Autun in the 590s: see chapter 11, note 38.
[6] For the rise of the see of Ravenna and its relations with Rome, see Chapter 10 below. For dissent in Ravenna, see below, p. 136.

We have little detailed evidence for the state of affairs during the pontif-
icates of Pelagius I's successors, until the last years of Pelagius II (579–590).
The principal change in the situation had been brought about by the
Lombard invasions since the late 560s. The history of the schism is closely
bound up with the Lombard occupation of Northern Italy. Dissent survived
in areas occupied by the Lombards as well as in places under imperial control. Its most visible results were the splits in the churches of Milan and of
Aquileia. These were the two great North Italian sees, intent on guarding
their traditional independence of Roman jurisdiction. Circumstances, as
we shall see, combined in such a way as to allow the pope to extend the
scope for intervention in the areas under imperial control in the North of
Italy, while losing his influence in schismatic areas, mainly within the
Lombard occupied lands. The outcome in Italy was, in effect, the gradual
emergence of two 'territorial churches'.

AQUILEIA

At the time of the Lombard invasion the patriarch of Aquileia had transferred his see to Grado.[7] Around 580 archbishop Elias built a new cathedral, significantly dedicated to the highly emblematic Chalcedonian St
Euphemia, at Grado; and he called a synod of bishops of the province
of Istria and Venetia to 'confirm, having laid all doubts to rest, all that
has been doubted about the Council of Chalcedon'.[8] The patriarch of
Aquileia and the churches of Istria remained firm in rejecting the Fifth
Council and severing communion with the Roman see.

Soon after an armistice arranged with the Lombards in 585 pope
Pelagius II resumed attempts to heal the schism. He wrote to Elias and the
Istrian bishops reaffirming the papacy's duty of care (citing Matt. 16:18)
for all the churches, summoning them tearfully to return to the 'bowels
of mother Church', reassuring them of the integrity of its faith. Like
Pelagius I before him, he passed in silence over the Second Council of
Constantinople and reaffirmed the faith of the four Councils and especially of Chalcedon. They had no reason, therefore, he urged, to persist
in their separation.[9] A second letter shows how embittered the schism
had become.[10] It was written in reply to their rejoinder (which has not
survived), which the pope described as 'a list of indictments or rather

---

[7] Paul Diac., *HL* II.10.
[8] *Chronicon patriarcharum* 1–2 (*MGH SSRL* 393). Significantly, it was the pope Sergius (see below, n. 74) who
    reconciled the Aquileian schismatics who also restored the Roman church dedicated to St Euphemia.
[9] *Ep.* 1 (*MGH Epp.* 2, App. III, 442–5).
[10] *Ep.* 2 (*MGH Epp.* 2, App. III, 445–9).

anathemas ... indeed a judgement'.[11] The pope added a compilation of testimonies taken from the papal archive to substantiate the claim that the Fifth Council had decreed 'nothing about the Council of Chalcedon but that the definition of its faith be inviolably upheld'.[12] Quotations from the scriptures and Cyprian followed to recall them to unity.

This appeal, too, failed, and a third, long, letter followed. There can now be no doubt that this letter was written by Gregory as deacon in his predecessor's service and on his behalf, probably before or just after his return from Constantinople.[13] In this letter we find faced, for the first time, the argument used by the Istrians in support of their opposition: that initially the apostolic see along with all the Latin Church had opposed the condemnation of the Three Chapters.[14] And, again for the first time we have a careful defence of the change of mind on the part of the papacy:

Dear brethren, do you think that to Peter, who was reversing his position [*sibi dissimilia docenti* – 'contradicting himself'], one should have replied: We refuse to hear what you are saying since you previously taught the opposite? If in the matter of the Three Chapters one position was held while truth was being sought, and a different position was adopted after truth had been found, why should a change of position be imputed a crime to this See which is humbly venerated by all in the person of its founder? For what is reprehensible is not to change one's stand, but to entertain fickle opinions [*non enim mutatio sententiae sed inconstantia sensus in culpa est*]. Now if the mind remains unwavering in seeking to know what is right, why should you object when it abandons its ignorance and reformulates its position?

Remarkable words for a pope, the more so for having been written for him by a deacon who was to become pope Gregory the Great.[15] After a lengthy

[11] *quasi capitularem vel interdictum potius ... velut iudicatum ...* : *Ibid.*, 446.

[12] *Ibid.*, 446. As Caspar (*Geschichte*, 2, 369–70; 372 n. 1) notes, the pope evidently treated only the first six sessions of Chalcedon as authoritative, thus excluding its approval of Theodore, Theodoret and Ibas from its binding decisions, which he described as *privatae causae quae illic post definitionem fidei actae sunt*, which were to be the subject of further discussion.

[13] *Ep.* 3 (*MGH Epp.* 2. App. III, 449–67). On it, and especially on its authorship and the controverted history of its attribution to Gregory, see now Meyvaert, 'A letter', who argues convincingly that its author is Gregory, and that letters 1 and 2 are not from his pen. (Caspar, *Geschichte*, II, 371 nn. 4 and 5 reached the same conclusion.) As Baluze noticed (Mansi, x.164), the documentation in the letter is drawn from the Latin translation of Sessions IV and V of the council (cf. *ACO* IV / 1, 39–136). I am nevertheless inclined to accept Meyvaert's arguments on Gregory's access to and use of Greek documents. This would imply that the letter was written, or at least begun, in Constantinople, or very soon after Gregory's return to Rome. On the Greek material, see also Schieffer, 'Zur Beurteilung', especially his 'Excurs: Zu einem falsch bezeichneten Zitat bei Papst Pelagius II', *ibid.*, 189–92.

[14] *Ibid.*, 455, ll. 3–8.

[15] *Ibid.*, 455, l. 48_456, l. 7. I have quoted the translation by Meyvaert, 'A letter'. Cf. Caspar, *Geschichte*, 373: 'Wie sehr hoben sich diese Ausführungen nicht allein von dem Schlusse des letzten Briefs Pelagius' II., sondern von allen stolzen Primatsthesen der päpstlichen Vorgänger ab!'

reply to the Istrians' arguments about the condemnations the letter appeals to their generosity of mind:

> You know, beloved brethren, that a thing subject to uncertainty should always be interpreted so as to give it the benefit of the doubt [*in parte semper est interpretanda meliore*]. What is to prevent [Theodore & co.] being praised by one Father while his error was still obscure and subject to doubt, and, when his error later became known, being shot through by the judgements of almost all the great Fathers like a wild beast by a growing shower of missiles?

– and the letter concludes with a final appeal for peace and unity.[16]

As pope, Gregory was immediately drawn into the problems of the Istrian schism, at a peculiarly difficult moment. At the end of his second letter Pelagius II had hinted that he would invoke the support of the Exarch, at that time Smaragdus, if the Istrians were to prove obstinate and refuse to send accredited representatives to discuss the issue at stake between them, either to Rome, or to Ravenna, where a meeting might more easily be held in these difficult times.[17] The pope's invitation had evidently been declined, and the Exarch's men used force against the Istrians, thus further inflaming the situation. At their request, the emperor issued an order forbidding the Exarch from molesting the schismatic bishops. Paul the Deacon recounts how Elias's successor as patriarch of Aquileia, Severus, had been dragged from his cathedral by the Exarch, taken to Ravenna with three of his suffragan bishops, where they were compelled to enter into communion with bishop John of Ravenna. After a year, returning to Grado, they were repudiated by their own people and fellow-bishops. A council of Istrian bishops was called, which received the patriarch's recantation and restored him to communion with his schismatic colleagues.[18] All this had taken place on the eve of Gregory's accession to the see of Rome, in 588–89.

Attempted coercion and the ensuing violence had embittered the schism, and renewed Lombard incursions modified the government's attitude. The Exarch Smaragdus had been recalled – he was said to have gone mad – and Romanus appointed as his successor, evidently charged to deal with the schismatics in a more conciliatory manner in these troubled times. Gregory seems not to have been aware of a shift in the official policy when he wrote to the patriarch Severus within four months of his accession, reprimanding him severely for his relapse into schism after his reconciliation

---

[16] *Ibid.*, 466, ll. 10–14; 467.
[17] *Ep.* 3 (*MGH Epp.* 2. App. iii, 449, ll. 4–16).
[18] *HL* iii.26.

(forcibly exacted in Ravenna, under pressure from the previous Exarch).
Again, Gregory summoned the patriarch, as had Pelagius II previously, to
come with his followers to Rome for a council to judge these contentious
matters, in accordance with imperial orders, and sent two officers to
enforce his demand.[19] The Istrian bishops assembled and sent a submission to the emperor Maurice.[20] Subjected for their sins, they wrote, to the
barbarian yoke, they had steadfastly kept the integrity of the Catholic
faith intact. Now deprived of the peace that imperial rule had formerly
secured for them, they wished with all their strength to return to it. Having
thus carefully prepared their ground, the bishops went on to rehearse the
sad history of the division that had arisen in the Church: they recalled the
'execrable' condemnation of the Three Chapters, the resistance of the
Western churches and their subsequent capitulation under imperial bully-
ing (*imperiali pondere*), and their own inflexible fidelity. They reminded
Maurice of the harassment of archbishop Elias by Smaragdus, and the
emperor's order issued in response to their appeal that he should cease to
bother any of the bishops on this score, and to desist from forcing anyone
into unwilling communion. Then they recounted the recent history of
Severus. They went on to complain of Gregory's recent summons to their
patriarch, with the alleged backing of an imperial order – one they knew,
they said, to have been obtained from the emperor by devious means – to
go to Rome. Reduced to utter despair (*ad ultimam desperationem*) that their
metropolitan should be required to submit himself to the judgement of
the opposing party in the dispute, they discreetly pointed out that their
archbishop was, anyway, not authorised to commit their Church in this
matter and that the people would never tolerate being 'driven from the
ancient catholic communion'. They professed their loyalty to the Empire
and asked to be left in peace; for otherwise they foresaw a wholesale deser-
tion by the Istrian bishops, whose loyalty might be deflected from the
Empire towards the 'archbishops of Gaul'. The letter had its desired effect
at the court. Predictably, in his reply to Gregory the emperor forbade him
to afflict the Istrian and Venetian bishops in the present troubled state of
Italy, until peace, and with it the Church's order, might be restored.[21]

 Gregory had no choice but to acquiesce; but he did so reluctantly, com-
plying with imperial policy only to the extent that he had no alternative.
Not much later he told archbishop John of Ravenna that he would never

[19] *iuxta christianissimi et serenissimi rerum domini iussiones*; *Ep.* 1.16 (16, l. 11). The sending of a *tribunus* and an
   excubitor is mentioned in *Ep.* 1.16b (*MGH Epp.* i. 22, l. 12).
[20] *Ep.* 1.16A (*MGH Epp.* i. 17–21). The two other letters referred to in I.16b (*MGH* i.22, ll. 9–11) have not
   survived.
[21] *Ep.* 1.16b (*MGH Epp.* i. 22–3).

cease to remonstrate strongly and openly (*summo zelo et libertate rescribere*) with the emperor on this matter; and he consoled John – who had evidently had some tussle with the Exarch – telling him not to let himself be worried by his hostility: for a bishop had to tolerate maturely and with dignity offences done to him by people placed beneath him in order and precedence. John had also proposed sending alms to the schismatic Severus, whose city had been burnt down; but Gregory would not have it: should succour not be sent first to the faithful, rather than to the Church's enemies, who had been spending money in promoting their case at the court?[22] Gregory could be harsh: some schismatic bishops of an unknown province, who had informed the pope of the persecution they had undergone for their steadfastness, were peremptorily reminded that their affliction would be of no avail to them for salvation, since, as St Cyprian had written, 'it is not the suffering but the cause that makes the martyr'. Let the integrity of their faith lead them back to the Church, their mother which gave them birth.[23]

   During Maurice's reign Gregory could not hope to enlist the support of the secular authorities in this matter. His concern about the Exarch's obstructive tactics seems to have been well founded. Under the two Exarchs between Smaragdus's two tenures of the office, that is to say between 590 and 602/3, the pope's plans were constantly being frustrated in Ravenna; and the bishops and clergy of the city were drawn into anti-Roman activities.[24] After Maurice's overthrow in 602, however, Smaragdus returned to the office he had held before, and Gregory could once again look to the Exarch for support. Now, however, his request was a modest one: he asked for protection by the Exarch's officers for the bishop of Trieste. This bishop had been reconciled to the Catholic communion and then exposed to harassment in riots allegedly engineered by Severus, the head of the schism, when he had failed to win him over by persuasion. To this specific request Gregory added a plea for the protection of all schismatics wishing to return, and followed this up with a reminder of the zeal Smaragdus had previously shown in this affair, and a wish that it would burn with renewed fervour, so that the enemies of God might find in him a guardian more intent on the good of souls than on the good of bodies: 'Let the righteousness of the faith that is strong in you arm you against the dissenters; let the body of the Church [*scissum corpus ecclesiae*] that has been

---

[22] *Ep.* II.38.
[23] *Ep.* II.43, quoting Cyprian, *De unitate*, 14. The lacuna in the address must remain dubious, despite many attempts to fill it.
[24] On Ravenna and Gregory's dealings with officials, see below, chapter 10.

rent be made whole. In this work you will have One who will reward you, who is the Author of righteousness and integrity.'[25] Perhaps there is a hint here of more ominous expectations from Smaragdus – expectations that his reputation might well have justified.

Within imperial territory, under the constraints of official policy, Gregory was not in a position to do much to heal the schism. He had to be content to help and protect schismatics who either had returned or were trying to return to the Catholic Church. They often encountered difficulties, created by local opposition, either by administrators or by lay people. In 599 Gregory remonstrated with the Exarch Callinicus that the imperial order ('though of course', Gregory wrote, 'fraudulently obtained' – *subrepta*) prohibiting compulsion of the schismatics did not mean that he had to obstruct those wishing to return to the Church; he should inform the emperor that people were doing so spontaneously.[26] Several non-schismatic Istrians made their way to Sicily, some passing through Rome; the pope took care that they should be adequately provided for.[27] Some courageously decided to return to Istria; they were commended to the archbishop's, and, with some justifiable apprehension, to the Exarch's, good will and assistance.[28] Bishops willing to come to Rome for discussion of the split were encouraged to do so and offered safe conduct, without prejudice to their return, should they fail to be reconciled.[29] It is hard to judge the extent of this flow of converts from the schism. Despite obstacles evidently created by the civil administration,[30] it seems to have continued throughout Gregory's pontificate. The appearance of a formula for the reception of a repentant schismatic in 602 cannot be taken as evidence for a steady trickle of converts, still less for a flood; it was devised for the return of a particular bishop, Firminus of Trieste.[31] We have ample reason to believe the claim that there, as elsewhere, the schism had strong roots among the local people.

After the assassination of Maurice and the return of Smaragdus to Ravenna, despite the new Exarch's more aggressive disposition – or, rather,

---

[25] *Ep.* XIII.34.

[26] *Ep.* IX.155. The immediate reference here is probably to the people of *insula Caprae* who returned from schism, together with their bishop who then defected again: *Ep.* IX.156. The remonstration made to the Exarch in the previous letter is here repeated, and the pope's representative at the court was also to be alerted.

[27] *Ep.* IV.14; VI.38, 47; IX.151. In one case, a woman whose husband was in Rome and had made himself indispensable to the pope, was bidden to join him there: VII.34; IX.117–118 cast further light on her case. See also IX.161, 162.

[28] *Epp.* IX.142, 149; apprehension: IX.149.

[29] *Ep.* V.56.

[30] The role played by the civil administration in Ravenna is discussed below, chapter 10.

[31] *Ep.* XII.7, 13. Cf. above.

perhaps because of it – the schism was set to continue. Soon after Gregory's death, on the death of the patriarch Severus (607), a pro-Roman patriarch was installed in Grado, now called 'the new Aquileia', with the backing of the Exarch Smaragdus. Under the protection of the Lombard king and the duke Gisulf, an abbot John was made bishop of Aquileia. He wrote to the Lombard king complaining: 'The unhappy suffragans of our church, the bishops of Istria, have been abducted by the Greeks with great force and compulsion from Grado to Ravenna, and there denied freedom of speech; and the worthless Candidianus . . . was ordained bishop.' Three of the Istrian bishops had been dragged by soldiers from their churches with grave offence and injury, and made to assist in his consecration.[32] This forcible imposition of a bishop unacceptable in 'old Aquileia', now under Lombard control, sealed the schism: henceforth there were, as Paul the Deacon sadly says, 'two patriarchs in Aquileia'.[33] In 628 pope Honorius I made use of another unhappy occasion to give papal recognition to the archbishop of Grado and to tie him more closely into the orbit of Rome by bestowing on him the pallium. Fortunatus, the bishop of Aquileia, had raided the church of Grado, and taken its treasure to his own see; this 'Judas', as the pope called him, was to be replaced by Primogenius, whom he was now sending to them to be consecrated.[34] The province of the Aquileian church was now definitively split between a Lombard and a Roman part, until almost the end of the seventh century.[35]

The bishops of Aquileia-Grado had long been using the title of "patriarch", and it had been recognised at least within the region. Thanks to the independence the see gained in the course of the schism, and its subsequent separate development outside the framework of the Western orthodox churches, it was able to preserve the title – alone among Western sees which had at one time or another claimed it – until well into the twelfth century.[36]

MILAN

The other North Italian province which experienced the schism sharply was the metropolitan province of Milan, Liguria and Aemilia. In the

---

[32] *Epp. Langobardicae collectae*, 1 (*MGH Epp.* 3, 693); cf. *Chronicon patriarcharum* 3. Bertolini, 'Riflessi politici', 744–5 has commented on the significance of the reference to compulsion by the Greeks.

[33] On these events, see Paul Diac., *HL* iv.33 and *Chronicon patriarcharum* 3–4 (394); cf. Bertolini, 'Riflessi politici', 736–41.

[34] *Epp. Langobardicae collectae*, 3 (695); cf. *Chronicon patriarcharum* 5–6.

[35] See below, p. 139.

[36] See Fuhrmann, 'Studien II', 43–61, especially p. 50.

period preceding the Fifth Council Datius, the bishop of Milan, had been among the staunchest defenders of the Three Chapters in Constantinople, seeking to strengthen pope Vigilius's will to resist imperial pressure. Datius died in Constantinople; but his successor, Vitalis, allied with the archbishop of Aquileia, kept up the resistance.[37] As the Lombards were rapidly gaining control of Northern Italy, in 569 bishop Honoratus took refuge in Genoa, with a large number of his clergy.[38] His successor, bishop Laurence, allowed himself to be won over from the schismatics, and became a firm ally of the papacy and the Empire.[39] Milan itself was now under Lombard control; in Genoa, isolated from his community, among refugees, he was dependent on the income of his church's Sicilian property, and thus very exposed to Byzantine and papal pressure.[40] He had given a strict undertaking to the apostolic see, signed by a number of great men including Gregory himself, at that time Prefect of the City, in effect submitting to its jurisdiction over his church. As pope, Gregory lost no time to remind Laurence's successor, bishop Constantius, of this submission. It should be stressed that the pledge exacted from Laurence was not simply for assent to the condemnation of the Three Chapters, but, further, for permanent submission to Rome: 'after returning from such a split [in the Church] over no real cause [the Three Chapters], it was just that the apostolic see should take charge [of the Church of Milan], in so much as it always guards unity in the minds of all the bishops of the universal Church'.[41] In a carefully staged official ceremony, the Roman see obtained a formal acceptance of its authority by the ancient metropolitan church of Milan.

Gregory had long (*dudum*) known Constantius, the bishop elected – in obscure circumstances which we shall consider – to succeed Laurence. They had been colleagues as deacons in Constantinople, representing their respective sees at the court; and Gregory professed close friendship

---

[37] Pelagius I, *Ep.* 59.

[38] Paul Diac., *HL* II.25.

[39] For his relations with both and the Frankish king Childebert II, see *Ep. Austr.* 46, and Bognetti, 'Milano langobarda', 95.

[40] As Gregory reminded the Milanese clergy resident in Genoa, their income was safe, being derived from their church's Sicilian and other possessions under imperial control: *Ep.* XI.6 (cf. below, n. 59). See on this Bognetti, *L'età*, 2, 202, and 'La continuità', 428. On the property being managed for the church of Milan by agents of the Roman church, see Gregory, *Ep.* I.80. Some overlap in the management of Sicilian lands belonging to the Roman and to the Milanese churches is also implied by *Ep.* IX.187, if the lands referred to were from the estate of Italica (the likeliest reading at p. 743, l. 19, adopted by Norberg). Cf. Pasini, 'Chiesa di Milano', 371–2. On the lands of the Genoese priest Magnus, see p. 141 below.

[41] *Ep.* IV.2: *Inter quos [sc. uiri nobilissimi] ego quoque tunc urbanam praefecturam gerens pariter subscripsi, quia postquam talis scissura pro nulla re facta est, iustum fuit ut sedes apostolica curam gereret, quatenus unitatem in uniuersalis ecclesiae sacerdotum mentibus per omnia custodiret.*

for Constantius.[42] Constantius could be expected to side with Rome over the issue of the Three Chapters. Gregory wished to make quite sure that no difficulties would be raised about this in the future: writing to the electors about their choice, he told them to be quite sure they knew what they were doing, for once the bishop was elected they would no longer be able to judge him but would have to obey him.[43] He also took steps to ascertain that Constantius's election had proper support; and, evidently apprehensive about the final outcome of the election, he asked the Exarch Romanus to give his assistance to Constantius, whether he was elected or not.[44] In the event, the clergy resident both in Milan and in Genoa concurred in electing Constantius.

But unity was precarious. Resistance in Milan was not extinct.[45] There are symptoms of dissent, both within the Milanese church, and among its suffragans. Three bishops within the metropolitan province of Milan, including the bishop of Brescia, were about to sever communion with Constantius, alleging that he had condemned the Three Chapters and given an undertaking (*cautionem*) on this matter.[46] Gregory confirmed that although this had been done by Constantius's predecessor, bishop Laurence,[47] he did not recall any mention of the Three Chapters between Constantius and himself, 'neither in writing nor in words'.[48] We shall consider below (pp. 139–40) the outcome of this split; what is important for our present purpose is the evidence this provides about the position of both bishops. It had been possible to believe – at any rate at a distance from Genoa – that Laurence had been an upholder of the Three Chapters; but in Milan doubts about Constantius were beginning to surface within a year of his election. His orthodoxy remained suspect.[49] Tensions existing in the time of his predecessor were evidently by no means resolved in Constantius's time; and the conflicts provoked by Laurence's adopting the papal and imperial orthodoxy had not been laid to rest. It is very likely that this conflict also lies behind the curious quarrel between Laurence and

---

[42] *mihi magna familiaritate coniunctus* – *Ep.* III.31; cf. *Ep.* III.29.

[43] *Ep.* III.29. The suggestion made (in a personal communication) by Claire Sotinel that Gregory feared that the clergy had not consulted the *honorati* who had also fled to Genoa and wished them to remedy this omission is attractive.

[44] *Epp.* III.29, 30, 31. The letters present a difficult problem concerning the interpretation of the election. For discussion, see the additional note appended to this chapter.

[45] Milanese records preserve the name of a bishop Fronto, whose existence is not certain; if there was such a bishop, it is unlikely that he represented a dissenting part of the Milanese church, unless there was a schism so brief that neither Gregory, nor Paul the deacon knew of it.

[46] *Ep.* IV.2; 3. cf. IV.37.

[47] See above, p. 134.

[48] *Ep.* IV.3.

[49] The rumours were still circulating late in 596: *Ep.* VII.14.

one of his clergy, the priest Magnus, but this must remain uncertain. All we can know is that the enemy of the bishop's predecessor was clearly a trusted agent of the pope.[50] All this suggests that Laurence's act of adhesion to Rome and its orthodoxy may not have been permanent and unambiguous, or, if it was, that it had not been seen as such, or even known, by all his clergy. It was possible for both supporters and opponents of the Three Chapters to connive in accepting him.

The tensions which existed under bishop Laurence were inherited by his successor, Constantius. It is clear that Constantius's position as bishop depended on carefully maintained ambiguity on this subject; an ambiguity which Gregory's advice recommended him to adhere to. He told Constantius to stick to affirming his unwavering adherence to Chalcedon, saying nothing about the Fifth Council[51] – following, in this, the advice Constantius had given him about writing to queen Theodelinda.[52] Ambiguity, silence and obfuscation were essential tactics in the dispute. Even on his own doorstep, the bishop faced opposition; silence was his best protection. There was opposition to the bishop's custom of including the name of archbishop John of Ravenna among those commemorated in the mass:[53] he, above all others, was seen as an upholder of the imperial orthodoxy. Naturally, he was objectionable to opponents of the condemnation. Dissent had not died out even in Genoa.

In the areas under imperial control, Gregory exercised the rights bestowed on him by bishop Laurence's submission[54] without constraint. Constantius had himself been very ready to comply with Gregory's expectations, apparently accepting the consequences of his predecessor's surrender to the Roman see, and consulted the pope on questions that metropolitans would normally have settled on their own authority.[55] In the province traditionally under the metropolitan authority of Milan, Gregory exercised his authority in a manner not substantially different from the way he governed his own metropolitan area, southern Italy.[56] Most significantly, on Constantius's death in 601, Gregory supervised the election of a

---

[50] *Ep.* iii.26; and on his possessions, xi.6. On Magnus, see Bognetti, *L'età*, 203; see also the Additional Note appended to this chapter. Was anything similar involved in the case of Fortunatus, the bearer of *Ep.* iv.37 (*Epp.* iv.37; v.18)?

[51] *Ep.* iv.37.

[52] See below, p. 138.

[53] *Ep.* iv.37. On archbishop John, see below, ch. 10.

[54] See above, n. 41.

[55] E.g. *Ep.* v.18, on various matters of clerical discipline. *Ep.* x.11 for the deposition of a bishop, whose case Gregory felt unable to judge for lack of sufficient information. *Ep.* xii.14 on the enforcement of a will.

[56] *Epp.* iv.21, 22; viii.5, ix.115 (Luni).

successor.[57] The pope was in a position to exercise what was in effect a metropolitan authority in subsequent episcopal elections: whereas in former times the archbishops of Milan and of Aquileia had traditionally consecrated each other,[58] in 601 Gregory could take over the arrangements for the election of a successor to Constantius. The division of the see between Milan and Genoa again created a problem; but Gregory acted quickly and decisively. A candidate had emerged, who met with unanimous approval, evidently in Genoa. Gregory hastened to confirm the election. There was however, some apprehension that king Agilulf would put forward his own candidate in Milan: 'Do not worry about the letter which you report having received from Agilulf. For we would on no account consent to a man being chosen by non-Catholics, especially by Lombards.' He went on to dismiss out of hand the possibility of a schism if a rival candidate were to be presented from Milan by the Lombard court; for after all, the Milan Church's income, derived from its lands in Sicily, was safely under Roman control.[59]

CATHOLICISM AMONG THE LOMBARDS

In the province of Aquileia, as we have seen, the schism was perpetuated by the creation of a schismatic patriarchate, under Lombard protection, competing with a patriarch, with some suffragans, in communion with the Roman see. The church of Milan, previously a metropolitan province proud of its ancient prestige and tradition, was now also pulled apart, on the one hand, into submission to Rome, on the other into the orbit of the Lombard kingdom.[60] But the fortunes of the churches in the provinces under Milan's metropolitan authority were more closely bound up with the Lombard court. The bishop resided in exile, as we have seen, in Genoa. It was through his confidant, bishop Constantius, that Gregory established relations with the Catholic, albeit schismatic, queen, Theodelinda. Gregory seems to have been drawn into communications with the queen in the course of the diplomatic negotiations in progress at the Lombard court, of which he had been informed by Constantius;[61] he now took

---

[57] *Epp.* xi.6, 14.
[58] Pelagius I, *Ep.* 24.
[59] *Ep.* xi.6. Cf. above, n. 40, and Bertolini, 'I papi', 342, n. 44. It is notable that the agent Gregory sent (*Ep.* xi.6; 14) to arrange the episcopal ordination of Deusdedit was the notary Pantaleo: he was almost certainly one of Gregory's most trusted agents, used in particularly delicate missions; and he had close ties with Sicily (on his identity, see Hartmann's note (*MGH Epp.* 2, 274, *ad loc.*). He also had instructions concerning lands in Sicily managed by the late Magnus, priest of their Church: cf. below, n. 82.
[60] For a very full treatment of the bishoprics under Lombard rule see Bognetti, 'La continuità'.
[61] *Ep.* iv.2.

advantage of his contacts with the court to admonish the queen to enter communion with him, sending her a letter which Constantius was bidden to 'transmit without delay', sending, at the same time a plea to the three bishops who had separated themselves from communion with him.[62] His letter to the queen was a rebuke for her adherence to the schism.[63] Both letters affirmed Gregory's unswerving fidelity to Chalcedon, which is to be held in its integrity, adding nothing, taking nothing away; but the letter to the queen also said that the 'council held in the time of Justinian of happy memory' had enacted nothing against the decisions of Chalcedon, and summoned her – somewhat imperiously – to enter communion with Constantius without delay.[64] Constantius was alarmed to receive this letter, as he told Gregory, and did not send it on, as it had mentioned the fifth Council, which would have scandalised the queen. He had done well not to forward the letter, Gregory replied; and he sent a substitute omitting mention of the Council, confining himself to the first four Councils.[65]

Among the Roman advisers in favour at the court was the Tridentine monk, Secundus, a firm adherent of the schism. He appears to have been close to the queen, was to become god-father of her son Adaloald, born in 603, and a determined and informed opponent of the condemnation of the Three Chapters.[66] One of the last of Gregory's letters congratulated the queen on the Catholic baptism of her son. It is a friendly, even cordial, letter, accompanied by gifts to the queen and the prince. Gregory refers to his correspondence with Secundus, but he seems less concerned now to attack the schism than to defend his own orthodoxy. He seems to have come to accept that the queen's and her circle's adherence to the schism could not be remedied.[67]

In the churches within Lombard-held territories, dissent flourished unchecked. Within a year of Constantius being established in Genoa, three of his Northern suffragans were renouncing his metropolitan authority,

---

[62] *Ep.* IV.2. The letter concerning the schismatic bishops must be IV.3. See above, pp. 103–4.

[63] *Ep.* IV.4.

[64] *Ep.* IV.4.

[65] *Ep.* IV.37; (33). Gray and Herren, 'Columbanus', regard this 'concealment of the real issues' as a change effected by Gregory in papal policy. It is, however, exactly in line with Pelagius I and Pelagius II's arguments: see above, pp. 127–8. He followed the same practice with Queen Brunhild: *Ep.* VIII.4. Gregory mentioned the Fifth Council when this could not be avoided: e. g. *Epp.* I.24 (his *Synodica*); III.10.

[66] Paul Diac. *HL* IV.27. He sent Gregory a *libellus* to which Gregory replied at length: *Ep.* IX.148. His identity with the 'Secundus abbas' mentioned in Gregory's letter to Theodelinda, *Ep.* XIV.12 is not certain.

[67] *Ep.* XIV.12. Bognetti, *L'età longobarda*, 2, 232, remarks on *una larga tolleranza nei rapporti colla corte longobarda* – one very different from his attitude to schismatics in Byzantine territory (233).

and transferring their adherence to the patriarch of Aquileia.[68] The church of Como, subject to Milan, renounced communion and also sided with the patriarch of Aquileia.[69] The ecclesiastical province subject to the metropolitan authority of Milan, Liguria and Aemilia, was thus rent between a Lombard and a Roman sphere of influence. The community which remained in Milan, now under Lombard rule, and others within its metropolitan territory outside imperial control, remained separated from Rome. Within this Lombard sphere, Gregory seems to have underestimated the depth of feeling about the issue, and never ceased to entertain the hope of reunification, or of drawing schismatics back into the Roman communion. He entertained unrealistic hopes of their speedy return, and unrealistic views of the seriousness of their commitment. He was anxious not to do anything that might alienate schismatics, and discourage them from returning to the fold. Thus he wrote to bishop Constantius asking him to restore property rights to schismatics at Como – within his metropolitan province though within Lombard territory – so as not to prejudice their willingness to return to the 'womb of their mother the Church'.[70]

It was a decade after Gregory's death that an initiative was made to heal the schism. The dukes of Trent and Friuli were now united with the king.[71] The Lombard court enlisted the recent immigrant, the Irish monk Columbanus, now at Bobbio, to try to unite the churches of Italy under the Lombard kings and a pope who was urged to call a council to resolve the schism. 'Thus the king [Agilulf] asks, the queen asks, all ask you that as soon as may be, all should be made one, that as peace comes to the country peace should come quickly to the Faith, that everyone may in turn become one flock of Christ.'[72] The reconciliation Columbanus and his royal patrons sought to bring about in 613 – the first attempt to detach the Italian Church from its Byzantine orbit[73] – had to await the end of the century.[74]

The conditions of the schism allowed, on the one hand, the consolidation of something like a territorial Church within the Lombard sphere. Based on the Tricapitoline form of Catholicism, the Lombard kingdom was christianised in the main by Tricapitoline clergy. The main centres in which manuscripts preserving the dissenting tradition were being produced and

---

[68] See above, p. 138, n. 62.
[69] *Ep.* IX.187.
[70] *Ep.* IX.187.
[71] Paul Diac. *HL* IV.27.
[72] Columbanus, *Ep.* 5.17, trans. Walker.
[73] Delogu, 'Il regno longobardo', 44.
[74] *LP*, Sergius, 86.15 (I. 376); Paul the Deacon, *HL* VI.14, based on Bede's confused notice *Chron.* 4659 (*MGH Chron. min.* 3, 317).

circulated were located in the schismatic areas of Northern Italy.[75] On the other hand, the schism allowed Gregory to blur the distinction between the nature of papal control in Northern and in Southern Italy. It helped him to consolidate Roman jurisdiction outside the Lombard territories within a more homogeneous Italian orbit. Until the end of the century the Catholic Church in Italy was clearly divided between a papally controlled sphere and its counterpart under the Lombard court.[76]

ADDITIONAL NOTE: THE ELECTION OF BISHOP CONSTANTIUS

The process of this election, involving the two communities in Milan and in Genoa, is obscure. It is profitable to elucidate it, to shed important light on the state of public, and especially clerical, opinion, and on Gregory's ability to manipulate the situation.

Gregory, as we know, received notification that the Milanese deacon Constantius had been elected unanimously, although some doubt hung over the election as the document reporting it to the pope bore no signatures.[77] The question that principally needs to be investigated is where the initiative came from – Milan or Genoa – and what part Gregory and his agents – whoever they were – played in the process. Hartmann recognised the difficulty of both alternatives, and in his edition of the *Registrum* suggested that *Ep.* III.29 (to the Milanese clergy in Genoa, addressed *diaconibus et clero*, omitting the usual *ordini et plebi*, who would, presumably, be in Milan) was one of two identical letters, the second being a copy sent to Milan, now lost or never registered; that the initiative for the election had been taken in Milan, communicated to the clergy resident in Genoa and to Gregory, and confirmed by both.[78] This reconstruction has been generally favoured. The main objection to it is that this seems highly unlikely. Constantius would seem an unexpected choice for the Milanese clergy to have made or the Lombard rulers to have endorsed. The clergy resident in Genoa, however, may be assumed to have been far less, if at all, opposed to the condemnation of the Three Chapters, and could well have elected a candidate favoured by Gregory. They would have been more inclined to agreement with the pope and would have less reason to regard his friend with suspicion.

---

[75] See Schieffer, 'Zur Beurteilung'.
[76] Bobbio accepted papal obedience after Columbanus.
[77] *Ep.* III.29.
[78] See his note on *Ep.* III.29, *MGH Epp.* I, 186. I see no good reason to accept Hartmann's view that the priest Magnus resided in Milan (*ibid.*, 183, note) if his reconstruction is abandoned.

This alternative scenario (of an election initiated at Genoa) can in fact be reconstructed quite convincingly, if we note the provenances of the various persons involved in the proceedings. The news was brought to Gregory by the priest Magnus and the notary Hippolytus.[79] Hippolytus was evidently an intermediary in Gregory's dealings with Queen Theodelinda, and will certainly have been resident in Milan;[80] he seems to have come to Rome with Magnus, having, perhaps, joined him in Genoa. The role of the priest Magnus in the election is more interesting, and more difficult, to determine. His past is the only thing that can throw light on the question. Magnus had been excommunicated by bishop Laurence 'for no good reason' (*nullis ... culpis extantibus*).[81] He had evidently gone to Rome to appeal against the sentence, had been rehabilitated by the pope, and now brought him the news of the election of Constantius. Had he come from Genoa, or from Milan? Bishop Laurence had, as we know, lived in Genoa. Where had Magnus incurred his enmity? Unfortunately, all we know about Magnus is that he had held or managed a little land, probably in Sicily;[82] he was evidently orthodox in the pope's eyes and innocent of whatever charges had been laid against him; so he must have been a supporter of the Fifth Council. Could this be what brought him into collision with Laurence? Of course, Laurence, too, had fallen in line with the papal position. But, as we have seen (see above, pp. 135–6), it was vital for him to maintain a careful ambiguity on the question. Magnus could have made himself objectionable to Laurence by challenging him to a less ambiguous commitment than he was prepared to make, jeopardising his position which depended on a carefully maintained ambiguity on this score. If this is what got Magnus into trouble with his bishop, then Genoa is far more likely to have been the scene of the trouble than Milan. In any case, hostility, like affection, is more likely to grow in proximity than at a safe distance. Though we cannot be certain, it seems likeliest that Magnus had been in Genoa, had probably had a hand in engineering the election of Laurence's successor, and came to Rome from there, accompanied by Hippolytus who had come from Milan, and returned to Genoa.

John the subdeacon was on Gregory's staff and is almost certainly to be identified with Gregory's official in charge of the Roman church's

---

[79] *Ep.* III.29 (174, l. 4. *notarius*: *Ep.* IV.2, 4).
[80] *Ep.* IV.2 (218, ll.15–19); cf. *Ep.* IV.4 (221, l.29).
[81] *Ep.* III.26 (171, l. 5).
[82] *Ep.* XI.6: *de possessiunculis quas Magnus quondam presbyter commissas habuerat* ... ; the context and the link with the notary Pantaleo who was sent to Genoa after Constantius's death to deal with matters concerning it, suggest that the lands were in Sicily. In any case it is clear that Magnus's link was with Genoa, not Milan. Cf above, n. 59.

patrimony in Liguria.[83] He was sent to Genoa to obtain confirmation (April 593);[84] by September the same John had returned to Rome from Genoa with good reports about the new bishop;[85] so had the notary Hippolytus and an abbot (not the subdeacon) John, with news from the Lombard court, presumably from Milan.[86] They were also to take Gregory's correspondence to the Lombard court and were charged with the task of explaining it to the queen, having first called on the bishop in Genoa.[87] John the subdeacon was the pope's man; Magnus, almost certainly his Genoese confidant, was evidently an emissary of the clergy resident in Genoa, whereas Hippolytus and abbot John belonged to the Milanese rump.

This procedure would also be very much in line with the strategy adopted by Gregory at the time of the next election, in 601. Then he wrote to the Genoan clergy telling them not to worry about a nomination by king Agilulf, for, he reassured them, 'we should never give our consent to a man not chosen by catholics, and especially by Lombards . . .'; the clergy in Milan, if defiant, could be starved into submission, as all their revenue came from property safe in imperial territory.[88] The principal difference between the two elections is that Gregory's control over the affairs of the church of Milan in exile in Genoa were now more consolidated, as was that of the Lombard court over the rump left in Milan.

The election indicates not only the complications of electing a bishop in a see divided between two cities, one in Roman the other under Lombard control. More importantly, it also allows us to glimpse the way Gregory consolidated his power in the church still within an area under imperial control, and the widening gap between this and its sister-church outside imperial control, a gap which was both a reason for and one of the consequences of the division between the two parts of the Milanese church.

---

[83] As suggested by Hartmann, *Ibid.*, 187 n. 7.

[84] *Ep.* III.30 (176, ll. 8–10).

[85] *Ep.* IV.1 (217 l. 17).

[86] *Ep.* IV.2 (218, l. 18).

[87] *Ep.* IV.4 (221, ll. 28–9). On abbot John, see Hartmann's note 10 to *Ep.* IV.2. *Ep.* IV.37 to Constantius indicates that the two messengers must have called on him in Genoa and consulted him over the correspondence with queen Theodelinda before proceeding to Milan.

[88] *Ep.* XI.6.

CHAPTER 10

Ravenna and Rome: *and beyond*

ASPIRATIONS AND MYTH

Churches have always been proud of their antiquity and jealous of the prestige and the status that went with it. Their past was seen as the promise of future glory, and – more important – as the foundation of aspirations legitimated by their origins. Among the major sees scattered around the Mediterranean, Ravenna was a comparative newcomer. That did not prevent it staking claims to ancient rights and privileges; but a past to legitimate them had to be freshly created. Inevitably, myth came to overlay the historical record. In the case of the church of Ravenna, fact and myth are especially hard to disentangle.[1] Its relations with the see of Rome were determined by its comparatively recent rise to importance on the one hand, and the compensating myth it propagated about itself and its ancient traditions and status on the other. Happily, it is over the earlier history which does not concern us here that the haze of legend lies most impenetrably. It dissolves sufficiently to allow us to see the facts of Ravenna's more recent rise.

In AD 400 Ravenna was a minor bishopric, subject to the metropolitan authority of the Roman see. In 402, however, the imperial court took refuge among its marshes from Milan, too exposed to the threat of invasion. This was to be the start of a rapid advance in its secular prestige, and of a corresponding ascent only a little slower in its ecclesiastical status. It remained an imperial residence until 476, when the Western ruler Romulus Augustulus was removed from the imperial throne by the German war-leader Odoacer. Ravenna remained a royal residence under the Germanic régimes. From the second quarter of the fifth century the city had acquired an architectural and artistic wealth in keeping with its new importance. The imperial family, lay officials, bishops and clergy vied

---

[1] The great work of Deichmann, *Ravenna*, is somewhat cursory on the history of the Church (vol. 1, 11–19; 11/3, 169–71). For its history, see generally Testi-Rasponi, 'Annotazioni'; *Storia*, 2/2, especially Orselli, 'La chiesa' and Morini, 'Le strutture'. For an outline, with bibliography, see Markus, 'Ravenna'.

with each other to enhance its beauty; and the Germanic kings followed their example. The high point came in archbishop Maximian's (see below) time, when some of the greatest and finest churches were built; by wealthy laymen as well by his own initiative.[2] After the reconquest from the Goths Ravenna continued to be the centre of the imperial administration in the West, and the headquarters of the emperor's supreme representative in Italy, the Exarch, as he was known by Gregory's time. The pope maintained a representative (*responsalis* or *apocrisiarius*) at the Exarch's court in Ravenna, as he did at the imperial court in Constantinople, to look after the interests of the Roman Church and to make representations with the authorities as appropriate. But Rome had never subscribed to the principle – dear to Byzantine hearts – that civil and ecclesiastical rank should coincide.

Roman refusal to bow to secular reality could not, however, halt – though it could slow down and disguise – the rising status of the Church of Ravenna. The removal of the imperial court from Milan at the beginning of the fifth century cleared the ground for the rise of more than one church: Aquileia and Arles both shook off the ascendancy of Milan. From the 370s Aquileia and Milan had risen to a rank higher than that of ordinary bishoprics, and by the opening years of the fifth century Aquileia joined Milan as the second metropolitan see of Northern Italy.[3] But soon Ravenna began to take over some of the metropolitan privileges and authority of Milan. It was to become the chief beneficiary of Milan's decline. Its importance grew fast with the establishment of the imperial court, when it took refuge there from the threat of barbarian invasion in 402, and especially during the second quarter of the fifth century, during the episcopate of Peter I (Chrysologus) and the residence of the empress Galla Placidia in the city. In the teeth of strong opposition from Milan, but not without the connivance of the see of Rome, Ravenna assumed authority over a number of churches in the province of Aemilia, previously under Milan jurisdiction, as well as churches in its own province of Flaminia. The church of Ravenna, however, while soon seen by distant outsiders such as Eutyches in Constantinople and Theodoret of Cyrrhus as one of the four great churches of Italy – along with Milan and Aquileia – remained subject to Roman jurisdiction.[4] With imperial backing and

---

[2] See on this generally, Von Simson, *Sacred fortress*; on Maximian, Mazzotti, 'L'attività'; Bovini, 'Giuliano', and Id., 'Massimiano', 27.

[3] The best survey of the emergence of metropolitan structures in Northern Italy is Menis, 'Le giurisdizioni'.

[4] Theodoret, *Ep.* 112 (*PG* 83.1312) included Ravenna with Milan and Aquileia as the great Western churches he consulted.

papal connivance, something like a sphere of metropolitan jurisdiction was beginning to be carved out for the new imperial city, while the bishops of Rome continued to treat it as an ordinary bishopric subject to their metropolitan authority.[5]

But this did not satisfy the corporate pride of the Ravenna clergy. Local tradition gradually built up a body of legend to support their church's antiquity and a fictitious association with the apostles. By the fifth century the legend of St Apollinaris, a confessor who had suffered in Ravenna, already had currency.[6] In the sixth and seventh centuries these small beginnings were inflated by forged documents and elaborate legends to justify much larger claims. An enhanced version of the myth gave St Apollinaris, and the church of Ravenna, an association with St Peter; and the emperor Valentinian III (425–455) was credited with granting a privilege to the church of Ravenna, in keeping with the city's new status as a capital: 'so that', as the ninth-century historian of Ravenna, Agnellus, wrote, regretting the failure of Ravenna to shake off the supremacy of Rome, 'with Rome removed, Ravenna should be the head of Italy'.[7] To buttress its association with the apostles, a cult of St Andrew was also fostered in Ravenna. It was already known in the time of Peter Chrysologus, but it was archbishop Maximian (below) who came to be particularly associated with the veneration of St Andrew at Ravenna. He certainly did much to promote the cult and to enhance its shrines, and he was credited with more in later legends. One of these is especially revealing: the relics of St Andrew, brother of the Prince of the Apostles, were known to be venerated at Constantinople, the 'new Rome'; according to a charming later story, archbishop Maximian tried, on one of his visits to Constantinople, to procure the body for Ravenna. The emperor, however, thought that the bodies of the brother-apostles should stay in the sister cities, Rome and Constantinople, and that 'where the imperial seat is there the body of the apostle should be'. Maximian therefore resorted to a ruse to steal the relics. He had to be content with St Andrew's beard, secretly cut off during a night vigil; 'and indeed', Agnellus ruefully comments in the ninth century, 'if only the body of St Andrew, the brother of St Peter, Prince of the Apostles, were buried here, the Roman bishops would never have been

---

[5] On the creation of Ravenna's metropolitan authority, see Massigli, 'La création'. As late as 495 Gelasius I could refer to Ravenna as one of the bishoprics which had an imperial residence in the city but had not exploited the fact to usurp ecclesiastical privileges: *Ep.* 26.10 (Thiel, 405–6).

[6] Peter Chrysologus, *Sermo* 128.3.

[7] Agnellus, *LP eccl. rav.* 40 (305): *ut absque Roma Ravenna esset caput Italiae.* Valentinian III is also credited there with bestowing both the archiepiscopal authority (*archigeratica potestate*) and the pallium on bishop John, along with the metropolitan authority given to the see of Ravenna. On the forged diploma attributed to Valentinian III, see Brandi, 'Ravenna und Rom'.

able to subjugate us'.[8] In Ravenna memories Maximian was – as indeed he
had been in reality – one of the outstanding champions of its prestige.

By the time of Gregory's pontificate the see of Ravenna had held
archiepiscopal status for almost fifty years. This status was not yet clearly
defined, but was generally understood to imply an honour somewhat
higher than that of an ordinary metropolitan see. It was held principally
by the bishops of the patriarchal sees.[9] The church of Ravenna had been
edging towards something like metropolitan status ever since the time of
Peter Chrysologus; now, suddenly, with bishop Maximian (546–554/7?) it
leapt to super-metropolitan, quasi-patriarchal status. In this it was assisted
by the constellation of imperial politics, both secular and ecclesiastical.

Ravenna had returned to imperial control in 540. From the time of its
military reconquest in 540 it had been cast for a special role in Italy by
Justinian: along with the church of Rome it was to be a pivot for the spiritual unification of Italy.[10] From the time of bishop Victor (537–544)
Ravenna had been singled out for imperial favour. At a time when the controversy over the Three Chapters gave the imperial court much anxiety,
Constantinople intervened dramatically in Ravenna affairs. The see was
kept vacant after bishop Victor's death in 544/5. Late in 546 Maximian, an
outsider from Istria, was appointed.

Milan and Aquileia, the two northern metropolitan sees, were in open
revolt. Imperial policy required a solid ecclesiastical base in Northern
Italy. The appointment of bishop Maximian was a key element in the
emperor's efforts to secure the consent of the Eastern and the Western
churches to his project; and to boost Maximian's standing, he was
endowed with the pallium, a ceremonial token of singular honour,
bestowed on him by pope Vigilius, at the emperor's initiative, at Patras,
where the pope's eastward journey crossed Maximian's westward route.

Vigilius was on his way to Constantinople, where under strong pressure
by the court he eventually, as we have seen, approved the imperial formula
endorsed by the Council in 554. The imperial orthodoxy had been fiercely
contested in the Western churches, including those of Italy.[11] Along with
Rome – once Vigilius's successor, pope Pelagius I had come into line with
the court and the Council in condemning the Three Chapters – Ravenna

---

[8] Peter Chrysologus, *Sermo* 133; Agnellus, *LP eccl. rav.* 76 (329): *si corpus beati Andreae, germani Petri principis,*
     hic humasset, nequaquam nos Romani pontifices sic subiugassent.
[9] See *DDC* i.927–34; *LThK* iii.1066f, and Testi-Rasponi, 'Archiepiscopus'. But the looseness of the
     vocabulary allowed, for instance, the bishop of Caralis to be called *archiepiscopus*. It is striking that
     despite this precedent the popes did not use the title for the bishop of Ravenna. Cf. below, n. 13.
[10] On this see my articles 'Carthage', and 'Justinian's ecclesiastical politics', with the references there
     given.
[11] See above, chapter. 9.

was to be the bridgehead of imperial orthodoxy in the tide of opposition already flowing strongly in Italy. The new privilege granted to the see of Ravenna was to assist the rise of a counterweight to the centres of dissent in Italy: Milan and Aquileia. Before long Maximian assumed the title of 'archbishop'.[12]

The title and corresponding rank were not acknowledged by the popes; they were neither disputed nor conceded; they were simply passed over in silence.[13] At the low point of papal prestige, however, when the churches of Rome and Ravenna found themselves in shared isolation among the major churches in Italy and the West, pope Pelagius I was prepared to go so far as to include Ravenna among the 'apostolic sees'.[14] Ravenna being Rome's principal ecclesiastical ally in these conditions, especially at the time of Rome's greatest weakness in the 550s, tensions and rivalries between the two churches were kept in check. By the 590s, however, the long discredited papacy had emerged from the trough of its fortunes. Gregory could afford to be less compliant with Ravenna aspirations.

GREGORY AND RAVENNA

At the time that Gregory assumed office in 590 the bishop of Ravenna was an old friend of his, John II (III). He was a Roman by origin, consecrated to the see of Ravenna by Pelagius II in 578. To be sure, there was, as we shall see, some friction (whose causes will turn out to be most instructive). But nevertheless John evidently enjoyed Gregory's trust, perhaps friendship. An inscription recorded the gift of Roman relics provided by Gregory at John's request;[15] and almost certainly he was the dedicatee of Gregory's *Regula pastoralis*.[16] In 592 Gregory entrusted to his supervision, albeit in carefully restricted terms, the affairs of churches subject to Roman

---

[12] Following Deichmann (Ravenna II/2 13–15) who dates the assumption of the title to between 547 and 549, I have suggested ('Carthage', 296–8) 548–9. He was officially using it by 553.

[13] The archbishops of Ravenna continued to be addressed by the popes as bishops until the midseventh century. John is never addressed as 'archbishop' in Gregory's correspondence; and Marinianus once, *Ep.* IX.139; probably by oversight in the papal *scrinium* (as suggested by Hartmann, *ad. loc.*)? The use of the title occurs in the report included in Gregory's *Registrum* (Ewald and Hartmann, VIII.36), which originated in Ravenna, and is rightly relegated to an Appendix (v) by Norberg in his edition. Papal recognition of its metropolitan jurisdiction, however, is implied by the inclusion of its bishop among the addressees of *Ep.* VIII.10. Cf also *Epp.* III.54; V.15.

[14] Pelagius I, *Epp.* 10 (32); 19 (60); 24 (74, 76); 35 (98, 99); 39 (111); 52 (137); 60 (160). On this and what follows, see Markus, 'Ravenna and Rome'; and Orselli, 'La chiesa'.

[15] Agnellus, *LP eccl rav.* 98 (342, ll. 21–2). This was at one of the monasteries over which there was to be friction between Gregory and Marinianus, that of SS Mark, Marcellus and Felicula: see below, pp.152–4.

[16] I have presented the argument for this in summary form in 'Ravenna and Rome', 570, n. 20. See also most recently B. Judic's note in *Grégoire le Grand. Règle pastorale*, I, 16–17.

jurisdiction but at the time, on account of the hostilities with the Lombards, not easily accessible from Rome.[17] Even in letters critical of John's actions, Gregory speaks with notable directness, even affection; his tone is one of friendly bantering rather than peremptory asperity.[18] Gregory instinctively turned to him to enlist his support in his quarrels with the Exarch and the civil administration, and to seek his help in obtaining their aid; and as we have seen, Gregory regarded him as an ally in the cause of the Three Chapters.[19] On his death in 595 John was succeeded by Marinianus, a man even closer to Gregory. He was to hold the see during the remainder of Gregory's pontificate. He had been a member of Gregory's community at St Andrew's, and he was Gregory's man, in more senses than one. His reception at Ravenna was less than unanimously friendly; but, to judge by Gregory's effort to allay local fears, this was not due so much to hostility to an appointment made in Rome, or to the habitual suspicion with which the Ravenna clergy tended to treat outsiders, bishops 'not from our own flock',[20] as to sympathy felt among a section of the Ravenna clergy for the defenders of the Three Chapters.[21]

Gregory clearly had a decisive part in securing his election to the see of Ravenna. John had died in January 595, and Gregory, according to custom, set up the standard procedure, appointing a neighbouring bishop as visitor to look after the church's affairs and to superintend the election of a successor.[22] Quite naturally he also wrote to his representative in Ravenna, urging him to do what he could to ensure the election of a suitable candidate to so important an office, without allowing private or selfish interests to influence the choice of the clergy and the people. In the event of an unclear or disputed election, he was to send a delegation of ten Ravenna electors to Rome.[23] Gregory was evidently concerned to avoid local interests exercising undue influence over the election; and according to custom, the elected candidate was to be consecrated in Rome.

Gregory's fears of local pressure were well founded: the Exarch had his own favoured candidate, the archdeacon of Ravenna, whom he wished to be elected. Gregory cited 'many reasons' (which he did not specify) that made him unsuitable for the office;[24] and he also rejected another

---

[17] *Ep.* II.25.
[18] See especially *Epp.* III.54; V.15; and, of course, the dedicatory letter to the *RP* (Ewald and Hartmann, *Ep.* I.24a).
[19] *Epp.* I.32; 35; II.38; on the Three Chapters and Ravenna, see above, chapter 9, esp. at n. 22.
[20] The phrase is common in Agnellus: e.g. *non ex hoc ovile* (Maximian, 69); *non de ovibus istis* (John, 98), etc.
[21] *Ep.* VI.2. See chapter 9, n. 53.
[22] *Epp.* V.21; 22. On the procedure, see above, p. 108.
[23] *Ep.* V.24.
[24] A clue, however, is given in *Ep.* VI.31.

candidate, a local priest, put forward apparently by the Exarch, ostensibly on the grounds that he did not know the psalms. As no other candidate was presented to him, Gregory took the initiative of appointing, 'with common consent and acclamation' by the delegation from Ravenna (presumably chosen by his representative there) Marinianus, the monk from his own community who came to ecclesiastical office as unwillingly as had Gregory himself.[25] The warmth of Gregory's affection for Marinianus appears as late as 601, when he wrote to him on receiving the news that his friend had been vomiting blood. Gregory had taken the best medical advice he could find in Rome; Marinianus was to give up fasting and keeping vigils, and find substitutes for the discharge of his episcopal duties. Gregory, too, was 'very weak'; let Marinianus come to him to be looked after, so that, if he could not return to his see cured, whichever of them God was to call first might die in the other's arms.[26]

The close personal friendship between Gregory and both the men who held the see of Ravenna during his pontificate contrasts sharply with the frequently tense official relationships between the two churches during the same time. To understand this contrast we need to examine both the issues at stake in their quarrels, and – more important – their social and institutional context.

The problems over which there was friction were those which arose from negotiating a peace, or a truce, with the Lombards;[27] the policies to be adopted over the schism of the Three Chapters, especially in the church of Aquileia;[28] the archbishops' use of the pallium; and disputes about some Ravenna monasteries and their property. Here we shall consider the last two problems, the more specifically ecclesiastical questions: the use of the pallium, and the monastic matters which seem to have been running sores in the relationship of the two churches. To conclude we shall consider what light social alignments at Ravenna may shed on some of the other tensions between them. To understand these tensions we shall need to take into account the persons involved.

Apart from his own representatives, Gregory could rely on trusted supporters in Ravenna: well-disposed clergy, monks, and lay people: among them his trusted friend abbot Claudius; the mayor (*curator civitatis*) of the city, Theodore, of whom he often made use in diplomatic and other

[25] *Ep.* v.51: *communi concordantique voce atque consensu.* Agnellus's statement (*LP eccl. rav.* 99) that Marinianus was a nephew of his predecessor John is unsupported and may not be reliable.

[26] *Ep.* xi.21.

[27] See chapter 7.

[28] See above, chapter 9.

matters,[29] and the abbot Probus who was often associated with Theodore in these affairs.[30] There were, however, also individual officials in the Exarch's administration at Ravenna whom Gregory felt he could trust. Sometimes he appealed to one or other for support. Thus, for example, we encounter the *scholasticus* Severus who is asked to persuade the Exarch to accept Gregory's views on peace with the Lombards;[31] the *scholasticus* Andrew, who is to smooth the way for Marinianus as Gregory's nominee for the office of bishop;[32] an unknown *vir gloriosus* at the Exarch's court on whom Gregory felt he could always rely 'not to neglect his business' at Ravenna;[33] the Basil who was asked to assist Gregory's representative with his business (in the Three Chapters affair) with the Exarch;[34] the military man Gulfaris and one Mastalo who earned Gregory's approval by their conduct, notwithstanding the uncooperative Exarch under whom they were serving, in the matter of the Istrian schismatics.[35] These, apart from his own representatives, and – as we shall see, to a very limited extent – the two archbishops, were the people on whose cooperation in Ravenna Gregory felt he could rely. It is, however, significant that in most cases they were asked to intervene on his behalf, or to assist him, in circumstances which were unpropitious and with persons whom Gregory thought hostile. One of his correspondents at Constantinople felt it necessary to warn Gregory about two members of the new, and less hostile, Exarch's staff.[36] The overwhelming impression created by his correspondence is that Gregory felt he was fighting with few allies against heavy odds at Ravenna.

One issue over which the two sees came into conflict was the use of the pallium. The pallium had been bestowed on Maximian, as we have seen, by pope Vigilius on Justinian's orders in 546, on his way to Ravenna to take up his office.[37] He is shown wearing it in the famous mosaic in the church of S. Vitale, where he appears alongside the emperor, surrounded by their

---

[29] See *Epp.* IX.44, 93; 117; 134, and chapter 9.

[30] *Ep.* IX.44; See chapter 7, notes. 53 and 54.

[31] *Epp.* V.34. On *scholastici*, see Brown, *Gentlemen*, 80.

[32] *Ep.* V.51; see above, pp. 148–9. *PLRE* 3, ANDREAS 15; also the recipient of *Epp.* IX.102(?); 152 (commending his representative Castorius to him). But in *Ep.* VI.31 — if he is the same 'Andrew' — he was on the 'wrong' side in the controversy over the pallium.

[33] *Ep.* IX.96.

[34] *Ep.* IX.154. He may be identical with *PLRE* 3, BASILIUS 6.

[35] *Epp.* IX.161; 162.

[36] *Ep.* VII.26.

[37] Agnellus says (70) that the electors of Ravenna had requested the pallium for the person elected to succeed Bishop Victor. That election had been quashed by the emperor, who kept the see vacant until Maximian's appointment. Agnellus's suggestion is possible, but it is more likely to reflect a tradition which gave Ravenna credit for the honour. On the date of the grant and the sequence of privileges, see Markus, 'Carthage', 296–7.

retinue. The mosaicists of Ravenna also bestowed the pallium – anachronistically, projecting Ravenna's glorious present into its past – on bishop Ecclesius, shown as the founder and donor of the church of San Vitale in the great mosaic in its apse; and on the legendary founder of the Church of Ravenna, St Apollinaris himself, in his church in Classe. Both churches were completed between 547 and 549; the stress that came suddenly to be laid on the pallium shows that it was a recently acquired and highly valued distinction. It was apparently confirmed by pope John III in 569, in a grant made to archbishop Peter III.[38] But soon after Gregory's accession to the see of Rome, reports were reaching him that archbishop John was claiming the right to wear the pallium beyond the strictly limited ceremonial periods for which the pope was prepared to sanction its use. Gregory wrote reprimanding John for this breach of the universal custom of metropolitan bishops, which was an offence against the 'way of humility' that was proper for bishops to follow.[39] In his answer John professed obedience to the authority of the Roman see, but denied having done anything contrary to what had long been normal usage in Ravenna, which he asked the pope not only to confirm, but to amplify.[40] By the time of the next exchange of letters a year or so later, the issue had evidently become a matter of public concern in Ravenna. A concession on the use of the pallium had been urgently solicited by the 'most excellent Exarch and the most eminent Prefect and by other noblemen of the city'. The fact that the local aristocracy were involved in the dispute is of far more interest to us here than the details of its course. Gregory now accused his friend, bishop John, of double-speak, and of having been corrupted by secular influence; but he still professed himself not to wish to injure or diminish the Church of Ravenna, only to curb the excesses of pride, and to purge John's 'duplicity'.[41] John did not live to satisfy the pope's admonition to 'allow [Gregory] to love him', and 'to reply by deeds, not words'.

The archbishop had not been acting on his own but represented the corporate aspirations of the clergy of Ravenna, supported by the local civil administration and lay nobility. This is confirmed by the sequel under archbishop Marinianus. Here, at last, was a bishop truly after Gregory's

---

[38] It was entered in Gregory's Register as *Ep.* III.67 (Ewald and Hartmann; relegated to Appendix VII by Norberg) having been sent to him by Archbishop John with his letter of 593 (*Ep.* III.66, Ewald-Hartmann; App. VI, Norberg).

[39] *Ep.* III.54 of July 593; this letter indicates that the controversy had arisen before. It is interesting to note the hint in this letter of a suspicion that some clergy, apparently in trouble with Archbishop John, may have enjoyed the protection of powerful men (*maiorum ... patrocinium*).

[40] App. VI. I bypass here the related question raised over the use of *mappulae* by the Ravenna clergy, also a subject of controversy and taken up in the letter.

[41] *Ep.* v.15.

heart: a monk, trained in religious observance in his own school, a closer friend than even John can have been.[42] But neither his background nor the closeness of his friendship with Gregory were enough to make him immune to the pressures he encountered in Ravenna. Local traditions proved stronger, and the pallium continued to be abused.[43]

The strength of these pressures is no less evident in the disputes that arose over some monastic communities in Ravenna. Monastic matters are a frequent subject of Gregory's correspondence; he was anxious that monastic life should be carried on without undue interference from out-side, whether by bishops and clergy or lay people.[44] Problems of this kind cropped up repeatedly, especially in Ravenna. Gregory wrote to arch-bishop John in September 594 asking him to make sure that monasteries be kept clear of clerics and lay people, as their vocations and ways of life were too different to be pursued under the same roof.[45] A letter such as this would cause no surprise, being quite normal in Gregory's correspon-dence,[46] were it not that in the case of Ravenna it fits into a pattern that emerges from a survey of monastic affairs as disclosed by Gregory's corre-spondence. Two monasteries, both in Classe, seem to have had a particu-larly close relationship with Rome: one was the monastery of SS Mark, Marcellinus and Felicula, founded by archbishop John;[47] the other the monastery of SS. John and Stephen under abbot Claudius. It appears to be archbishop John's monastery into which the papal agent had placed a monk for penitence; he was instructed in February 595 to keep him there, as if the community were under the pope's jurisdiction.[48] Soon after the death of archbishop John, Gregory intervened in a dispute between this monastery and the archbishops. It seems that the dispute had its roots in some disagreement back in the time of archbishop John. Gregory was par-ticularly anxious that John's endowments and dispositions for this monastery, which Gregory had promised him in his lifetime to safeguard, be faithfully observed by his successor.[49]

But it is especially the affairs of abbot Claudius's monastery that give us

42 See above, p. 149.
43 *Epp.* VI.31; IX.168.
44 See chapter 5. On monasteries in Ravenna, see also Morini, 'Le strutture'. It is noteworthy that it is in the case of Ravenna monasteries that Gregory came closest to contemplating granting 'exemption' from local episcopal authorities. See chapter 5, p. 71.
45 *Ep.* V.1.
46 E.g. *Epp.* I.40 (Campania); IV.11 (Sicily); in Ravenna, Gregory wrote several times on these lines, with-out identifying specific monasteries: in addition to *Ep.* V.1, see *Epp.* VI.28; VII.40.
47 Agnellus, *LP eccl. rav.* 98. See above, p. 147.
48 *Ep.* V.25.
49 *Epp.* VI.1; 24; VIII.17; IX.169.

an insight into the problems Gregory was faced with in Ravenna. Claudius was a close friend of Gregory's, who spent long periods with him in Rome and helped with the revision of his Homilies.[50] Gregory regarded his monastery as particularly closely bound to the pope. When he wanted Claudius to join him in Rome, he took great care to secure a suitable person to take charge of his monastery.[51] On Claudius's death Gregory assumed personal responsibility for appointing a successor.[52] In a dispute that had arisen between the monastic community and the archbishops Gregory intervened on behalf of the community: it had 'suffered much injustice and oppression under your predecessor', Gregory wrote to Marinianus;[53] and he commended the abbot to the archbishop's protection.[54] Gregory was aware of the hostility of local public opinion towards Claudius and to Roman intervention, and he was anxious that the matter be settled not in Ravenna, but by himself. To avoid offending the sensibilities of the church of Ravenna, Gregory had to tread carefully; to justify his intervention in Ravenna, he drew the archbishop's attention to the Roman see's appellate jurisdiction recently exercised in a case affecting so eminent a see as that of Constantinople. If Constantinople, why not Ravenna? So Marinianus was to submit to his jurisdiction and to send accredited representatives to Rome, and not to listen to 'the words of stupid people', to ignore 'silly talk'.[55] But Marinianus was obdurate. Gregory professed himself astonished by the rapid transformation of his (monastic!) 'discretion', so that Marinianus was now setting higher store on the words of 'evil persuaders' than on the wholesome precepts of the scriptures. Gregory wished to absolve Marinianus and to lay the blame on 'people who give bad advice' to which the archbishop was too ready to listen.[56] As in the dispute over the pallium, Gregory's correspondence reveals an unholy local alliance of lay and clerical interests at work.

In the case of archbishop John's foundation of SS. John and Stephen, the difficulties may have arisen from irregularities in archbishop John's will; but it is striking that curtailment of monastic privileges and property rights by the clergy and bishop and lay interference seem to be so recurrent a feature in Ravenna. The problems which had arisen under the

---

[50] Claudius was evidently one of Gregory's trusted agents in Ravenna: see *Ep.* II.38; XII.6; on abbot Claudius, see Meyvaert, 'The date'.

[51] *Ep.* IX.180.

[52] *Ep.* XII.6.

[53] *Ep.* VIII.17.

[54] *Ep.* VIII.18.

[55] *Vos autem ibi stultorum verba non moveant; ...verba inania non audire: Ep.* VI.24.

[56] *Ep.* VI.28: *sic in brevi ... tuae fuerit immutata discretio. . . plus apud te verba male suadentium valuisse quam divinae lectionis studium profecisse . . . incongrua dicentes audire non rennuis . . .*

archiepiscopate of John continued under his successor Marinianus, despite his impeccable monastic background. What the documentation reveals are the pressures of local society, the lay and clerical establishments, which engulfed both bishops, despite their Roman origins and links of friendship with the pope.

Resentment of papal intervention and control evidently played its part in the case of abbot Claudius's monastery. There were occasions when such resentment manifested itself publicly. This happened in 596 when the policies promoted by Gregory and by his representative at Ravenna were notably unpopular. Gregory had been urging peace with the Lombards, and despatched his representative with orders to press for peace;[57] the Exarch was opposed, and public opinion in Ravenna sided with him. To Gregory's indignation, under cover of darkness posters were put up which lampooned his representative; he addressed a strong protest against the anonymous libel to the *duces*, nobles, clergy, monks, soldiers and people of Ravenna.[58] It is hardly likely that the archbishops would have been associated with such public opposition to the pope; but, it is significant that at this same time Gregory complained that bishop Marinianus appeared to 'have gone to sleep', and asked a correspondent to prod him into action.[59] As we have seen both in the disputes over the use of the pallium and over monastic rights, bishops and clergy could easily be drawn into solidarity with local interests and often yielded to local pressures.

This seems to hold the clue to the interpretation of an anonymous document recently published for the first time.[60] It is contained in a collection of material to support the papal side in the schism, most of it long known. The dating of the collection to *c.* 600 has been generally accepted. The piece in question [*Epistola*] is a plea from an anonymous repentant sinner for forgiveness and restoration to communion. Most of it is an appeal to the authority of the scriptures and to that of Gregory, with texts of both either quoted or alluded to in the course of the entreaty. It is followed by an appendix, consisting of excerpts from Gregory's *Pastoral Care* and his *Homilies* on the Gospels. The *Epistola* itself is addressed to a bishop John of Ravenna, plausibly identified as John II (III) (578–95). The likeliest date for the letter then would be 593–595, after the composition of Gregory's

---

[57] See chapter 7.

[58] *Ep.* VI.34, restored to its correct place in the papal Register by Norberg.

[59] *Ep.* VI.33. The specific point on which Marinianus was accused, however, concerned different matters.

[60] See Sotinel, *Rhétorique*; for the interpretation of its circumstances, with detail and references, see my review in *JTS* 46 (1995) 360–5.

Homilies on the Gospels and before the death of archbishop John in 595.

The author was himself a bishop. All we know about him and his case is what the *Epistola* allows us to infer. He was separated from the unity of the Church, detained in captivity, possibly even threatened with death. There is a hint in the letter that some other, perhaps trumped up, charge had been brought against him. He had written before to archbishop John, appealing to be released and to have his case referred to a synod due to assemble at Rome. But John had repeatedly refused even to receive his request – thrice repeated – and refused to consider re-admitting him to communion, and disdained his appeal to the pope. Legates sent by the pope had brought orders to the effect that if he confessed his fault he should receive immediate absolution; having humbly and openly confessed, he wrote, he did receive absolution and wished to hasten with the returning legates 'to the womb of the holy Roman church'; but he was prevented from doing so for some unstated reason which, he says, was – tantalisingly! – well known to all. The anonymous petitioner is entreating the bishop for his mercy. He protests tearfully against his treatment, addressing what appears to be a vaguely defined group around bishop John, lay and clerical, who seem to be 'great men' who had decided that the petitioner should not be rehabilitated. Throughout this 'open letter' its author is pleading, in meekly submissive terms, not disputing the justice of whatever the sentence had been, protesting only against the withholding of absolution to a penitent. He pleads repentance, not innocence. Though the Exarch is not mentioned, it seems highly likely that the 'great men' who were involved in his imprisonment belonged to the civil administration. There is a close parallel with the equally shadowy case of a bishop detained in Ravenna about whom Gregory wrote to the Exarch in 591.[61] The case referred to in this *Epistola* evidently belongs to a well established pattern of resistance to papal policies in leading circles of clergy and lay people in Ravenna, by cabals prepared to frustrate them. In 599 emissaries of some Istrian converts from the schism complained at the court in Constantinople about the corruptness of unnamed bishops 'in those parts'; and, as we have seen, already when Marinianus arrived in Ravenna to take up his see he met opposition in both lay and clerical quarters on the grounds of being an upholder of the condemnation of the Three Chapters.[62] The mood among the ruling circles in Ravenna, ecclesiastical and administrative, was not likely to be unanimously sympathetic to the author of our *Epistola*.

[61] *Ep.* 1.32.
[62] *Epp.* IX.202; VI.2. See above, n. 21.

We should not, however, exaggerate the conflict of interests and the solidity and coherence of local groups. The alliances and enmities in such groups were often tangled. The tensions between the two churches had not yet crystallised into actual conflicts over jurisdiction, and had not reached the pitch that they would reach at their climax, with the declaration of the Ravenna church's autocephaly in the seventh century. What we can observe in the more mundane and sporadic quarrels in Gregory's time, is the increasingly coherent sense of local pride and the corporate sense of the Ravenna clergy, aided and abetted by important elements in the civil and military administration established in the Exarch's capital. Their links with the local clergy and the archbishops were close, if sometimes unpredictably erratic in direction.[63] It is interesting, for instance, that the Exarch Romanus patronised a delinquent priest in defiance of the archbishop whom he was supporting in the quarrel over the pallium, and that Gregory should be appealing to the Exarch in this and other monastic matters.[64] The ease with which the two 'outsider' archbishops from Rome were sucked into this whirlpool of local aspirations is significant: it is one of the many symptoms that have been recognised to point towards the emergence of powerful alignments of ecclesiastical, administrative and military groupings in local society. French and Italian historians have familiarised us with what they have called *régionalisme* or *campanilismo*;[65] what the tensions between the churches of Rome and Ravenna show is a stage in the growth of this phenomenon, observable in many parts of the Western Empire around AD 600.

Ravenna occupied a special position in the civil and the ecclesiastical structure of the Western Empire. The closeness of its links with the imperial court prevented its church from drifting out of the imperial and into the Lombard orbit, and thus precluded its outright opposition on the question of the Three Chapters. The same circumstance also enabled its (arch)bishops to repudiate subjection to the Roman see. The church of Ravenna, alone in Italy, emerged from the struggle over the Three Chapters on the Roman side and, at the same time, greatly strengthened against Roman domination.

DALMATIA; AND BEYOND

The Balkan provinces had long been an ambivalent area, where the margins of the eastern and the western parts of the Empire overlapped.

---

[63] For a puzzling case, see *Ep.* v.19.
[64] *Ep.* III.54. The oddity is noted by Ewald in his note 1 to the letter.
[65] See Chapter 1, above p. 7.

Culturally, they were divided between Greek- and Latin-speaking areas. Their administrative, as well as their ecclesiastical, status had undergone a series of changes since the re-organisation at the beginning of the fourth century. In the sixth century Slav settlers were beginning to create enclaves, undermining the existing network of administration.[66] The more eastern areas, the provinces of *Illyricum orientale*, were distinct in the administrative geography of the empire from their Western neighbour, Dalmatia. In the conditions of the later sixth century the Western part of the area, Dalmatia, was drawn into the sphere of the Exarch's authority, centred on Ravenna. The ecclesiastical divisions largely corresponded to the secular boundaries. Gregory's relations with the churches of Dalmatia were closer than with those of Illyricum, even though his links with Dalmatian churches, as well as much of his communications, passed through Ravenna.

The metropolitan see of Dalmatia was Salona (just North of Split). It was a source of difficulties throughout Gregory's pontificate. Its incumbent in 590 was Natalis, a pleasure-seeker and gourmet who disliked reading and had given it up for high living,[67] which he liked to justify by quoting good scriptural authority.[68] Natalis had been opposed by an abrasive archdeacon of notably austere life-style, Honoratus. He had had a long quarrel with his bishop, which Pelagius II had tried and failed to resolve.[69] The bishop had hoped to undermine his opponent's power as archdeacon, by forcibly ordaining him a priest.[70] The bishop defied Gregory's orders to restore him; Gregory threatened reprisals: withdrawal of the right to use the pallium, suspension from communion, in the last resort deposition, if he persisted and failed to send a representative to Rome where the case could be heard. He also asked the Praetorian Prefect not to give Natalis his support.[71] On receiving a reply he must have seen as facetious self-justification, Gregory – aware of the limits of what could be achieved – was ready to forgive; but the matter was cut short by the bishop's death early in 593.

It was not, however, the end of the affair. Division in the Church of Salona had hardened in the course of the conflict, and there was now a party bitterly opposed to Honoratus;[72] a small party rallied to Honoratus, but Gregory was cautious; he wanted more general consent, hoping his

---

[66] *Ep.* I.43; II.20; IX.155; X.15 on the insecure conditions of the area; Paul the deacon, *HL* IV.24 on Slavs and Avars.

[67] *Ep.* II.17.

[68] *Ep.* II.44. Caspar, *Geschichte*, 2, 431 n. 5 comments on Gregory's good-tempered and ironical reply.

[69] *Epp.* II.18; 19. Gregory tried to get them to be reconciled: *Epp.* I.10; 19.

[70] *Ep.* I.19; II.18; 19.

[71] *Ep.* II.20.

[72] *Ep.* III.32. Honoratus's complaints were to be investigated by the rector, Antoninus.

agent would be able to secure it.[73] His rector in Salona, the sub-deacon Antoninus, was instructed to arrange an election with great care, avoiding factional patronage and obtaining Gregory's consent to the choice made, meanwhile making an inventory of the Church's assets.[74] That more was at issue than the quarrel between the archdeacon and the deceased bishop and their supporters is evident from the fact that the suffragan bishops had taken side against Honoratus; Gregory admonished them not to consecrate anyone without his approval, on pain of excommunication; and he warned them against electing their preferred candidate, one Maximus, whom he would disallow on the grounds of 'the many bad reports' he had had of him.[75] Maximus and the opponents of Honoratus had the support of local notables and imperial officials; he was enthroned, with the use of armed force, by men of the Exarch, whom, Gregory alleged, Maximus had bribed. Gregory's representative, Antoninus, would have been killed, had he not fled.[76] Maximus had somehow managed to obtain from the emperor an order for his consecration, countermanding a previous order prohibiting it. Gregory thought – this time perhaps not without reason – that the emperor's permission had been obtained in an underhand way, and may have hoped to get it reversed.[77] Maximus was strictly forbidden to exercise the office until Gregory obtained confirmation from the emperor. He was, as always, prepared, however reluctantly, to abide by imperial orders.[78] The emperor eventually ordered Maximus to appear in Rome to sort out his differences with the pope; but the effect was spoiled by the emperor's insistence that Gregory should receive him 'with honour'. The instruction reached Gregory in the spring of 595, at a moment when his troubles were overflowing:[79]

It is a very grave thing that a man of whom so many and such serious crimes are reported should be honoured, before the matter is looked into and examined. And if the affairs of bishops committed to my charge are to be settled by our most pious lord [the emperor] through others' patronage, what shall I, a wretched man, do in this Church? That my bishops should spurn me and take refuge with lay judges, I give thanks to God and I attribute it to my sins. But this I submit briefly: that I shall wait a little; but if he [Maximus] puts off coming to me too long, I shall certainly not desist from applying strict canonical sanctions against him.[80]

---

[73] *Ep.* iii.46.
[74] *Ep.* iii.22.
[75] *Ep.* iv.16.
[76] *Ep.* v.6.
[77] *Ep.* iv.20; V.6.
[78] On Gregory's attitude, see above, chapter 6, pp. 89–90.
[79] See above, chapter 6, p. 92 and chapter 7, pp. 104–6.
[80] *Ep.* v.39. On lay patrons: *Epp.* iv.38 (Marcellus, Proconsul of Dalmatia); V.29: the 'wishes of the palace and the love of the people' are said to be behind Maximus; viii.24 (the Exarch).

But the conflict dragged on; repeated summons failed to bring Maximus to Rome;[81] and he enjoyed the support of the Dalmatian bishops, of local clergy, notables and officials: only two members of the Salonitan clergy, one of them being the deacon Honoratus, paid any attention to Gregory's sentence suspending Maximus from communion.[82] Gregory was unable to make any headway in the face of such powerful opposition. It was only when support for Maximus began to break up that a possibility of compromise began to appear. In 597 Dalmatian bishops began to turn against Maximus;[83] more important may have been the departure from office of the Exarch Romanus, not a lover of the pope, and certainly the remarkable conversion of the Proconsul Marcellinus.[84] Perhaps with the mediation of the latter, the new Exarch and the pope agreed on a compromise: the case was to be heard in Ravenna, by archbishop Marinianus assisted by Constantius, the bishop of Milan.[85] Gregory's representative was to hand over a document re-admitting Maximus to communion provided he satisfied the conditions laid down by the pope. In the end, however, Maximus was re-admitted to communion without a trial, having been allowed to purge himself in Ravenna.[86]

The long drawn-out and bitter affair of Salona does not reveal the alignment of local groupings as clearly as do the tensions between the churches of Rome and Ravenna; but in a more shadowy manner, they allow us to see similar forces at work in Dalmatia, too. Dalmatia was closely linked to Ravenna, both in its secular and in its ecclesiastical affairs. Illyricum, bordering it on the East, was much less so.

The provinces of Illyricum were nominally within the orbit of Roman jurisdiction. Always on the margins of Greek and Latin-speaking areas, the churches, too, had a history of changing and uncertain allegiance. Early in the fifth century, after the Empire had been divided between the sons of Theodosius I, imperial legislation assigned them to the jurisdiction of Constantinople.[87] In the course of subsequent development they were drawn into the orbit of the Roman patriarchate, an arrangement modified by Justinian's legislation. The pope's authority was, in theory, mediated here by his vicar, the bishop of Thessalonica, which appears to have

---

[81] *Epp.* VI.3; 25 (the latter contains the charges against him).

[82] *Ep.* VI.26.

[83] *Epp.* VII.17 (Iadera); VIII.11 (Epidauros).

[84] *Ep.* IX.159; cf. IX.237: he seems to have put his weight behind the pope's efforts at Ravenna, both in the case of Maximus and that of the Istrian schism.

[85] *Epp.* IX.150; 156; 177–9.

[86] *App.* V.

[87] *CTh* XVI.2.45. Cf. Fuhrmann 'Studien', 1, 173–5; Beck, *Kirche*, 60–98. Duchesne, *Autonomies ecclésiastiques*, 233–9, though dated, is still useful.

survived in Gregory's time. The situation had been complicated by
Justinian's foundation of an episcopal see in Prima Iustiniana, a 'great and
populous city, blessed in every way', built to mark the place of his birth
(near modern Skopje).[88] Justinian based this innovation on the need for
an administrative realignment of the praetorian prefecture of Illyricum
northwards, and a corresponding shift in ecclesiastical jurisdiction. This
see, too, was given the status of a papal vicariate, without its relations with
the old vicariate of Thessalonica being precisely defined. Justinian had
hoped to be able to rely on the new archbishopric as a fulcrum of his ecclesiastical power; a hope which was only partly disappointed in the debate
over the Three Chapters, when, in 549, the archbishop of Prima Justiniana,
though alone among the bishops of Illyricum, supported the emperor's
policies.[89] The Illyrian metropolitans were reckoned by Gregory as subject
to his authority in the same way as the other Western metropolitan bishops,
and he enumerated them along with the bishops of Ravenna, Cagliari and
Sicily.[90] In fact, however, the Illyrian bishops were called to attend the synods of Constantinople, an arrangement that Gregory did not challenge.[91]

Gregory had few dealings with Illyrian bishops, and we need not follow
them in detail.[92] One episode arose from the disturbances in the Balkans:
refugee clergy and people from Slav occupied territories were settled in
areas under imperial control by edict of the emperor, and given certain
rights. This sometimes created friction and conflict with local bishops.
Gregory's attempts to defend what he saw as just according to the canons
were once more frustrated by the court. Characteristically, Gregory wrote
to his representative in Constantinople, the deacon Boniface: Gregory
had made his decision on the matter, but he would not publish it, 'for fear
that I should appear to be doing something against the orders of the most
clement emperor, or, which God forbid, spurning him'; and he instructed
Boniface to make the necessary representations at court to convince the
emperor that his order was 'altogether wicked (*pravum*), altogether unjust,
altogether illegal and contrary to the sacred canons' and to get the order
reversed.[93] This episode ended in amicable agreement; others, some of a
highly complicated nature, also indicate conflicts between imperial interests and what Gregory saw as the requirements of the canons; and the

[88] Procopius, *Aedif.* IV.1.15–27, description at 24. On its ecclesiastical status, Markus, 'Carthage, Prima Justiniana, Ravenna', 289–92.
[89] See Markus, 'Carthage, Prima Justinana, Ravenna', 291.
[90] *Ep.* VIII.10. There are, however, some oddities about this address list.
[91] *Ep.* IX.157: he exhorted them not to sanction the use of the title of 'ecumenical patriarch'.
[92] See Dudden, *Gregory the Great*, 1, 467–75; Caspar, *Geschichte*, 2, 437–42.
[93] *Ep.* XIV.8; the case is dealt with in *Epp.* XIV.7, 8 and 13.

narrow limits within which he had to be content to assert his authority. Gregory was very prone to blame the Illyrian episcopate's troubles on the prevalence of simony.[94] If this means anything at all other than an ingrained suspicion of the state of affairs in distant churches enshrined in the formulae in use in the papal *scrinium*, it may have been Gregory's way of explaining to himself the ubiquity of government influence in the area, and the readiness of the bishops to turn to the court rather than to the pope for resolution of their conflicts. The papal vicariates, at any rate, offered little foothold for the exercise of any effective papal influence.

It would be hazardous to make any generalisations about Gregory's dealings with churches even further afield, within the areas under the eastern patriarchs' jurisdiction. He clearly took for granted the five Justinianic patriarchates: his synodical letter was addressed to the patriarchs of Constantinople, Alexandria, Antioch (and the former, deposed patriarch Anastasius) and of Jerusalem.[95] The only correspondence with them which is more than occasional in character is that with the patriarchs of Constantinople (which we have considered sufficiently, above, pp. 91–4), and with the patriarchs of Antioch and of Alexandria. Both the latter were friends of Gregory's, with whom he liked to exchange news, on whom he sometimes called for support, but with neither of whom he had occasion to conduct routine ecclesiastical business. The same is true of his exchange of letters with Domitianus of Melitene, a friend from Constantinople days.[96] His actual dealings with other patriarchs or bishops belonging to them were very few. Gregory had somehow got involved – probably through his *apocrisiarius* in Constantinople – in a long-standing quarrel between the bishop of Jerusalem and a local monastery, which he bade them resolve.[97] It was also in Constantinople that his only other contact with Jerusalem originated: an acolyte under the authority of Gregory's *apocrisiarius* there had fled from his discipline and took refuge in the Church of Jerusalem; Gregory asked the patriarch to apprehend him and send him to Rome.[98] Iberia, on the Black Sea coast, to whose bishops Gregory addressed a letter concerning problems about receiving converts from heretical groups, is the most remote area reached by his correspondence.[99]

This is a small harvest, and tells us little about Gregory's exercise of the authority he conceived as residing in his office over the eastern churches.

[94] *Ep.* vi.7. On the interpretation of this theme, see chapter 11, pp. 171–3.
[95] *Ep.* 1.24; in II.44 he speaks of four patriarchates (plus Rome?).
[96] *Ep.* iii.62; cf chapter 1, n. 55.
[97] *Ep.* vii.29.
[98] *Ep.* viii.6.
[99] *Ep.* xi.52: the letter raises many problems.

That Gregory upheld the traditional teaching of the Roman see on its primacy is not in doubt. An errant bishop had professed himself to be subject to the apostolic see; Gregory's rejoinder was sharp: 'when a bishop is guilty of a fault, I do not know any bishop who is not subject to it'.[100] In Gregory's language the 'apostolic see' was the see of Rome; Pelagius I had – at a time when the papacy was at the lowest ebb of its fortunes – regularly used the phrase (in the plural) in reference to the patriarchal sees; Gregory returned to the more exclusive usage of Leo I:[101] the Roman see was the only 'apostolic see', which he governed as the 'vicar of Peter the prince of the apostles'.[102] The see of Alexandria was bound to the Roman see by peculiarly close ties, as Peter had sent his disciple Mark there; though Gregory was prepared to allow that Peter's authority was now shared by three bishops,[103] he never spoke of Antioch or of Alexandria as 'apostolic' sees. The Roman Church was the only one, and it was 'the head of all the churches'.[104] In practice, as we have seen, this authority was subject to severe limitations; especially when it came into conflict with imperial authority, or in ecclesiastical cases in which secular authorities took sides and gave their support to Gregory's opponents. But, as we have seen (chapter 6, p. 90) Gregory had his principles with which to meet such cases.

[100] *Ep.* IX.27; cf. IX.26, of Constantinople.
[101] See above, p. 126.
[102] *Ep.* II.39.
[103] *Ep.* VII.37; X.14. Cf. *HEz* II.6.10–13.
[104] *Ep.* XIII.49.

CHAPTER 11

In cunctis mundi partibus: *the far west*

We have now considered Gregory's pontificate within the sphere of the
Empire and of the imperial Church, and on its borders, where it overlapped with barbarian Europe, in Lombard-occupied Italy (chapters
6–10). We have already seen something of Gregory's work in the context of
a Germanic people, the Lombards. Their settlement, however, was of
recent origin, and had developed far less towards a consolidated kingdom
(or more than one) than had the kingdoms of the Franks in Gaul and that
of the Visigoths in Spain. The English kingdoms, at a more fluid stage
of their development, were also older than that of the Lombards. The
Germanic kingdoms entered the orbit of Gregory's *cura* in different ways;
but whatever the nature of the pastoral care that he saw himself called to
exercise in each, he saw them all within a perspective determined by his
Roman and imperial heritage.

An index of this is the diplomatic language he adopted in his dealings
with the Germanic rulers of Western Europe and the emperors respectively. The traditional modes of addressing the emperor were redolent
of deference, even veneration, towards him. The normal practice of the
papal writing office echoed imperial protocol. In contrast, barbarian
rulers were addressed by titles corresponding to those assigned to top-
ranking imperial officials, as 'glorious' or 'most excellent'. Gregory often
calls them – if they were Catholic Christians – his 'sons' or 'daughters':
something he never did with emperors, always his 'lords' (though he did
refer to the emperor as 'his son', albeit only writing to third parties).[1] This
habit of administrative routine is not as trivial as it may appear. What it
reveals is not a pretension to papal *principatus* over barbarian kings and
their kingdoms, but a readiness to continue using the established forms of
administrative procedures in use in official quarters, and to share the now
somewhat anachronistic perspective on Germanic rulers implied by them.

---

[1] See chapter 6 above, and Markus, 'Gregory the Great's Europe', 28–9, especially n. 24 for details on
titulature.

Gregory adhered to the Byzantine representation of the Germanic nations as subjected by divine providence to the universal Empire and to the 'most Christian emperor', the supreme representative of God's authority on earth.[2] Byzantine conservatism had never found it easy to come to terms with Germanic state-building, and preferred to disguise the facts beneath the fictions of federate settlement within the imperial system. Unrealistic hopes still kept alive in Maurice's Constantinople of an eventual reconquest of lands in Western Europe did not, however, prevent the imperial government from dealing with their kings as the rulers of autonomous nations. Gregory's perspective on the Germanic nations was not very different from the official image held in Byzantine government circles. And like the imperial government, he too, in his dealings with their rulers, could show a realism at variance with the fiction. What he knew far more about, and what made the greatest claims on his time and his energies, was his own Church of Rome and the churches of the Empire; but his pastoral zeal embraced Western Europe.[3]

THE VISIGOTHS AND SPAIN

Gregory's first contact with the affairs of a barbarian kingdom had been with Spain. His friendship with Leander, bishop of Seville, began when Gregory was in Constantinople as his predecessor's ambassador. Leander was in the capital on diplomatic business connected with the affairs of the Gothic kingdom around 580. The precise nature of that business and the extent to which Gregory was acquainted with its details must remain unknown; but that he must have been aware of what was happening in Spain can hardly be doubted. And this was the time of one of the great turning-points in the history of the Gothic kingdom.

The Visigoths had established a foothold in Spain in the fifth century, where they were the neighbours of Suevi settled in the North-West of the peninsula, and of Vandals, until their departure for Africa in 429–30, in the South. Defeated in battle by the Frankish king Clovis in 507, the Goths were driven out of Gaul, keeping only a narrow strip of territory in the South around Narbonne. The greatly weakened Visigothic kingdom survived, for a time under divided kingship between the North and the South, for a period under Ostrogothic protection. Royal authority remained

---

[2] It is also significant that some barbarian rulers were ready to speak of themselves in the same way: e. g. Childebert II, engaged on a delicate diplomatic campaign, wrote of the emperor as *sacratissimi patris nostri imperatoris . . .* : *Ep. Austr.* 46 (*MGH Epp.* 3, 151).

[3] For a fine summary statement, see Wallace-Hadrill, 'Rome', 117.

weak, constantly threatened by the power of local 'tyrants' and of important cities.[4] The turning-point in the history of the kingdom is the reign of
king Leovigild (569–86). A single kingship was now re-established,
embracing the northern and the southern parts of the kingdom; before the
end of Leovigild's reign the Suevic kingdom was incorporated into the
Visigothic. Conquests in the area in the South occupied by Byzantine
forces since the 550s extended the king's control over most of the peninsula. Most important, perhaps, to the stabilisation and consolidation of
royal authority was the suppression of local rebellions. Leovigild adopted
characteristically imperial symbolic expressions to enhance and display
the new style of kingship: his coinage, his legislation, the court ritual and
the founding of a capital city, named Reccopolis after one of his sons, were
all designed to underline the kingdom's newly revived condition: it could
be seen as an answer to Byzantine *renovatio*. The assimilation of the Goths
into Roman society had advanced a long way, and was in full tide.

Goths were, however, still divided from their Roman subjects by religion. Christianity had been established among them before their entry
into Roman territory in the late fourth century. In an Arian version it had
become the Gothic national religion. Initiatives by the king to seek a *rapprochement* of Arian and Catholic on the basis of Arian religion, reformed
to be more accessible and less objectionable to his Roman subjects, had
limited success. Pressure was exerted on some Catholic bishops, especially
Gothic converts from Arianism, to conform. But the tide towards full
assimilation between the two nations was not to be reversed; and it was
desirable to end the Goths' international isolation as the only remaining
Arian nation in a world of Catholic Franks and their Roman allies. In 587
Leovigild's son Reccared was converted to Catholicism, and in 589 a geat
council of bishops, nobility and court, held at Toledo, marked the public
conversion of the kingdom. Like Constantine at Nicaea or Marcian at
Chalcedon, king Reccared now brought his people to orthodoxy and 'cut
off' Arianism in his kingdom. After 280 years, as the chronicler computed
it, Arianism, originating in the twentieth year of Constantine's reign and
ending in the eighth year of the emperor Maurice, the Catholic Church
had overcome the heresy which had infested it so long.[5]

Before this, however, Gregory's friend Leander had been involved in a
conflict, a revolt by the king's son Hermenegild against his father.

---

[4] See Collins, 'Mérida and Toledo'; generally, Thompson, 'The conversion', and *Goths in Spain*, 57–113;
Collins, *Early medieval Spain*, 32–58; Vilella Masana, 'Gregorio Magno', and Ramos-Lissón, 'Grégoire
le Grand'.
[5] John of Biclarum, *Chron. s. a.* 590, 1.

Leovigild had built up a network of alliances through dynastic marriages. As a part of this policy, he had married Hermenegild to a Catholic Frankish princess, Ingundis, and sent him to rule the southern province of Baetica on his behalf. It was there that Hermenegild came to associate himself with bishop Leander. His unilateral declaration of independence flared into war between father and son in 582, which ended with Hermenegild's defeat in 584. He was exiled by the king and killed by a Goth – with or without his father's connivance – in the following year. The reasons which led Hermenegild to revolt are by no means clear, but it is now generally accepted that religion was not at the roots of the attempted secession.[6] Gregory, when he received information about the events long after Leander's departure from Constantinople, interpreted Hermenegild's death as that of a Catholic martyr rebelling against the tyranny of an Arian father. His Spanish contemporaries saw Hermenegild as a simple usurper, until a much later time when a cult of Hermenegild the martyr emerged under the influence of Gregory's *Dialogues*.[7]

By the time of Reccared's conversion the tensions between Arian and Catholic had lost much of their importance; Goth and Roman were now rapidly united in a Catholic kingdom with surprisingly little resistance. The chronicler John of Biclarum commends Reccared for having persuaded the Arian clergy to accept the Catholic faith 'by reason rather than by command', thus bringing 'all the Gothic and Suevic people to the unity and peace of the Christian Church'.[8] This was the final outcome of the 'widespread move towards the Romanization of the kingdom that took place in the reign of the Arian Leovigild as well as the Catholic Reccared'.[9] It was the beginning of the Visigothic golden age. In his *History* Isidore of Seville, its outstanding representative, could celebrate the prosperity of a Spain united within the territory ruled by its kings from Toledo as a single nation, comprising Roman and Goth.

Of these momentous events Gregory appears to have received news from his friend Leander in the first year of his pontificate. In the midst of

---

[6] Thompson, *The Goths*, 67–8 interprets it as 'essentially a conflict of Goth against Goth, not of Goth against Roman'. Cf. *ibid.*, 103.

[7] Gregory received the news from Spanish travellers *nuper* come to Rome. His view (*Recharedus non patrem perfidum sed fratrem martyrem sequens...*: *Dial.* III.31.7) of Hermenegild as a martyr is tellingly rejected by the Mérida *Vitas patrum* (v.9.2), which alters the text copied from Gregory, substituting *Christum dominum* for *fratrem martyrem*. See Thompson, *The Goths*, 76–8; Collins, *Early medieval Spain*, 46–7. Ramos-Lissón, 'Grégoire le Grand', 189 n. 9, following J. Orlandis, attributes the late-seventh-century reputation of Hermenegild as a martyr (e. g. by Valerius of Bierzo) to the survival of a local popular tradition.

[8] *Chron. s. a.* 587, 5. Collins, *Early medieval Spain*, 58, notes the ease with which Arianism was replaced and the rapidity of its disappearance in Spain (and Burgundy), compared with Lombard Italy.

[9] Thompson, *The Goths*, 109.

all his cares, feeling himself to be struggling among the swelling billows of this world, doubting his ability to steer into a safe port the rotting old ship whose command God had unaccountably confided to him, Gregory could hardly express his joy at the news that 'our most glorious son king Reccared had been converted to the Catholic faith with most complete devotion'.[10] But as the wiles of the ancient enemy of mankind never cease, let Leander watch over him, that he might be constant in his good works and firm in faith; let the king display in his actions service of the eternal kingdom that he could now hope to enter after many years of ruling his earthly kingdom. Then Gregory went on to speak about baptismal rites used in Spain (see Chapter 5), and sent Leander, in response to his request, a part of the revised version of the homilies on Job he had begun in Constantinople.[11] Despite their friendship, no further communication seems to have taken place between Gregory and Leander, or anyone else in Spain,[12] until an exchange of letters and gifts in 599. A batch of letters had arrived from Leander and king Reccared, and Gregory replied to both.[13] The correspondence appears to be little more than an exchange of formal courtesies, but allows us to glimpse diplomatic activity (which it is beyond my scope to discuss here)[14] between the Gothic king and the imperial court. Writing to the king, Gregory commends the king's faith and life; acclaims the conversion of the Goths as a 'new miracle wrought in our time'; commends the king for refusing to repeal legislation against the Jews (see Chapter 5), despite the offer of bribes; and he ends with a little 'mirror for princes', sketching the qualities of a good ruler, and sends the king a cross and a relic and Leander the pallium.[15] A postscript was appended to the letter when Gregory, on having his original dictation read back to him before despatch, remembered that some time ago Reccared had asked him to write to the emperor requesting him to search the archives for copies of treaties with the Gothic kingdom, a request Gregory declined. For one thing, the archives had been destroyed in a fire in Justinian's time, and

---

[10] *integerrima … deuotine conuersum*: *Ep.* 1.41. Gregory was fond of the nautical image: e. g. *Ep.* 1.4.

[11] On this see Meyvaert, 'Uncovering', 63–5, and Vilella, 'Gregorio Magno', 175–6.

[12] Except *Ep.* v.53, when Gregory sent Leander his *RP*; and the letter of bishop Licinianus (*Ep.* 1.41a, Ewald and Hartmann, *MGH Epp.* 1, 58–61, dated to between 591 and 595). No reply by Gregory is preserved. On it, see Meyvaert, 'Uncovering', 62–3. Three years after his conversion Reccared had sent gifts with his announcement of the news, but the messengers' shipwreck prevented them reaching the pope: *Ep.* ix.227a (Ewald and Hartmann, *MGH Epp.* 2, 220–21).

[13] *Ep.* ix.228, 229.

[14] See Thompson, *The Goths*, 332.

[15] Vilella, 'Gregorio', 180, concludes that Leander was thereby made a papal vicar; this cannot be assumed. Ramos-Lissón, 'Grégoire', 192, is more guarded. On the gift of *benedictiones* and relics, cf. Vilella, *ibid.*, 179–80, who refers to Cracco-Ruggini, 'Grégoire le Grand', 87 to note Gregory's 'propagandistic' use of such Petrine gifts.

besides, Gregory added with some asperity – justifiably resenting being asked to carry out the king's diplomatic dirty work – nobody should be asked to provide evidence against himself. So let the king carefully observe the peace for his own good and that of his kingdom.[16] At the same time as this exchange of letters, taking advantage of the carrier, Gregory wrote to a *dux* Claudius, a faithful follower of the king who may have had a part in suppressing a rebellion against Reccared at the time of his conversion, commending abbot Cyriacus to him and asking him to facilitate his work and speedy return to Rome.[17] The only remaining contact between Gregory and Spain concerned a case in the Byzantine occupied area, where the *defensor* John was sent to adjudicate in a dispute involving two bishops and a provincial governor. Gregory's emissary was given very full instructions, supplemented by a large dossier of legal material.[18] The jurisdiction of the Roman see was evidently still regarded as extending to imperial territories in the West. The contrast between Gregory's readiness to intervene in Byzantine Baetica and his keeping at arm's length from the Visigothic kingdom has often been noted. It may be that he thought the affairs of the Spanish Church were in good hands. But it is also true that with its highly centralised character under strong royal control from Toledo, where great councils – 'national institutions'[19] – of king, nobility and bishops were to meet regularly, it constituted a comparatively self-contained world closed to outside intervention.[20]

THE FRANKISH CHURCH AND KINGDOMS

The battle at which the Frankish armies of Clovis overcame the Visigoths in 507 rounded off a series of victories in which the Frankish king obtained control over most of Gaul, as far as the Rhine. Within a quarter of a century the absorption of the Burgundian kingdom brought the whole of Gaul (apart from a narrow coastal area in the south) into the Frankish kingdom. Gaul had the good fortune – the foundation of modern France – to be taken over as a whole by a single conquering nation. After Clovis (d. 511) this kingdom came to be divided between members of his dynasty, the Merovingian royal family. A series of further divisions between his sons and their heirs, sometimes preceded, accompanied or followed by feuds

---

[16] *Ep.* IX.229. To describe their relation as one *de grande cordialité* (Ramos-Lissón, 'Grégoire', 196) seems over-enthusiastic.

[17] *Ep.* IX.230. On Cyriacus see below, n. 43.

[18] *Ep.* XIII.46–9. XIII.47 concerns a monastery in the Balearic islands.

[19] Thompson, *The Goths*, 279.

[20] Cf. Vilella, 'Gregorio Magno', 177.

which so horrified Gregory of Tours, did not prevent the survival of a sense of a single Frankish kingdom shared between members of the Merovingian family, embracing the part-kingdoms (at various times) of Neustria in the North, Austrasia in the East, Burgundy (and Aquitaine) in the South.[21] The Church in Gaul, especially when gathered in council, was well on its way to becoming a truly national institution and helped to maintain a conception of unity encompassing a divided kingdom.

The sons of Clovis and their sons and grandsons inherited not only his lands, but his religion. Alone among the Germanic conquerors, in the course of his wars of conquest, at a much controverted date not many years before or after 500, Clovis had accepted the religion of his Roman subjects, Catholicism. The bishops were the men who mattered in Gaul; and, as one of them, Remigius of Reims, advised Clovis at the start of his victorious career, the king would do well to heed them. Quickly, even before his baptism, Clovis learnt to value the support of the Gallo-Roman bishops. As his success was to prove, his new religion did not destroy the royal *fortuna*. His kingship came to serve the cause of Christianity: Clovis was seen as the champion of Catholicism, as a new Constantine.

Gregory of Tours saw the period since Clovis as a time of decline. Considering his own times he came close to dismay. And yet, despite the civil wars and the violence, and despite the undoubted difficulties in which they involved the Church,[22] much had been achieved in the Frankish Church in the sixth century. The legacy of the Gallo-Roman Church provided a solid foundation. Although by Gregory's time men of Frankish descent began to appear among the bishops, most of them were still Gallo-Romans; and traditional Roman ecclesiastical order was what the bishops sought to extend throughout Gaul. Beginning with Orléans in 511, the series of Frankish councils extends through the sixth century. There is no apparent break between the preoccupations of the councils held under Caesarius of Arles (bishop 502–42), the great pastoral reformer in Roman and Gothic southern Gaul, and the later councils attended by bishops from the whole of the Frankish kingdom.

Caesarius' councils, however, involved only southern bishops. By the time of his death in 542, Arles had come under Frankish rule and the Merovingians had extended their authority over most of Gaul. His work was continued by the councils held in the Frankish kingdom from the 540s. The councils which met in Orléans in 541 and 549 drew bishops from all over Francia. Their concerns were those of Caesarius. As the centre of

---

[21] For a fine account, see Wood, *The Merovingian kingdoms*, 33–70.
[22] See for instance the Council of Paris between 556 and 573: *Concilia Galliae*, I (*CC* 148A, 205–6).

gravity of the Frankish Church shifted northwards, it was the old Roman South that provided the model; it could show them 'how bishops in unity could define the purposes of their Church; they could apply the wisdom of the canons and the Fathers to a new situation'.[23] With the northward shift, the problems of adjustment to a society more deeply Germanic became more urgent. Marriage, the relations between a warrior-aristocracy and clergy, monks and nuns, conflicts brought about by royal influence and control, property-rights, all raised delicate and worrying problems for the bishops. They were anxious to deal with all major ecclesiastical matters. Nourished by Roman tradition, they sought to shape the religion and the life of a society becoming less and less Roman, in accordance with received Christian norms. Their record, as seen in the work of the sixth century councils, is impressive.

How much Gregory knew about the affairs of the Gallic Church can only be inferred from his correspondence, and that suggests he was more impressed by its shortcomings than by the remarkable achievements of its bishops over two or three generations. Before 596, the year in which he sent his mission to the English (see below, pp. 177–87), Gregory's contacts with Gallic bishops were effectively confined to Provence.[24] After 596 they were greatly extended, and the opportunities for communication multiplied, by the Roman missionaries sent to England in the course of their passage through Gaul on their way. Even in his later years, when he had more extensive contacts, Gregory's correspondence was preponderantly with Provence, the area most easily accessible. Here the Roman Church had some possessions, whose management involved the pope in correspondence with local aristocrats and others.[25] It was not until the summer of 595 that the priest Candidus, soon to be caught up in bigger things, could take over the administration of the patrimony. He was to be one of the channels of Gregory's communication with the court.[26] Interestingly, Gregory's first contact with any Gallic bishops was through Jewish merchants from Provence, and concerned the treatment of Jews.[27]

[23] Wallace-Hadrill, *The Frankish Church*, 99. His chapter on 'The Church in Council' is by far the best account of conciliar activity. Pietri, 'Grégoire le Grand', is a useful general survey. Vaes, 'La papauté', remains useful.

[24] Only six of his letters addressed to Gaul are preserved in the first five books of the Register and all these were sent to destinations in the region of Provence. *Epp.* V.59 and 60 are only partial exceptions: addressed to all the bishops in Childebert's kingdom and to King Childebert himself, they must in fact have gone to Arles with *Ep.* V.58 (a reply to a request emanating from Arles) with the intention of being sent on from there. In 593 Gregory used the bishop of Milan as a source of information for news about the Frankish kingdom: *Ep.* IV.2.

[25] See above, p. 113. Later letters of commendation: *Epp.* IX.212; 213; 226; XI.43; 44.

[26] *Epp.* VI.5; VIII.4.

[27] *Ep.*I.45; on Jews, see above, chapter 5.

It was one of the two bishops with whom Provençal Jews had established Gregory's relations, Virgilius the bishop of Arles, who four years later (595) took the initiative to write to the pope requesting the privilege of the renewal of a papal vicariate and the use of the pallium. The request had respectable precedents: the bishop of Arles had been made a vicar of the apostolic see in 417 by pope Zosimus, and Caesarius and several of his successors in the sixth century had received the pallium. The bishop's request came with the support (and perhaps at the initiative) of Childebert (II), the son of queen Brunhild and now king over Austrasia, Burgundy and Aquitaine, and Gregory gladly granted it. Virgilius was to bear the authority of a papal vicar in the realms ruled by king Childebert; he was to respect the honour due to each metropolitan; he was to authorise their journeys; he was to settle the more difficult cases that might arise with the advice of twelve bishops, and refer the most difficult to the pope.[28] To the bishops under Childebert's dominion Gregory wrote demanding their obedience to his dispositions, since in the Church, as in the world of creatures in heaven and on earth, order and hierarchy must be maintained among unequals, in order to secure peace and mutual charity. So Virgilius has been placed in charge over them, to arbitrate in their disputes in accordance with the canons. Any doubts in matters of faith or serious problems will be referred to the pope; let them all obey his vicar, and attend the synods to be called by him.[29] King Childebert was notified at the same time that, in view of his faithful service of God and the love and respect he showed to His priests, Gregory was pleased to grant the requested privileges.[30]

In doing so, Gregory expected two conditions to be met: that vicar and king both devote themselves to the elimination of simony, and to the abolition of the practice of ordaining laymen unqualified for the priestly ministry. He had already stipulated something like this among the pastoral requirements he imposed on John, the bishop of Prima Justiniana, when granting him the privileges of a papal vicar and the use of the pallium: it should be his chief concern 'that [he] should never make illicit ordinations, but if there were occasion to promote somebody to clerical orders, or to higher rank, he should be ordained not on account of presents or patronage (*non praemiis aut precibus*) but of merit. In no ordination must he allow presents to be slipped to [him] in any manner, lest he become entangled in the snares of the heresy of simony.'[31] Here Gregory voices under a

---

[28] *Ep.* v.58.
[29] *Ep.* v.59.
[30] *Ep.* v.60.
[31] *Ep.* v.16.

single head, without distinguishing the two things, the same anxiety that was to haunt him later: simony, and ordination on merit only.

Gregory's insistence would raise no problems if it stood by itself, or if it recurred only in his letters addressed to Gaul. But in fact it is one which not only recurs in many of his letters elsewhere, but does so in a stereotyped form which hardened into a more or less fixed formula used by the papal *scrinium*.[32] What are we to make of this? Are we really to believe, as Gregory sometimes asserts, that he has had reports that 'nobody can receive holy orders' in Gaul, or in the churches of the East – all of them? –, 'without giving presents'? It is possible, but unlikely. Or is Gregory simply assuming the worst when he knows little about distant churches and has little direct communication with them? Modern readers of papal letters have learnt to be on their guard against making inferences as to the facts from the formulae utilised; they will look for independent supporting evidence. Royal influence and control over episcopal appointments in Gaul cannot be doubted; Gregory may well have become aware of its extent. We cannot be sure; Gregory was apt to attribute wickedness in the Church to corruption by payment or favour.[33] The fact that he first used the formula in his correspondence with Gaul makes it seem likely that he had become aware of the prevalence there of practices he interpreted as simony (though they might have been seen by Gallic clergy as social nicety), and that the habit of suspecting simony in unknown churches took root in his mind, and the formula in his correspondence.

To 'simony' he gave a wide sense. Commenting on the sin of Simon Magus (Acts 8:18) he said: 'some there are who although they accept no money for ordination nevertheless confer holy orders from human favour (*gratia*) and seek only praise in return: these do not give freely what they have freely received; for the sacred office they have conferred, they expect payment in esteem.'[34] It was far more than esteem that Frankish kings would have expected from their bishops. Bishops were the leaders of their communities. Their support, especially in the troubled times that Gregory of Tours records, was an indispensable requirement for royal authority. On the whole, Gregory does not seem to have questioned the rulers' reasonable exercise of patronage. The Gallic councils, too, were trying to restrict its practice, ruling out the more blatant practices of

---

[32] It recurs, with variations, in *Epp.* v.16 (Prima Justiniana); 58; viii.4; ix.216 (Gaul); v.62; 63; vi.7 (Illyricum); ix.136; xi.28 (churches of the East).

[33] In addition to the letters cited in n. 32 above, see *Epp.* i.82; ii.39; iii.22; iv.13; v.24; v.59; vi.3; ix.214, 219; xi.38, 40, 42, 47, 49, 50, 51; xii.8, 9. Gregory admonished the bishops against simony in *HEv* i.17.13; and it was condemned at the Roman synod of 595: *Ep.* v.57a.

[34] *HEv* i.4.4.

simony.[35] Gregory did not go into detail; what he wanted to rule out was, presumably, the overt corruption that was generally seen as objectionable, even when practised.[36] Indeed, for the enactment of the reforms Gregory wished to see in the Frankish Church, he could not have excluded the influence, and the control, of the court over the bishops. The bishops could have achieved nothing without royal sponsorship. Recognising this, he continued to appeal to queen Brunhild, to king Childebert,[37] and, after his death in 596, to his young sons, Theudebert and Theuderic, and to the Neustrian king Chlothar II.

Queen Brunhild, regent in Burgundy and Austrasia on behalf of her grandsons, became, especially after 597, the pivot of his hopes for reform. She and Syagrius, the bishop of Autun who stood very close to the Burgundian court, had been particularly helpful to Augustine on his way to England. They were rewarded by the grant of the pallium for Syagrius in response to their joint request. It was to be conferred by the rector Candidus when Syagrius's petition had been received.[38] But gratitude for what they had done for Augustine will scarcely account for Gregory's compliance. He was usually more cautious: neither the request for the pallium by Desiderius, the bishop of Vienne,[39] nor that of bishop Etherius of Lyon for confirmation of the privileges of his see,[40] were granted, as no documentary evidence was available in support. Moreover, Syagrius had failed to request the favour in person, and Autun was not free of the taint of schism; Gregory will have had special reasons for acceding to the request. He had evidently come to centre his hopes for the Frankish Church on the queen and her confidant, the bishop of Autun. In his letter, one of several praising the queen's devotion and service of the Church,[41] Gregory asked the queen to take care that 'nobody under [her] rule be allowed to receive holy orders in return for a gift of money or any personal patronage or family connection', but only for personal merit. The heresy of simony will

---

[35] Paris, 556–73, c. 8; Orléans, 549, c. 10 rules out simony, though it allows royal confirmation.

[36] As, for instance, in the stories told by Gregory of Tours, *HF* vi.38–9 (584). On Brunhild's practice, see Nelson, 'Queens', 54–5. On Gregory's attitude, Pietri, 'Grégoire le Grand', 122–5.

[37] *Ep.* v.60.

[38] *Ep.* viii.4. The grant had had to be delayed: no request had been received from the bishop in person; the messenger turned out to be a schismatic; the emperor's consent had to be sought – perhaps because there was no precedent in this instance? It was finally conferred in 599, together with the privilege granted to the Church of Autun of ranking second after Lyon, the metropolitan see: *Ep.* ix.223.

[39] *Ep.* ix.221.

[40] *Ep.* xi.40.

[41] *Epp.* ix.213; 214; xi.48; 49; xiii.5. How much the pope's apparently extravagant praise was therapeutic flattery, and how much he knew about her, cannot be guessed. For a balanced assessment, see Nelson, 'Queens'.

weaken her kingdom. Similarly, only properly tested clergy are to be promoted; for how is a man to assume leadership in the Lord's flock who has not undergone the discipline of a subject? The extirpation of simony and of the promotion of laymen to clerical posts continued to be central in Gregory's requests to the Frankish rulers and their bishops. In later years this demand took a modified form: Gregory urged that a council be called by the rulers to enact these reforms in the Frankish Church. From about 599 or 600 the position of Queen Brunhild was weakening; the pope may have been aware of this, and, if so, his new emphasis on councils as the agents of reform would have been a realistic response. He may also have come to appreciate that councils would be likely to call out the best from the bishops. But as Gallic councils had already outlawed simony and lay ordinations, it is not clear just how Gregory expected a new council to deal with the problem.[42] At any rate, this becomes the refrain of his letters from about 600. In his request to the queen in 599 he proposed that she should call a council, chiefly to root out these twin evils, to be held in the presence of his representative, the abbot Cyriacus and under the presidency of Syagrius.[43] He was still requesting the queen's permission to send a legate to a council in 602;[44] the council was never held.

There were, of course, many other things on which Gregory wanted to see action: he asked Brunhild to dispel the lingering suspicion about the papacy's fidelity to Chalcedon; to restrain the cult of idols, of trees and demons,[45] with 'healthy coercion' and to repress violence, adultery, theft and other depravity.[46] King Childebert was not to punish without proper trial;[47] and especially as Gregory's contacts with Gaul extended, and more information and more complaints reached him and furnished more opportunities, in his later years he intervened on specific matters. He took up – fruitlessly – complaints by the bishop of Turin about parishes within his area being incorporated in a diocese within the Frankish kingdom;[48] he sought to remedy clerical irregularities and breaches of canonical

---

[42] In his letter addressed to the metropolitans and Syagrius, *Ep.* IX.219, Gregory wished for at least one, if possible two, annual diocesan synods to be held. This had also been laid down by the Council of Tours in 567, c. 1.

[43] *Ep.* IX.214; cf. *Epp.* IX.216; 219; 220; 223; XI.38; 40; 42; 46; 47; 49; 50; 51. Cyriacus had evidently arrived in Marseille in July 599 with the expectation of attending as Gregory's legate; he was a busy man and not to be detained: *Epp.* IX.209, 214, 216, 219. He seems to have had a wide-ranging brief, from Marseille to Spain: *Epp.* IX.230; XI.10. On Cyriacus, see Pietri, 'Grégoire le Grand', 118. Bishop Aregius of Gap was to join Cyriacus as Gregory's legate: *Ep.* IX.220.

[44] *Ep.* XIII.5.

[45] On 'paganism' in Gaul, see Markus, 'From Caesarius'.

[46] *Ep.* VIII.4.

[47] *Ep.* VI.6.

[48] *Epp.* IX.215, 227.

observances;[49] he prohibited a bishop teaching the Latin classics;[50] and he concerned himself, as always, with monastic foundations and monastic life and discipline.[51] There was correspondence concerning the treatment of Jews (see Chapter 5); and on diplomatic relations with the court of Constantinople.[52]

Among the pope's rebukes to Gallic bishops one administered to Serenus, the bishop of Marseille, is of particular interest. Gregory's contacts with Marseille had revealed that the bishop, 'seeing people adoring pictures, had them [the pictures, not the people] broken up and thrown out of the churches'. Gregory, while commending such zeal in prohibiting the worship of anything made by human hands, objected to the treatment of the pictures: 'For pictures are placed into churches so that those who cannot read might at least read by seeing on the walls what they are unable to read in books.'[53] But Serenus proved obstinate; he refused to believe that the prohibition had been an authentic letter of Gregory's, and attributed it to its bearer, the abbot Cyriacus. To Gregory's remonstrance he pretended to reply 'with priestly goodwill', but the later parts of his letter revealed something very different. So, ignoring Gregory's admonition, he used this pretext to continue, 'fired by thoughtless zeal', to break up pictures of the saints (*sanctorum imagines*). Has any priest ever been heard to do such a thing? If nothing else, should this not have dissuaded Serenus, who, spurning his brother-bishops, stuck out, affecting to be the only holy and wise one among them? Gregory went on at length:

> It is one thing to adore a picture, another to learn from the story of a picture what should be adored [*per picturae historiam quid sit adorandum addiscere*]. For what writing presents to those who read, that the picture provides to the unlearned; so even the ignorant can see in it what they should follow; even the illiterate read. Hence especially for the barbarians [*gentibus*] pictures are a substitute for reading [*pro lectione pictura est*].

Ancient tradition sanctions pictorial representation of stories of the saints; let Serenus humbly conform and gather his flock and explain his over-zealous breaking up of the pictures to them, and teach them that nothing made by human hands must be adored, but that it should be used in the worship of the One almighty Trinity. For good measure, Gregory

---

[49] *Epp.* IX.219; 224; 225; XI.10; XIII.5; 6.

[50] See above, p. 37.

[51] *Epp.* VII.12 (privileges for St Cassian's monastery in Marseille); IX.158; 217; XIII.5; 9–11 (Queen Brunhild's and Syagrius's foundations).

[52] *Epp.* XIII.5; 7.

[53] *Ep.* IX.209. This large and important topic has received a good deal of discussion recently. For references, see Markus, *Signs and meanings*, 62, n. 39. (I discuss Gregory's views on reading and seeing there, 62–5.) Here I need refer only to the fine study: Chazelle, 'Pictures'.

added a warning against keeping bad company, associating with fallen priests.[54]

This episode elicited from Gregory what was to become a classic statement on the use of images in worship. In his letters to Serenus Gregory affirmed what had become, and remained, the Roman view on the use of images: not for adoration but for the instruction of ignorant minds. But the correspondence seems also to allow us a glimpse of a rather different view beginning to take shape in Gaul.[55] In the sixth century there was nothing uncommon about figural decoration on the walls of churches in Gaul, as elsewhere. But there are grounds for thinking that in the later sixth century new attitudes were beginning to focus on pictures. Bishop Serenus had evidently tolerated the pictures on his churches' walls until he noticed people 'adoring' them. The correspondence does not give us any indication as to what was involved in the *adoratio* of pictures that bishop Serenus so hated. There is, however, a fair body of evidence of a new streak in popular piety, which tended to erode the distinction between the image and its original. The merging in worship of the image and the person represented has been diagnosed as a trait of Byzantine piety from the later sixth century, and described as a 'magic' quality with which icons were being endued.[56] Its clearest manifestation is in miracle stories in which icons take on the character of living persons, demand to be fed, clothed, moved, or bleed. In the sixth century such stories began to circulate in Gaul. Moreover, other hints suggest that a new fashion in piety did not by-pass Gaul. An obscure and controversial canon of a council held in Tours in 567 is best interpreted in this context: 'Let the Lord's body be placed on the altar not amid an arrangement of images, but under the sign of the cross.'[57] The canon has often been understood in a different sense, as prohibiting some bizarre magical ritual which involved an arbitrary or fanciful arrangement of the consecrated elements of the eucharist; but its language does not fit this interpretation easily. It is far more likely that something like the Byzantine iconostasis had made its appearance in Gaul; perhaps as arrangements of images on the *cancelli* around the altars of Gallic churches, inspired by the prestigious model of the new chancel-screen in the church Hagia Sophia in Constantinople. That something like

[54] *Ep.* XI.10. Cf. *Ep.* XI.38.
[55] On the following, see Markus, 'The cult', where details are given.
[56] Kitzinger, 'The cult', 101.
[57] C. 3 (*CC* 148A, 178): *Ut corpus Domini in altari non imaginario ordine, sed sub crucis titulo componatur.* I have argued that *imaginario ordine* should be understood not as 'fanciful', 'phantastic' or 'arbitrary arrangement', but as 'in an arrangement of images': as in normal Latin usage in Late Antiquity, e.g. in Diocletian's edict (where *pictor imaginarius* means not an 'imaginary painter', but a 'painter of images'). My translation has not, as far as I know, been refuted.

this is what the bishops were concerned about is suggested by the very next canon they enacted, which lays down that lay people should have free access to the Holy of Holies (the sanctuary) for prayer and communion, except during mass and vigils, when the space between the altar and *cancelli* is to be reserved for clergy.[58] There was no need for the further physical closing off of the sanctuary space by a screen of pictures.

Taken in this context, bishop Serenus's anxiety about the *adoratio* shown to the pictures on the walls of his churches in and around Marseille may have been rather better grounded than Gregory could have guessed. That Byzantium and Gaul should both have been affected by similar artistic fashions and similar currents of spirituality should not surprise us. A fragment of the True Cross had been exported from Constantinople to Poitiers in the 560s; we may assume that its cult flourished. Gaul and the Greek East both inherited a Mediterranean-wide Christian culture and were still in fairly frequent contact; they did not develop in isolation.[59] Augustine's arrival at Canterbury preceded by a cross and an icon of the Saviour – perhaps a Western copy of a Byzantine work – might serve as a reminder of how much in Gregory's world was still shared between the Constantinople of Justin II and the empress Sophia, the Poitiers of Venantius Fortunatus, and, despite Roman conservatism, Rome itself.[60]

THE FRANKS AND THE ENGLISH CHURCH

In the first few years of his pontificate Gregory knew little about Gaul. In his later years his contacts with Gallic bishops and the Frankish royal family were frequent. The watershed was the mission he had sent in 596 to convert the heathen English to Christianity. It was to turn out to do almost as much for Frankish as for English Christianity.

In September 595 Gregory instructed Candidus, about to take up his appointment as rector of the Roman Church's patrimony in Gaul, to use revenue from the lands which could not be transferred and spent in Rome on the purchase of 'clothes for the poor or English slave boys (*pueros Anglos*) aged seventeen or eighteen that they might be educated in monasteries'.[61]

---

[58] Tours 567, c. 4. (*CC* 148A, 178).

[59] See Cameron, 'The early religious policies', and her 'The Byzantine sources'; and Brown, 'Eastern and Western Christendom'.

[60] If Bede's report (*HE* I.25) is not in fact a retrospective and perhaps anachronistic reconstruction: see below, n. 67.

[61] *Ep.* VI.10. On the problem of currency convertibility, see Grierson, 'The *patrimonium Petri*'. But a convertibility crisis is hardly likely to account for Gregory's interest in English slave boys.

They were to be sent, apparently to Rome, still unbaptized, in the charge of a priest, to be trained there in the monastic profession. This letter is likely to have given rise to the stories told in Northumbria a century later about Angels and Angles (and other puns pleasing to English ears); and it may well indicate Gregory's first step towards putting into effect a plan for a mission to the English.[62] Less than a year later, a monk of his monastery in Rome, Augustine, was despatched with a group of companions to convert the heathen English to Christianity.

The kings Theuderic and Theudebert and queen Brunhild were asked to do what they could to promote their mission.[63] Their intended route can be traced by the letters of recommendation which they carried to bishops along the route. It would have taken them through Lerins and Marseilles, Aix, Arles, Vienne, Autun, Tours and perhaps others.[64] The route is not the most direct; Gregory seems to have wanted his emissaries to go out of their way to make contacts with the Church in Francia. He may also have wanted them to call at the shrine of the great monk and bishop Martin at Tours.[65] The monks were evidently frightened by the difficulties facing them, and Augustine went back to Rome. He rejoined them, having been made their prior (*praepositus*) by Gregory, with a letter of exhortation: it would have been better not to have started out on their great task than to give up for faintheartedness and fear of what they had heard reported.[66] They arrived in Kent, landing on the Isle of Thanet, in the spring of 597.

Though little now remained in Britain of the organised Christian Church of Roman times, except in the West and the North, Christianity appears to have survived in Britain in greater strength than Gregory was aware. In Kent, the English kingdom closest – and not only geographically – to the Franks, the king, Aethelberht, had been married to a Frankish princess, Bertha, who had brought a bishop, Liudhard, as her chaplain; Christianity was not unheard of at the Kentish court, and he is likely to have had more Christians among his subjects. Nevertheless, according to Bede's account, the missionaries were received with suspicion and reserve: on the island of Thanet, in the open air. As the king was won over, they received provisions, permission to stay, and freedom to preach. They were given old Roman churches in and just outside Canterbury to serve as the

---

[62] Bede, *HE* II.1 and, independently, Whitby *'Life'* 9. On the origins of the mission and Gregory's intentions, see below pp. 185–7.

[63] *Epp.* VI.51; 58.

[64] *Epp.* VI.52; 54; 55; 56; 57. Not all letters may have been preserved.

[65] As suggested by Mayr-Harting, *The coming*, 61.

[66] *Ep.* VI.53.

episcopal church and as their monastic dwelling respectively, and allowed to build and restore others.[67] Bede, telescoping a drawn-out history some of whose details remain obscure, recounts the success of their preaching and their exemplary monastic life. It brought many to believe and to be baptized, eventually including the king himself.[68] The following July Gregory wrote to his friend, Eulogius, the patriarch of Alexandria. In the middle of a troubled letter, he had good news:[69]

[Augustine], with my permission [*data a me licentia*] has been made a bishop by the bishops of *Germania*, and, with their help, reached the [English] people at the ends of the earth, and now we have received reports [*scripta*] of his well-being and his work. He and his companions sparkle with so many miracles that in the signs they have displayed they seem to copy the miracles [*virtutes*] of the apostles. At the festival of Christmas this last year, more than ten thousand are reported to have been baptized by our brother and fellow-bishop.

It is clear that Gregory had had news of success, though it seems to have been indirect, most probably through Autun,[70] perhaps through Arles, or some other Gallic centre. Augustine had been consecrated as a bishop, presumably because his mission now looked like taking root; for the rest, the letter raises difficulties. The figure of 10,000 baptized is clearly impossible; and what about the king, of whom no mention is made? And where was Augustine consecrated? To these questions there is no certain answer. Bede thought Augustine had returned to Arles for his consecration, and a case has been made for Autun; we cannot be sure either of its place or its time, nor of the date of the king's baptism.[71]

The missionaries had been frightened; they were going into the unknown, knew not what to expect, and rumour was not encouraging. Gregory shared their ignorance. There is no evidence in any of his letters up to this time that he had any definite information about the 'English people placed in a corner of the world and still faithless, worshipping sticks and stones'.[72] But Gregory's ignorance was soon to be remedied. In 601 a party of monks returned to Rome to report on the progress of the mission, and to fetch 'things that were needed for the Church's worship and

---

[67] Bede, *HE* I.25–6. Wood, 'The mission', 3 and n. 11 raises a doubt about the reliability of some of Bede's report. It seems far from decisive to me, and in any case leaves its main outlines unaffected.

[68] *HE* I.26.

[69] *Ep.* VIII.29.

[70] Gregory had an exchange of letters with Autun in September 597, in which Augustine is already referred to as a bishop: *Ep.* VIII.4 (*CC* 140A 520, l. 64–5).

[71] See on this Markus, 'Chronology', 24–8, and Mayr-Harting, *The coming*, 63 and 266–8; cf. Wood, 'The mission', 11; and Jenal, 'Gregor der Grosse', 799–800. Further, below, n. 79.

[72] *Ep.* VIII.29. The only possible exception is the statement that they had wished to be converted: *Ep.* VI.51. On this see below, n. 93.

ministry, such as sacred vessels, altar cloths and church ornaments, priestly and clerical vestments, relics of the holy apostles and martyrs as well as many books'.[73] Gregory sent reinforcements for the mission, led by abbot Mellitus and a priest Lawrence, with a large post-bag containing more letters to recipients in Gaul and in Kent. Again, they carried letters of recommendation; but to a strikingly larger number of bishops than five years before; and the kings addressed now included Clothar of Neustria.[74] Gregory's contacts with Gaul had multiplied, and he was now far better informed of its affairs.

The letters give a measure of how much had changed, both in Gregory's mind and in the world around him, since the first sending of the mission in 596. The English Church was now firmly established; in recognition, Augustine was given metropolitan status and authorised to ordain twelve suffragan bishops. The permanent metropolitan see of the province, however, was to be London. A second province with its own suffragans was to be established at York, once that region has received the word of the Lord; primacy should then be determined by seniority in consecration. Augustine was also to have jurisdiction over the British bishops.[75] In making these provisions Gregory failed to appreciate the strength of paganism in London, and his ecclesiastical map of England owed more to the ancient administrative geography of Roman Britain than to any grasp of sixth-century political realities. By 601 Gregory had been informed about the existence of British churches, but knew little more about them. He could not have appreciated their resentment of the alien and hostile conqueror, and their suspicion of a new ecclesiastical authority associated with it, imposed on its ancient churches. Bede's narrative, no doubt received from Canterbury, but in part coloured by British traditions and with a marked flavour of folk-lore, is an emblematic picture of the tensions between a continental model of the Christian Church, organised on a territorial basis with bishops in charge of dioceses, bearing the authority of their office, and a British model, monastic and charismatic in its emphasis. There is no evidence that Gregory knew anything

---

[73] Bede, *HE* I.29.

[74] Letters of recommendation: *Epp.* XI.34 (Vienne); 38, 45 (Arles); 40 (Lyons); 41 (Toulon, Marseille, Châlon, Metz, Paris, Rouen, Angers); 42 (Gap); 47 (King Theuderic); 48 (Queen Brunhild); 50 (King Theudebert); 51 (King Clothar). Altogether twenty-four letters preserved in the *Registrum* were sent to Gaul and England at this time (22 June 601); some dealing with matters that had come up before. The batch gives the impression that the *scrinium* was hard at work to meet a deadline, perhaps suddenly imposed: the departure of Mellitus and his companions.

[75] *Ep.* XI.39. Cf. Mayr-Harting, *The coming*, 265–6. Augustine would, of course, have had jurisdiction over British Christians within his area, such as those probably still living in Canterbury: cf. Brooks, *The early history*, 17–20.

about this Christian tradition.[76]

About the state of affairs at the Kentish court and the new Church among the English he was, of course, much better informed, though he may not have appreciated all the implications of what he was told. To Augustine he wrote congratulating him on success:

Who can be equal to telling of the joy aroused in the hearts of all the faithful here by the news that through the work of almighty God's grace and your labours the English people, having cast away the darkness of error, has been illuminated by the light of the holy faith; that it now tramples with a sound mind on the idols which it had previously worshipped with insane fear . . .

But it was all God's work, so let Augustine rejoice with trembling and tremble with rejoicing. He must resist the temptation to be elated by the miracles he had been granted by the grace of God to perform in order to draw English souls to faith in the Lord:

You should remember, dearest brother, amidst the outward things you do through the Lord's power, always to subject your inner self to the most meticulous judgement, and be aware of what you yourself are and how great is the grace shown to the people for whose conversion you have been granted the gift even of working miracles.[77]

Humility is endless.

At the same time Gregory wrote to king Aethelberht, and a separate letter to queen Bertha. The king was told to

guard zealously the grace [he] has received from God [*eam quam accepisti divinitus gratiam*] and to strive to extend the Christian faith among the people subject to [him]. [He] should increase [his] righteous zeal for their conversion; persecute the cult of idols [*idolorum cultus insequere*]; overthrow the shrines [*fanorum aedificia everte*]; strengthen the morals of [his] subjects by great purity of life, by exhorting, by terrifying, by enticing [*blandiendo*], by correcting them, and showing them an example of good works; so that [he] will find [himself] rewarded in heaven by Him whose name and knowledge [he] had spread on earth . . .

A comparison follows with Constantine:

the most religious emperor who converted the Roman state [*rempublicam*] from the false worship of idols and subjected it along with himself to almighty God and our Lord Jesus Christ, turning to Him with all his heart together with the peoples

---

[76] *HE* II.2. He may have received Columbanus's *Ep.* 1, but no reply survives. The *sacerdotes e vicino* of Gregory's *Ep.* VI.51 who made no attempt to convert the English to Christianity are certainly Frankish, as are the *sacerdotes in vicino* of *Ep.* VI.60 (and those *e vicino* whom Augustine was to take with him from Gaul), not British clergy: cf. Wood, 'The mission', 8.

[77] *Ep.* XI.36. On miracles as appropriate in times of conversion, see chapter 4, pp. 56, 62–6.

subject to him . . . And now let [the king] hasten to bring to the kings and peoples under [his] rule knowledge of the one God, the Father, Son and Holy Spirit . . .

Gregory was evidently aware by now that Aethelberht was more than an ordinary king, one of several, in Britain; he had kings, as well as peoples subject to him, and he was expected to exert himself in the effort of their christianisation. The king was then bidden to listen to and to follow Augustine's advice and exhortation; and finally, the letter ends with a reminder of the closeness of the end: the king should not worry about signs that may appear in his land heralding the end, but treat them as spurs to care for his soul and perform good works.[78]

The letter assumes that the king was already a Christian;[79] its chief burden, however, underlined by the use of Constantine as a model, is to encourage the king to promote the spread of Christianity among his subjects, by coercion, by favour and by example. The letter to the queen follows similar lines: in her zeal for the faith of the English she should follow the model of Helena, 'the mother of the most religious emperor Constantine, who kindled Roman hearts to the Christian faith'. She ought indeed, as a true Christian, already long ago (*iam dudum*) have exerted herself to incline her husband's heart to follow her own faith, for his own and for his people's eternal good; it would not have been difficult for her, fortified as she was by the right faith and by knowledge of letters. But now is the time to make compensation for missing that opportunity, and to do so 'in greater measure' (*cum augmento*): let her 'strengthen the mind of [her] glorious husband in the love of the Christian faith with unremitting exhortation; let [her] zeal bring him an increase in the love of God, and so kindle his concern for the fullest conversion of the people subject to his rule . . .'[80] The imperial model is again invoked to teach the same lesson: a true Christian ruler will promote and enforce the faith among his subjects. So the queen was asked to encourage her husband to do all he could in this cause.

The emphasis Gregory lays on this suggests that the reports he received about the progress of christianisation of the kingdom told him that the part taken in it by the king left something to be desired. This is, indeed,

---

[78] *Ep.* XI.37. Cf. above, p. 82. On the eschatological perspective of the English mission, see below, pp. 186–7.

[79] Though this has been disputed by Brechter, *Die Quellen*, 243–6. I have discussed this more fully in 'The chronology', 22–4. I am not now, however, convinced that the king was actually baptised: he may, like Constantine, have identified himself with Christianity but deferred his baptism.

[80] *Ep.* XI.35. Brechter, *Die Quellen*, 246–7 asserts that the letter implies that Aethelberht was not yet a Christian. I have discussed this in detail in 'The chronology', 18–21.

highly likely; only rather than being the king's failure, it was his position that was difficult. Bede's narrative suggests a tenacious pagan tradition in Kent: the king could not afford to be seen to favour the newcomers too much, and too openly – they had to be received with caution. He could not compel his pagan subjects to abandon their old religion; in Bede's words, he could only 'rejoice at their conversion', and 'hold believers in greater affection as his fellow-citizens in the heavenly kingdom'.[81] And the wave of pagan reaction that followed Aethelberht's reign in Kent and in Essex after his protégé, Saberht,[82] confirms the extent to which Christianity depended on the Kentish court, upheld in the face of strongly entrenched paganism.

Gregory, however, did not at first appreciate this, and attributed the slow progress to insufficient zeal and energy on the king's part. But soon, as the significance of the reports he had received began to dawn on him, or perhaps in the light of further information imparted by messengers who may have stayed behind in Rome, Gregory changed his mind. In a remarkable letter written four weeks after the large batch of letters taken to Gaul and England by the returning missionaries, he wrote to abbot Mellitus 'somewhere in Francia' (*in Franciis*), en route for England, address unknown:

Since you and our brethren who accompanied you departed, I have been anxious, having heard no news about how your journey has prospered. However, when almighty God has brought you to our most reverent brother bishop Augustine, tell him what I have decided after long consideration of the case of the English: that by no means should the shrines of idols in that nation be destroyed [*fana idolo- rum ... minime destrui debeant*], but only the idols within them. Let holy water be sprinkled on these shrines, altars be constructed, relics be placed, so that the shrines, if they be well built, might be converted from the cult of demons to the worship of the true God. Thus, when the people see that their shrines have not been destroyed they will banish error from their hearts and recognising and adoring the true God, they will be more inclined to come to the places they are accustomed to . . .[83]

This is a carefully considered countermanding of the instructions given to Aethelberht. The despatch of a special messenger – unique in the Register[84] – to hurry after Mellitus more than three weeks after his departure; the close similarity of the language; the stress Gregory lays

<hr>

[81] *HE* I.27.
[82] Bede, *HE* II.5–6.
[83] *Ep.* XI.56. The letter is dated 18 July 601; the previous batch is of 22 June.
[84] See Appendix, p. 208.

on his 'long consideration' – leave no doubt that the letter was intended to reverse the instructions given to the king.[85] All his assumptions and a long tradition of thought about the duties of Christian rulers had combined to suggest Gregory's first response to the situation in England as he understood it: coercion by a Christian ruler. That was the policy he had himself advocated elsewhere; and this was the response that came instinctively to his mind. He only came to question this strategy when the impossibility of applying it in the present case became starkly evident to him. That he did so is powerful testimony to Gregory's pastoral flexibility, and constitutes a dramatic change of direction in papal missionary strategy.

The same qualities of mind appear in another document which, as we can now confidently say, was sent to Augustine in 601.[86] It is a collection of answers to nine queries Augustine had sent to Gregory. The first lays down the form of life Augustine and his companions were to follow: it should be the common life of monks, adapted to the needs of an active ministry. Two others concern doubts – especially acute for Roman clergy faced with a Germanic society – about prohibited degrees of relationship in marriage; one of them showed such generosity in its concessions to Germanic custom that it disturbed Boniface in the eighth century. Two others (VIII and IX) deal with problems about marriage, sexuality and ritual purity. Pollution by sex, menstruation and parturition did not preoccupy Gregory; it was Augustine's queries that made him confront them, and Gregory dealt with them with some impatience, as unncessary questions which Augustine could well have answered for himself. Augustine's doubts seem to have arisen fom his contacts with circles in England, perhaps of Christian *Angli* who had received Christianity from British sources.[87] In his answers Gregory rejects a literal and legalistic interpretation of the Old Testament sexual taboos in favour of a more liberal, spiritual, interpretation. They show a degree of good sense and humanity which made the *Responsa* an apt and useful counterweight to much less liberal prescriptions

---

[85] See above, pp. 181–2. For full discussion, see Markus, 'Gregory the Great and the origins'. Cf. A. Hauck in the discussion on Jenal, 'Gregor d. Grosse', 851–4. Chadwick, 'Gregory the Great', maintains that the two letters differ in 'tactics rather than in strategy' (203, n. 18). A story in the *Dialogues* (II.8.11) tells of Benedict breaking an idol, overturning the altar, cutting down the sacred grove, and then building a shrine of St Martin in a temple of Apollo. Augustine had discussed the private and the public, legally authorised, conversion of pagan cult buildings in *Ep.* 47.3.

[86] Bede, *HE* I.27. Of the extensive literature on the *Libellus Responsionum* I need only cite Meyvaert, 'Le Libellus responsionum', and 'Bede's text'. See also Chadwick, 'Gregory the Great'. Unpublished and uncompleted work by Paul Meyvaert confirms the presumption of authenticity. I deal with *Responsum* I and II in chapter 5; with *Resp.* VI and VII below.

[87] Meens, 'A background'.

that were to gain currency in the late seventh century.[88]

Two of Gregory's answers set out to regulate the relations between the churches of Gaul and of Britain. The first (VI) relaxed the rule that required three or more bishops to assist at episcopal consecrations in Italy. This was clearly impracticable in the new English Church, and, though Gregory wanted the English and the Frankish churches to work together as closely as distance allowed, the availability of visiting bishops from Gaul could not be counted on. The next response (VII) spells out more precisely what their relationship was to be: Augustine was to have no authority over Gallic bishops, over whom the bishop of Arles had received vicarial authority from Gregory;[89] but they should consult and encourage one another as necessary and when feasible. Conversely, Virgilius, the bishop of Arles, was asked to show kindness to Augustine if he should happen to receive a visit from him, and to consider and to take action on any criticism that Augustine might have to offer of Gallic episcopal and clerical life – for faults are often better seen by outsiders.[90]

In 596 Gregory had looked to the Frankish Church for assistance for his missionaries; by 601 the new English Church was to promote his cherished plans for the reform of the Frankish Church. It is beyond doubt that the English mission took shape in his mind in the context of a broad vision in which the English and the Frankish churches were to be in a mutual partnership of Christian renewal. That other considerations combined to form Gregory's intention cannot be excluded. His frustrations with the imperial government and with the patriarch of Constantinople have sometimes been thought to have turned Gregory's mind towards the West: but there is no reason to think that he sought an orbit for the exercise of papal *principatus* in an area where it would be untrammelled by Byzantine resistance.[91] He was on the one hand an unquestioningly loyal subject of the emperor and deeply preoccupied with the life of the Church within its imperial setting, on the other altogether too little legalistically minded to see a matter of such moment in terms of legal authority and jurisdiction. Inspired opportunism will surely have played its part, though the plan could hardly have depended on the availability of English slave boys as a suitable purchase with money that could not be easily spent outside

---

[88] Meens, 'Ritual purity'. Chadwick, 'Gregory and the Anglo-Saxons', 210, points out that Gregory's position on ritual purity and pollution 'in essentials' follows Augustine's (*De bono coniugali* 20, 23); cf. the parallels noted *ibid.*, 211.

[89] See above, p. 171.

[90] *Ep.* XI.45.

[91] See my discussion in chapter 6, p. 92. Chadwick notes that when one considers the situation in Italy and Gregory's anxieties about relations with Byzantium at this time 'it is amazing that the mission to Britannia was sent' ('Gregory the Great', 205).

Gaul.[92] Gregory may have been aware that Kent was ripe for a mission, may even have heard rumours from Gaul, whether true or unfounded, that a missionary initiative might be welcomed by some in England.[93] He may also have thought, in the Byzantine manner,[94] that English kings were in some way subject to Frankish authority.[95] Frankish kings would thus have a duty to bring them to the Christian faith. What is certain, however, is that he founded hopes for the Frankish Church on the English mission just as he had enlisted the aid of the Frankish Church to promote its work.

Writing in 599, Gregory referred to the mission he had 'long had in mind' (*diu cogitans*).[96] It is anybody's guess how far back in time this takes us. The legends current a century after his death about Gregory's alleged desire to go to Britain himself to convert the English are a Northumbrian creation. It is in the highest degree unlikely that Gregory would have entertained such a notion at a time when he was consumed with desire to retire into monastic contemplation.[97] Nevertheless, the mission had deep roots in his mind. The message of the Gospel was meant to be universal: 'God has made the preaching of the saints go out into all parts of the world [*in cunctis mundi partibus*] – the East, the West, the South and the North'.[98] 'By the shining miracles of preachers, the Lord has brought to the faith even the ends of the earth. Behold, He has now penetrated the hearts of almost all nations; behold, he has joined together in one faith the ends of the East and the West . . .' Barbarous tongues have long ago [*iam dudum*] begun to chant the Hebrew 'Alleluia' in God's praise, as far away as Britannia![99] But now the English nation, 'placed in a remote corner of the world', was still worshipping sticks and stones.[100] There was little time, the

---

[92] *Ep.* VI.10. See above, n. 61. Note that in any case Gregory's priority was then clothes for the poor; evidently already well established as a way of spending Provençal money forty years before: Pelagius I, *Epp.* 4; 9.

[93] Such a conclusion has often been drawn from *Ep.* VI.51, e. g. by Wood, who thinks 'the Angles rather than the pope . . . were the prime movers in the English mission . . .' ('The mission', 9–10). I would hesitate to rely on such vague evidence as indicating any specific request; though it is possible that some rumour of the English being ready for conversion had reached Gregory from Gaul. Cf. Wallace-Hadrill, 'Rome', 120.

[94] Cf. Procopius, *Wars* VIII.20.10.

[95] Gregory's praise in this letter of the Frankish kings' concern for the faith of their subjects (*subiectos vestros*) could well be normal flattery praising their Christian zeal, and need not refer to English subjects. On this see Wood, 'Frankish hegemony'.

[96] *Ep.* IX.223.

[97] Whitby *Life* 10; Bede, *HE* II.1. Cf. Markus, 'The chronology', 29–30.

[98] *HEz* I.3.7.

[99] *Mor.* XXVII.11.21. The passage may refer to the Welsh (cf. Fritze, '*Universalis gentium confessio*', 109); or it could quite easily be understood to mean simply that the Gospel had already 'long ago' reached Britain, as indeed it had in Roman times. In any case, the passage could easily have been interpolated into the text of the *Moralia* by Gregory after 597.

[100] *gens Anglorum in mundi angulo posita*: *Ep.* VIII.29.

end was near.[101] Gregory had warned bishops before, and in terms very similar to the apocalyptic language he addressed to king Aethelberht:

> You see how the world is being ravaged by the sword; you see what blows are daily destroying the people. Whose sin but ours has brought this on us? Behold, towns are laid waste, fortified places overthrown, churches and monasteries overthrown, fields turned into wilderness ... Multitudes have perished through our sin; through our neglect they have not been taught for [eternal] life. For what shall we call the souls of men but the food of the Lord, created that they might be turned into His Body, that is to say, to the enlargement [*augmentum*] of His eternal Church? We should be the seasoning of this food; for, as I have said before, "you are the salt of the earth" (Matt. 5:13) was said to the preachers being sent out.[102]

Gregory had in mind primarily the pastoral duty of bishops to care for souls. The Church's growth was only a part, or consequence, of this overriding obligation. And this is just the point: Gregory saw no division between pastoral and missionary activity. He knew English souls were at risk, and the time was short. He could wait only until the opportunity came to act.

Gregory was not obsessed with measuring success or failure. In the short term his plan for the Northern churches came to nothing. The Irish monk Columbanus made a greater impact in Burgundy than Augustine made anywhere in Gaul; the Irish and a variety of Gallic missionaries were at work in christianising Northern Gaul and its fringe lands; in the English kingdoms missionaries from the Irish West and Northern Britain established a more deeply rooted Christianity in Northumbria than Augustine and his immediate successors were able to found in the south. For all that, the English and the Frankish churches owed more to one another than their historians always noticed.[103] And he had established a model for missionary work, no longer confined to the Roman Empire as the natural milieu of Christianity, but to 'all nations' (Matt. 28:19).[104]

[101] As Gregory reminded Aethelberht: *Ep.* XI.37; cf. chapter 4, p. 54.
[102] *HEv* I.17.16. Cf. also chapter 5, n. 86.
[103] On this, see Wallace-Hadrill, 'Rome'.
[104] See Fritze, '*Universalis gentium confessio*', and Markus, 'Gregory the Great's Europe', 25 n. 14.

CHAPTER 12

Inconcussam servare provinciam: *dissent in Africa*

In 590 North Africa had been re-conquered from the Vandals for almost sixty years. The quick and smooth course of the reconquest by the Byzantine armies had not, however, led to the re-establishment of a fully pacified Roman province. Incursions of African tribesmen, sedentary and nomadic, and rebellions of local chieftains, already troubling during the Vandal régime, now more often acting in concert, continued under Byzantine rule, and were to continue after the Arab conquest. They brought insecurity, sporadic fighting, and, in response, as in Italy, militarisation of government. Here, too, the civil administration, though it continued to function, was eclipsed by the supreme authority of an Exarch, stationed at Carthage. Under the reign of Maurice, Byzantine authority was consolidated in the North African core-provinces: Proconsularis, Byzacena and Numidia. Maurice's realistic reform here produced the basis for comparative prosperity and stability during the first half of the seventh century.[1]

A DONATIST REVIVAL?

One of Gregory's first letters to Africa, addressed to the Exarch, is a request that he should fight the 'enemies of the Church' with the same 'vehemence' he had applied to outside enemies. Gregory had heard reports that heretics had been 'lifting up their necks against the Catholic Church in defiance of the Lord, to subvert the Christian faith'; if not curbed, they will continue to pour their poison into the Christian body.[2] The heretics referred to are identified as Donatists, and Gregory went on

---

[1] The classic account, Diehl, *L'Afrique byzantine*, has not been superseded, despite the mass of new archaeological and other material. Pringle, *The defence*, is fundamental for the military history; brief summaries of ecclesiastical history are to be found in Cuoq, *L'Église*, and Schindler, 'Afrika I'. The best modern survey is Cameron, 'Byzantine Africa'. For Africa at Gregory's time, see Belkhodja, 'L'Afrique Byzantine'.

[2] *Ep.* 1.72. On Gregory and the Exarch Gennadius, see p. 85.

to recommend several measures he wanted the Exarch to get the bishops to adopt (see below pp. 193–7) to combat them. He thought that 'the heresy of the Donatists was growing daily',[3] 'as if unrestrained by any shepherd's control',[4] and he attributed their resurgence to Donatist bribes. 'The Catholic faith is being publicly sold', he was to complain to the emperor.[5]

Until quite recently, Gregory's reading of the situation has generally been accepted at its face value. Historians of Byzantine Africa, of North African Christianity, of the Donatist schism, of the papacy, biographers of Gregory the Great, have found themselves in agreement over the state of the North African Church: like Gregory, they have seen a revival of the old schism, the resurgence of Donatist propaganda, the negligence of local functionaries, the complicity of the governing and land-owning classes, corruption even among bishops, all conspiring to allow heresy to flourish, and to make the pope's task difficult.[6] Two things have combined to force a revision of this picture: a closer scrutiny of the evidence furnished by Gregory himself, casting a different light on the nature of African Christianity at the end of the sixth century; and a reassessment of the nature of the Donatist movement and of the African Christian tradition.[7]

The schism had its roots in the conditions which prevailed in the African Church during the last persecutions, in the early years of the fourth century, and, especially, in their immediate aftermath. With its ending, the new conditions of toleration revealed tensions within Christian communities produced by persecution. Reactions to the measures taken against Christians by the authorities had varied. The surrender of copies of the Scriptures to the authorities (*traditio*, 'handing over') by the clergy was generally condemned; but there was a wide range of attitudes towards

---

[3] *Ep.* II.39; cf. IV.32.

[4] *Ep.* IV.35.

[5] *Ep.* VI.64. Cf. *Epp.* I.82; II.39; III.47, 48; IV.32, 35.

[6] Three classic accounts on these lines: Diehl, *L'Afrique Byzantine* 2, 503–16; Dudden, *Gregory the Great* 1. 414–428, Frend, *The Donatist Church*, 309–12. Succinctly stated by Cuoq, *L'Église d'Afrique*, 95:

Par suite du laisser-faire des fonctionnaires, le schisme renaissait de ses cendres non complètement mortes. Des donatistes se flattaient de pouvoir renverser la religion officielle. Là où ils dominaient, ils expulsaient le clergé orthodoxe de ses églises, achetaient la bienveillance des évêques à prix d'or, menaient une active propagande et rebaptisaient les fidèles qui venaient à eux. Les plus hautes classes de la société, notamment de grands propriétaires, leur étaient favorables. Pendant six ans, de 591 à 596, la correspondance avec le pape est pleine de ce retour du donatisme et le Concile de Carthage, en 594, y est tout entier consacré. La situation était grave et urgente. La réaction paraissait difficile, car les évêques se heurtaient à la complicité de certains fonctionnaires avec le donatisme.

[7] The account that follows is based on my papers: 'Donatism: the last phase'; 'Reflections on religious dissent'; 'Christianity and dissent'; and 'Country bishops', which are summarised in 'The problem of Donatism'. I shall refer to them individually only when necessary. Such a view has been largely accepted. e. g. by Brown, review of E. Tengström, *Donatisten und Katholiken*, 281–3 (repr. 335–8); Schindler, *Afrika I*, 661; Cameron, 'Byzantine Africa', 49–53; Shaw, 'African Christianity'.

collaborators, or to people suspected of having failed to make a sufficiently determined stand in the resistance. The cessation of persecution brought the conflicting attitudes into the open, and sometimes led to splits between more and less rigoristic factions, fanatics and prudent compromisers. In Carthage the resulting split led to a double episcopal election, thus initiating the schism which came to be labelled 'Donatist'. The advent of Constantine gave the ecclesiastical division a new dimension. The Christian Empire could not recognise two rival churches; European bishops, and a council at Arles (314) decided on which of the two churches, both claiming to be the 'Catholic' Church in Africa, could rightly claim the title. Their decision, endorsed by the emperor, failed to end the division; the schism became firmly embedded in North African Christianity. Outlawed by legislation, sporadically repressed by imperial forces and by Roman landowners, the schismatics came to identify themselves as the true Church of the martyrs, persecuted by the worldly power of a godless Empire.

Theologically, little was at stake. The tangible issue was the Donatists' denial of the validity of baptism conferred outside what they considered to be the true Church, and their consequent insistence on re-baptism for those who entered their community from outside; and their rejection of episcopal consecration by *traditores*. But the tenacity of the division between the two ecclesial communities in Africa reveals a deeper division between Catholic and Donatist: it was over the question of what it meant to be the Church.

The African Christian tradition had long laid great weight on the separation of the Church from the world. It drew a very firm boundary around the Church, which enclosed the sphere of purity and holiness; outside lay a world of sin and pollution. The Church was a society alternative to the world, the refuge of the saints. Holiness was within; beyond lay the world ruled by hostile, demonic, powers. This model was deeply embedded in the theological and spiritual tradition of North African Christianity. In the post-Constantinian Church it was Donatist dissenters who could claim this legacy. Their opponents were defined as 'Catholic' by the decision and by the agreement of churches 'across the sea', as they liked to say. Almost overnight, the confrontation between the African and the overseas traditions, the latter recognised by the court and the government under Constantine and his successors, was transformed: the conflict between local (African) and universal (European) became a conflict between schismatic and Catholic. The Donatists claimed to be the ecclesial community which upheld, in the period after Constantine, the ancient African theological tradition. They were the champions of a regional Christian tradition asserted against the imperial establishment and against the consensus of the European churches. They saw the Catholics as the party prepared to sacrifice loyalty to the African tradition for the sake of agreement with Christianity 'overseas' and recognition by the government. 'Catholicism' was the form of Christianity imported into Africa and propagated with the support of the emperor, the rich landowners, and the army. Donatists represented the authentic Christianity of North Africa in the face of imperial pressure and apostasy, as they saw it, by the overseas churches. Their Church was a classic Church of dissent: dissent from the imperial orthodoxy as from that of the mainstream European churches.

Despite the measures taken against them, the movement flourished throughout the fourth century. In 411, at a conference in Carthage called by the government to settle their differences, the two rival churches faced each other across a deep gulf of mutual hostility. The schism survived well into the period of Vandal occupation from 430, though the fragmentary evidence does not allow us to trace its history. It appears to have lost some of its bitterness and violence, not surprisingly in a time when the division between the two churches was eclipsed by the tense and at times bloody split between Arian and Catholic. The Arian occupying power had little interest in discriminating between Catholic and Donatist; in the deeper chasm that had opened, the old conflicts lost much of their significance. It seems probable that the two communities initially continued in some more or less uneasy symbiosis, slowly and untidily losing their separate identities, and gradually moved towards some sort of fusion. The evidence from Gregory's time, as we shall see, lends strong support to such a retrospective reconstruction. At any rate, when the African Church re-emerged into the light of day after the Byzantine reconquest in the 530s, despite the existence of a fair body of material concerning Byzantine Africa, there is no trace of Donatists in any surviving evidence; not until Gregory's time, nearly sixty years later.

A Donatist revival on a grand scale, such as Gregory thought was taking place in Africa, would require a good deal of explanation. Why now? What developments in Africa or elsewhere, totally unknown to us, could explain such a resurgence, out of the blue?[8] Gregory's correspondence, however, provides ample evidence to show that he misread the information he had at his disposal concerning the Church in North Africa. What

---

[8] Cf. Markus, 'Country bishops', 10. n. 31, where I referred to S. A. Morcelli's astonishment (in *Africa Christiana* (1816)) that Donatism should have survived longer in Africa than Arianism, and his conjecture that it had been able to lurk in small village communities and remote areas provided it refrained from active proselytism.

emerges from his letters is the complete disappearance of the embattled hostility of two rival churches which had been so characteristic of Augustine's North Africa. The two churches – if indeed there were still two churches – seem now to have found a *modus vivendi*: Catholics, even devout Catholics, (*Catholici homines et religiosi*) we learn, often allow their families and their dependants to receive baptism from Donatists;[9] Donatist clergy are placed in charge of churches by Catholic bishops, and are even alleged to be promoted over the heads of their Catholic colleagues;[10] Donatists (or ex-Donatists?) could be made Catholic bishops, and were commonly permitted to become primates of their province;[11] Catholic bishops allowed the ordination of bishops for Donatist communities within their own diocese;[12] and they did nothing to check the spread of the poison.[13] If there were two churches, to an outsider like Gregory they seemed to be living together in remarkable, and objectionable, amity.

This portrait of North African Christianity furnished by Gregory's correspondence differs in a crucial respect from the state of affairs in Augustine's time. What has vanished in the course of the two centuries is the separate identity of two churches, altar against altar, church against church, facing each other in bitter hostility, as they had at the roll-call of the conference in Carthage held in 411, when Donatist bishops of each locality took their turn to identify their Catholic opposite number: 'I recognize my persecutor'. Instead, we have the oddly interpenetrating ecclesial communities coexisting, if not in complete harmony, at any rate in the untidy ways revealed by Gregory's correspondence. This situation would be exactly the consequence that one would expect of a historical development such as the schism underwent during and since the Vandal occupation: a slow blurring of the boundaries defining the separate communities; the attrition of local hostilities, often, perhaps, allowing episcopal vacancies arising on either the Donatist or the Catholic side not to be filled and thereby clearing the way for the gradual fusion of the two communities under a single bishop in many places. That such a fusion would produce local Churches which might often have preserved former Donatist traditions – particularly the practice of re-baptism – would not be surprising; nor would the prevalence of Donatist characteristics in the merged

---

[9] *Ep.* vi.36; iv.35.

[10] *Ep.* i.82.

[11] *Ep.* i.75. The phrase *qui ex Donatistis ad episcopatum perveniunt* is, as has often been noted, ambiguous: it could mean 'from among the Donatists' or 'from among former Donatists'. Cf. Duval, 'Grégoire et l'Église d'Afrique', 135, n. 15. If, however, in fact there were no two separate communities (see below), the distinction loses its force.

[12] *Ep.* II.39; see further below, nn. 15–17.

[13] See above, nn. 4, 5.

churches in areas such as Numidia, the province where Donatism had been especially strong and where Gregory's difficulties were concentrated.[14]

GREGORY AND THE AFRICAN CHURCH

This is precisely the state of affairs disclosed by Gregory's correspondence. It provides no evidence whatever of two rival churches with two separate hierarchies, or of even a single place with two bishops. On the contrary: a particularly instructive case reveals one way in which the coexistence of a merged community containing vestiges of two traditions could come about. A Numidian bishop had given permission for the appointment of a new Donatist bishop, not in his own see (*civitas*), but in the rural spot where he lived (*per villis*).[15] He was alleged to have been bribed to give his permission; he had evidently given way to a 'Donatist' pressure-group within his diocese to allow the consecration of a bishop for them. The procedure follows the lines of a long established mechanism of filling country bishoprics in recently reconciled former Donatist communities.[16] Gregory indeed says that this had been allowed by African custom, but he wished the custom to cease.[17]

Far from providing evidence for the continuance or the resurgence of the schism, Gregory provides evidence for a single North African Church undivided by schism, but one in which, apparently, Donatist features still survived here and there, and may have been – as Gregory thought they were – spreading. The only such feature mentioned is the practice of re-baptism. The prevalence of this is not proved by the use made of a formula by the papal notaries which prohibited the ordination of Africans arriving in Italy, on the grounds that they frequently turn out to be re-baptised (or Manichees). The formula originated in the 480s, when it referred to clergy fleeing from Vandal persecution who were suspect of having apostatised and re-baptised as Arians, not as Donatists. It continued in use until the eleventh century. The only evidence it provides is on the habits of the papal *scrinium*; not on realities outside its remarkably unchanging world.[18]

---

[14] In 411 the majority of Donatists in rural areas of Numidia was 'massive': Lancel, in *Actes de la Conférence*, I, 161; cf. 134–43, 154–64.

[15] *Ep.* II.39. I analysed the case of Pudentiana (the unidentified see in Numidia) in detail in 'Country bishops', 7–9.

[16] See Markus, 'Country bishops', 163 and n. 8 for details.

[17] *etsi hoc anterior usus permitteret*: *Ep.* II.39. The practice was also frowned on by Leo I: *Ep.* 12.10 (though this refers to Mauretania, not Numidia).

[18] Gregory, *Ep.* II.31 (III.11; IX.211). Origins: Gelasius I (JK 675; *PL* 59, 137–8) and Felix III (Roman Synod of 487; JK 609, *PL* 58, 924). Already stereotyped in Gregory's time, taken into the *Liber dirunus* (no. 6), it was still used by Gregory II writing to Boniface (Donatism in Thuringia!) in the eighth and Nicholas II in the eleventh century. Cf. Markus, 'Donatism', 124; 'Religious dissent', 145; 'Country bishops', 5–7.

Nevertheless, re-baptism is quite likely to have been the chief distinctive mark of African communities in which, despite their absorption in an undivided Catholic Church, Donatist traditions still survived,[19] and we may accept Gregory's view that it was still practised in Africa.

But this was not what worried Gregory most about the African Church. He interpreted what he knew about it in the light of what he knew – and that was very much more – about Augustine's North Africa. The Donatist revival he thought to be taking place was in reality something else, whose true nature he failed to understand, at any rate during the first six years of his pontificate.[20] But to this, too, his correspondence furnishes clues sufficient to allow us to describe it. There was much that caused him disquiet: the deviant customs of the African Church, especially prevalent in Numidia; and behind them, there was the almost monolithic resistance to Roman influence, aided and abetted by the local civil administration. Gregory's very first letter to Africa indicates the African Church's peculiar organisation as one source of his anxiety. North Africa differed from the pattern which had become the norm since Nicaea, which established a network of dioceses grouped into provinces, each with its metropolitan see. In Africa Carthage was the only metropolitan see, with an ill-defined preeminence over the other African provinces. The other provinces had no fixed metropolitan see; the primacy in each was determined by seniority among the bishops of each province, and the primate remained in his own episcopal see.[21] Gregory disapproved of this anomaly, and seems to have linked it with the distressing spread of Donatism.[22] In his letter he asked the Exarch to get the Numidian bishops to adopt a different system: the primate should not be designated by seniority without regard to the quality of his life, but should be chosen according to the merit of his conduct; and he should live not, as was customary, in the countryside (*per villis*), but in a city to be decided by the provincial council. It is not clear just how Gregory envisaged election by merit and the institution of a fixed metropolitan see; but in any case, perhaps appreciating the tenacity with which the Numidian bishops would cling to their ancient custom,[23] he conceded to them the observance of all the 'customs of former times'. He added, characteristically, that their way of instituting a primate was in no way contrary to the Catholic faith, provided only that bishops who have come

---

[19] We should recall, however, that (Arian) re-baptism was also practised and forced on Catholics under the Vandal régime.

[20] After 596 Donatism disappears from his correspondence.

[21] For details and references, see Markus, 'Carthage', 279–81.

[22] *Ep.* 1.72; see also above, n. 2.

[23] Which they had petitioned Pelagius II to sanction: *Ep.* I.75.

to the episcopate from the Donatists are not to be made primates even if it was their turn by seniority: that he absolutely forbade.[24]

This was not the only respect in which the Church in Numidia gave Gregory cause for concern. A whole cluster of problems is revealed by the case of a certain Paul, the bishop of an unknown see in Numidia. This bishop arrived in Rome in the summer of 596, complaining to Gregory about the treatment he had suffered in his province: he was said to have 'suffered harassment from persecution by Donatists'.[25] Two years before this, Gregory had heard of bishop Paul's troubles; he wrote with consternation of growing Donatist audacity, 'to such an extent that not only did they not shrink, with pestiferous assumption of authority, from throwing bishops of the Catholic faith out of their sees', but even from re-baptising them.[26] He assumed Paul to have been the victim of such audacity, and urged the Exarch, local officials and bishops to expedite his journey to Rome.[27] On his arrival in Rome, Paul complained that not only had he received no succour from the authorities in Africa, but that for two years he had been prevented by them from sailing to Rome. A letter from the Exarch to Gregory – giving, presumably, a different version of events – was read out to Paul, in response to which he explained that his complaint was not that he had become hated by some on account of his crusade of repression against the Donatists, but rather that he had incurred general 'ingratitude' 'on account of his defending the Catholic faith';[28] he mentioned further grievances which Gregory decided at this time to pass over in silence. A final, almost incidental, remark in Gregory's remonstrance with the Exarch reveals that Paul had been excommunicated by a provincial council in Numidia; a fact, Gregory complained, of which he should have been notified by the primate of the province, not the Exarch. Bishop Paul's case is the only one in which Gregory intervened directly; but as the secular authorities were involved, he sent him on to the emperor.[29] The outcome of the case is unknown; but Paul returned to Africa in 598, apparently to be dealt with by a provincial synod, armed with Gregory's – not notably optimistic – letters of support.[30]

The audacious Donatists who had driven Paul from his see turn out to

[24] *Ep.* I.75; on *ex Donatistis* see above, n. 11.
[25] *Epp.* VI.62: *a Donatistis insecutionis dicebatur molestiam sustinere.*
[26] *Ep.* IV.32; cf. IV.35.
[27] *Epp.* IV.32; 35. Gregory had asked the Exarch to allow free travel to Rome already in 591: *Ep.* I.72.
[28] *Ep.* VI.62: *respondit non se quorundam odio, quia Donatistas cohibebat, laborare, sed magis pro defensione catholicae fidei multorum perhibet ingratitudinem sustinere ...*
[29] *Ep.* VI.64: *causa ipsa saecularis iudicis intererat.* The Exarch's representative sent to Rome seemed ill-prepared to prosecute the case: *Ep.* VII.2.
[30] *Epp.* VIII.13, 15.

be the Numidian episcopate. Paul had clearly managed to unite the bishops and the civil administration in detestation of his anti-Donatist zeal; he had been regarded as a busy-body creating unnecessary trouble by his fussy intransigence. There were, we must assume, some grounds for Paul's – as for Gregory's – worries: perhaps re-baptism was being widely practised in Numidia. The crucial fact, however, is that whatever it was that gave grounds for concern, it was within the Catholic communion, and that efforts to disturb the coexistence of traditions which it had achieved were not welcome, either to the Church in Numidia, or to the civil administration. The bishops valued their independence, and sought to keep papal intervention at arm's length; and they had the support of local lay officials. They thought Paul's excommunication was their own affair, and saw no need to notify the pope. Gregory could not think of appointing a vicar in Africa, as he had done elsewhere.[31] He had to rely on a special unofficial agent, a Numidian bishop called Columbus, who was bound to 'St Peter, the prince of the apostles' by a special oath of loyalty.[32] Unsurprisingly, he was to complain to the pope of having become unpopular among his fellow-bishops on account of the frequent letters he received from him.[33] Gregory tried to get councils to concert action and to punish irregularities;[34] but neither the civil authorities nor the bishops were keen to promote his plans. Gregory suspected the orthodoxy of some officials, and wanted them to come to Rome to give an account of themselves; they had to be reassured that no violence would be used against them in Rome.[35] In other areas the pope could often make use of the rectors of the Roman Church's patrimonies as a further channel of his influence;[36] in Africa, however, in the face of such opposition the rector could achieve little. Gregory's diminishing expectations of him reveal how little power his agent could exert: whereas in 591 he was peremptorily ordered to arrange a council in Numidia,[37] and a year later he was to have supervised a council which was expected to right Numidian wrongs,[38] ten years later Gregory knew better: the Numidian

---

[31] Pointed out by Caspar, *Geschichte*, 2, 446.
[32] *Ep.* III.47. On the pope's agents, see Duval, 'Grégoire et l'Église d'Afrique'.
[33] *Ep.* VII.2.
[34] *Epp.* I.72; 82; II.39; III.47; 48. It is striking that Gregory seems to have preferred to issue his demands for action and complaints about decisions by Numidian councils to the Exarch: *Ep.* I.72 (cf. above, nn. 2 and 19) and *Ep.* IV.7, on uncanonical decisions by a Numidian council; or to his special agents, as in *Ep.* III.47; not to the bishops or primates concerned. The exception, *Ep.* III.48, shows the studious courtesy with which they had to be treated: the primate is requested to listen to bishop Columbus.
[35] *Ep.* IV.41.
[36] See above, chapter 8.
[37] *Ep.* I.82: *tuaque instantia in locis illis fiat ex more concilium* ...
[38] *Ep.* II.39 (with bishop Columbus).

bishops were politely asked to invite the rector to their deliberations, and the rector was instructed not to refuse an invitation if one were to come.[39] Over years of frustration Gregory had come to accept the limits on his influence in Africa.

Such attitudes were concentrated in Numidia, the province with the heaviest Donatist legacy. Donatism appeared in very different guise where it was not an immediate problem on the doorstep: both at the court in Constantinople and at Carthage. Whereas the local authorities in Africa were reluctant to disturb the Church's *modus vivendi*, the emperor issued orders against the Donatists;[40] but, as Gregory complained, they were flouted – inevitably – by the administration in Africa.[41] At Carthage the imperial order had been welcomed by an African synod; the bishop gave Gregory joy by the zeal he showed 'to keep the province of Africa unharmed [*Africanam inconcussam servare provinciam*], not sparing priestly fervour in coercing the deviousness of the heretical sects'.[42] Gregory went on, however, to express grave concern: although he wanted Catholic clergy to correct heretics both by force and by reason, he was worried about the decision of the synod at Carthage to impose heavy penalties on those who neglected the pursuit of heretics. This was easily said at Carthage; but it could well give offence to the primates of other provinces. It would be best, therefore, that in correcting what is wrong outside, charity should be served within. They will be better placed to combat heresy when they are united among themselves.[43] Gregory had seen enough of the determined resistance in Numidia and clearly feared the possibility of provoking a schism between the Numidian Church and the very differently placed province of Carthage.[44]

The pattern of resistance to papal intervention in both ecclesiastical and administrative circles, though most marked in Numidia, was not confined to this province. It characterises Gregory's dealings with the African Church. He found it necessary to send frequent reminders of the authority of the Apostolic see to Africa.[45] Carthage and its province (Proconsularis) was an exception, albeit only partial. Here he was on terms of friendship with the metropolitan bishop, Dominicus. Dominicus had written to him

---

[39] *Epp.* xii.8, 9. On similar problems about the rectors' authority in ecclesiastical matters, see Chapter 8, pp. 116–7.

[40] *Ep.* v.3; the *iussiones* have not survived.

[41] *Ep.* vi.64.

[42] *Ep.* v.3.

[43] *Ep.* v.3: *ut in his quae foris corrigenda sunt prius caritas interna servatur* . . .

[44] It is the great merit of Duval, 'Grégoire et l'Église d'Afrique', to have stressed Gregory's overriding concern for unity.

[45] *Epp.* ii.39; iv.41; viii.31; ix.27 (concerning the primate of Byzacena).

to congratulate him – after a delay which Gregory pointedly noted in his reply – on his accession to the see of Rome. The keynote of Gregory's reply is set by his profession of their indissoluble unity in charity. But, interestingly, in his letter Dominicus had taken the opportunity to remind Gregory of the ancient privileges of the Church of Carthage. Gregory answered with a long didactic letter and particularly eloquent praise of charity, 'this mother and guardian of the virtues', through which 'the unity of the universal Church, which knits into one the body of Christ, rejoices in its several individual members in their agreement, different as they may be in their diversity'.[46] Only in a brief final note did he advert, somewhat sharply, to the metropolitan's concern about the privileges of his see: he assured him that he always protected the traditional rights of all the churches, just as he defended those of his own; he would always seek to honour the rights of his brother-bishops without taking anything away from what was due to any other.[47] On the matter of Donatism the interests of the Carthaginian and the Roman churches coincided, and no conflict was to arise between Rome and Carthage during Gregory's pontificate; but Gregory was wary, and took care to pre-empt any possibility of conflict. This caution is a curious feature of much of Gregory's correspondence with the bishop of Carthage, and appears to show the care he took to assert the authority of his see in advance of any possible infringement from the side of Carthage.[48]

The tensions with Carthage were only potential, and beneath the surface. In the province of Byzacena the resistance of the episcopate to Roman intervention, though less blatant than in Numidia, was more overt. The primate of the province, bishop Crementius, had been accused of some misconduct whose nature the correspondence does not specify. He had appealed from his provincial council not to the pope, but to the emperor, who referred the case back to the pope; and his accusers, rather than challenging the appeal and invoking the pope, had flocked – to Gregory's great displeasure – to Constantinople to complain at the court and had held illegal gatherings. Gregory accused the official who reported the matter to him of having told him only half truths (*superficie tenus indicasti*), suppressing the 'root' of the matter; Gregory thought his information was insufficient for him to proceed.[49] It had been the emperor himself

---

[46] *Ep.* II.40: *Per hanc [dilectionem] universalis ecclesiae unitas, quae est compago corporis Christi, exaequatione mentis gaudet in singulis, cum sit ei disparitas in diversitate membrorum.*

[47] *Ep.* II.40. Compare the controversy over the title of 'ecumenical patriarch', above, Chapter 6, pp. 91–4.

[48] See Additional Note: Gregory's correspondence with Dominicus of Carthage.

[49] *Ep.* IX.24; 27.

who wished Gregory to settle this case, but a lay official – bribed, of course – obstructed action. Gregory had learnt from hard experience: 'seeing the perversity of men, we do not wish to enter into this business'.[50] He referred the matter, with an admonition, to the bishops of the province.[51] After 596 Gregory never again mentioned Donatism, and there is an air of resignation about his dealings with Africa. He had come to see its peculiarities as beyond the remedy of his influence, beyond the reach, even, of imperial legislation. It was a world as closed to Constantinople as to Rome.

THE AFRICAN CHRISTIAN TRADITION

In Africa Church and government were closing ranks against outside intervention from 'across the sea'. We should see neither this sense of regional autonomy, nor its obverse, the tension with the Roman see and the imperial court, as momentary aberrations. A centuries old native tradition of *Autonomiegefühl*[52] still contributed in Gregory's time to an African sense of identity. The historian of African Christianity must start, as Peter Brown has remarked, with 'the implications of two distinct views of the role of a religious group in society':[53] and one of them ('that the group exists above all to defend its identity – to preserve a divinely-given law, *Machabaeico more*'), the conception held by Tertullian, by Cyprian and his colleagues, was represented in the post-Constantinian Empire by the Donatists, opposed by the imperially recognised, protected and enforced Catholicism of the overseas churches. African Christianity was forced into Donatist schism by external pressure: the pressure of the overseas churches and the government. What was at stake was the survival of 'the autonomy of a provincial tradition of Christianity in a universal and parasitic Empire. It was Constantine who provoked this struggle [between Donatists and Catholics] by allying the Empire with the universal Catholic Church.'[54]

With the withdrawal of pressure, the schism gradually faded, leaving some of its features stamped on the merged churches that succeed the division. Of the schism we hear no more in Byzantine Africa; but the dissenting streak in African Christianity had not been extinguished. It came to a climax in the resistance to Justinian's edicts on the Three Chapters, which

---

[50] *Ep.* IX.27.
[51] *Ep.* XII.12.
[52] Caspar, *Geschichte*, 2, 446.
[53] Review of Tengström, *Donatisten*, 282–3 (338).
[54] Brown, 'Religious dissent', 97 (255). Cf above, pp. 190–91.

were seen by most of the Western churches as tyrannous meddling by
the emperor with Chalcedonian orthodoxy. The opposition was led by
African churchmen, who denounced the emperor's 'manufactured'
churches in the language of Tertullian and the Donatists. Its leaders, notably
Facundus, bishop of Hermiane, a distinguished theologian and follower of
Augustine, had to defend their resistance against the conformists' charge
that they were launching a new Donatist schism. In 550 a Carthaginian
council excommunicated the pope; African bishops had to be exiled or
rounded up forcibly, even with bloodshed, to be rallied to attend the council
Justinian was about to hold in Constantinople.[55]

In the course of the struggle over the Three Chapters the historian is
once more made aware of the fragility of the link between Rome and
Carthage, the potential for conflict. Half a century later, in Gregory's
time, we have seen both concord and tension. The tension was concentrated in Numidia, and, perhaps to a lesser extent, in Byzacena. At this
time, Carthage could stand aside: it was more aligned with Constantinople
and Rome. The concord between Carthage and Rome effaced the old
tensions, though signs of ancient suspicion still appeared, ready to flare
into conflict, given the occasion. Dissent was deeply ingrained in the
history of African Christianity. Its vitality was to appear once more in the
seventh century, when the resistance to the imperial attempts to impose
monothelitism on the Church, led by Maximus the Confessor, had its
mainstay in Arica. This time the African Church found itself alongside the
Roman in its defence of orthodoxy. But within half a century of the
African rebellion against Constans II (645) – a rebellion with wide popular
support – Carthage was in Arab hands.

The notion that weakness and division within African Christianity
undermined its resistance is not borne out by the evidence. The Church
which was submerged by the Moslem conquest was a singularly cohesive,
unified and vigorous Church. Local and cosmopolitan, urban and rural
traditions had coalesced to form a tenacious religious culture. Its vitality
rallied for a last moment in the fierce local resistance to Moslem rule
before the curtain finally descended. The African Christianity that
Gregory found so difficult to manage was the religion of Tertullian and
Cyprian, of Donatus and Parmenian, of Facundus and Maximus the
Confessor. And even Augustine, who took pride in being an African, was
not entirely a stranger to it.[56]

---

[55] On the whole episode, see Markus, 'Religious dissent' for details.
[56] See my *Saeculum*, chapter 5, *Afer scribens Afris*.

ADDITIONAL NOTE: GREGORY'S CORRESPONDENCE WITH
DOMINICUS OF CARTHAGE

Eight letters from Gregory to Dominicus are preserved in the *Registrum*.[57] Of these only two deal with specific matters. V.3 concerns a recent African council's decisions concerning the pursuit of Donatists (discussed above, p. 197); VII.32 is about a monastic problem which Gregory drew to the bishop's attention. The remaining letters are less specific. X.20 seeks to console the bishop on a recent outbreak of the plague in Africa; XII.1 greets his recovery from illness, and sends him relics. The four remaining letters, II.40, VI.19, VI.63 and VIII.31, are even less specific, and do not seem to arise from any particular occasion. They are akin to exchanges of Late Roman *amicitia*. This is, indeed, their overt purpose; but closer inspection reveals that this *amicitia* is tempered with something else.

The blend of praise and veiled warning in *Ep.* II.40 has been sufficiently described above (p. 198). *Ep.* VI.63 is also a hymn to charity, with particular emphasis on its power to heal division. *Ep.* VI.19 is a little more. It begins, again, as a simple exchange of courtesies. Gregory thanks Dominicus for his letter 'full of priestly charity' (*plena sacerdotali caritate*) and praises the charity that unites them. He ends with the hope that they might pray for each other: Gregory at the body of Peter the apostle, Dominicus at the body of Cyprian the martyr. A harmless enough reminder of the patrons of their respective sees; but not one that Gregory dropped casually into the correspondence. The care and reflection behind it is made more explicit in *Ep.* VIII.31. That letter, like the others in this group, lacks any specific occasion or subject. Like them, it is also a praise of charity, which is the bond of unity; here combined, briefly, with modesty. The letter closes with a reminder to Dominicus: 'Knowing whence sacerdotal orders in Africa have their derivation [*unde in Africanis partibus sumpserit ordinatio sacer-dotalis exordium*], loving the apostolic see as you do, you do well to return with wise recollection to the origin of your office, and to persist with praiseworthy constancy in your affection towards it.' This courteous but firm reminder of the ancient Roman claim over Africa is heavy with the overtones of more than 300 years. At the height of the Pelagian contro-versy, in 416, after two councils in Africa had condemned Pelagius and wished to spur the pope into action, several letters were sent from Africa to Rome. In one, Augustine and his friends among the African bishops, including Aurelius, the bishop of Carthage, wrote to pope Innocent I.

---

[57] *Epp.* II.40; V.3; VI.19, 63; VII.32; VIII.31; X.20; XII.1.

There was no conflict between them; they wrote to the pope with great deference, hoping he would support their condemnation of Pelagius. Speaking of the Church, they made use of the image of an irrigation system: the bishop of Rome has access to an abundant water supply; he will not need the contribution of their little trickle. They wanted only to be reassured that their trickle came from the same source as the pope's rich stream. Their image came from Cyprian. For Cyprian, as for Augustine and his co-signatories, it was meant to suggest that both the Roman and the African churches drew their supply of fertilising water from the rich well of the one Lord, the one faith and the one apostolic Church. That was not how the pope wanted to see Rome in relation to Africa; and he subtly altered the bearing of the image: 'just as all the streams which come forth from their common source flow through all the various parts of the world, retaining the purity of their source, so all the other churches draw from the authority of this source [the Roman see] the knowledge of what to teach, whom to absolve . . .'[58] The echoes of the conflict between Cyprian and pope Stephen; between the African Church in Augustine's time and pope Innocent I; not to mention the more acute conflicts in the more recent 550s (see above) cannot have escaped Carthaginian ears, and must have been the spice carefully sprinkled by Gregory into his exchange of *amicitia*. This is what gives definition to the context for what seems no more than unoccasioned praise of charity. If Gregory was Augustine's heir in much of his thought, one side of it that he did not share was Augustine's 'Africanity'. He was too well conscious of his Roman legacy.

---

[58] The African letter is among Augustine's, *Ep.* 177.19; Cyprian: *De eccl. unit.* 5; Innocent I: *Ep.* 181.1. The exchange has been memorably described by Caspar, *Geschichte*, 1, 330–7 with notes 605–7, which I summarised in my *Saeculum*, 128–9.

Epilogue

'Not Gregory but Gelasius I has rightly been described as the greatest pope between Leo the Great and Nicolas I. But if one were to ask about the greatest Christian personality, then the prize among all popes would have to go to Gregory.' This is how Erich Caspar, the great historian of the papacy, concluded his account of Gregory the Great.[1] Compared with Innocent I or Gelasius I before, Gregory VII or Innocent III after him, Gregory I, Caspar thought, played no part in the development of the papal 'idea'. His pontificate certainly made little impact on the development of the papacy as an institution. Immediately after his death there was a pronounced reaction against the ascetic ideals Gregory introduced. The groups in the clerical establishment whose dominance he had undermined (see above, chapter 8), in which opposition was concentrated to the new style he had brought to the Roman Church, reasserted their hold on it.[2]

Nor did his pontificate mark a change in the direction of papal concerns and policies. The English felt grateful to Gregory, their father and *magister*, and shared a veneration for the see of Peter and Paul with the rest of Western Europe. But the papacy was slow to exploit the new openings for Roman influence that Gregory's pastoral and missionary initiatives secured in Gaul and in Britain. Under his successors papal interests remained concentrated in, and to a large extent confined to, Italy and the Empire. It was only in the course of the eighth century that the popes embarked on the ideological re-orientation which prepared the papacy's alliance with the Franks.[3] By then, however, the world had drastically changed its shape. The great conflicts with Constantinople in the mid-seventh century over monothelitism, and later over iconoclasm, brought about a loosening of relations between Rome and Constantinople; a sense of alienation more ominous for the future than the sporadic tensions of previous times. Even

---

[1] *Geschichte*, 2. 514.
[2] See Llewellyn, 'The Roman Church'.
[3] Miller, 'The Roman revolution'.

more significant in the long term was the conquest of most of North Africa by the end of the seventh century by Islam. The submergence of African Christianity meant the loss to the Latin Church of an intellectually creative and vigorous regional Church. But this loss meant even more, and was in the long term even more subtly damaging to the Roman see itself; for North African Christianity had its own traditions of independence to which it clung with a tenacity with which popes and emperors had to reckon. By losing Carthage, Rome, increasingly isolated from the Greek East, was also cut off from the one great Latin see which could be a focus of fruitful tension. Rome's world became radically simplified; and the Roman see emerged as the single, isolated, religious centre of the barbarian West. No longer enriched by the creative tensions between a number of great sees ringing the Mediterranean, cut off from Africa and, gradually, from the Eastern churches, the Roman Church became the unchallenged mistress and teacher of the Western Germanic nations. And they were only too ready to learn.

In Gregory's time the Roman Church was still very much a part of the imperial system that had been given its shape by Justinian (see chapter 6). This was the unquestioned context of his pontificate; he could scarcely have imagined a differently constituted Church. It was within its framework that his work as a *rector* of the Church and a *pastor* of his flock was to be structured. The novelty of his pontificate was not any re-orientation of interest or policy; 'what was new was the persistence and moral fervour of the voice'.[4] What was unprecedented about Gregory's pontificate was the deeply pondered conception of the pastoral ministry which infused it. The *Pastoral care* is the key, as Gregory intended and knew it to be, to all his work. It represents that fusion of thought and action which gives Gregory his moral seriousness.

Gregory knew that he lived in a time of catastrophe.[5] It was not a passing crisis of conflict with government or with heresy, and it was not a crisis he could have described in specific detail. It was simply the impending end of the world he had known and could no longer take for granted. Its instability called for faith and energy. Gregory, faithful follower of Augustine that he was, did not underestimate the fragility of civilised order in his world. It was poised on the edge of chaos, in constant need of men's devotion, imagination and enterprise, dedicated to its preservation. Gregory was conscious of the sinister power of moral indifference, the scope it gives to

---

[4] Wallace-Hadrill, *The Frankish Church*, 118.　　[5] See above, chapter 4.

the growth of evil. In his practice, he relied on the established Roman order and legality and, supremely, on the ordering and healing power of Christian good sense informed by love. Perhaps beneath his praise of the 'discernment' of St Benedict's *Rule* there was also present more than a suspicion that it outlined a form of community 'within which the moral life could be sustained so that both morality and civility might survive . . .'[6] And his conviction that the end was near gave his voice its intensity and urgency.

[6] MacIntyre, *After virtue*, 244–5. On Gregory and the *Rule* see above, chapter 5, p. 68.

Appendix: on the distribution of Gregory's correspondence

There are too many uncertainties about Gregory's *Registrum* for any attempt to make a set of statistics reveal the pattern of his activities. In any case, it should be remembered that a very high proportion of his correspondence takes the form of 'rescripts', that is to say rulings made in reply to requests and queries originating with his correspondents.[1] We do not know, even approximately, the extent of his correspondence. There are references to correspondence which is not among the surviving letters in the *Registrum*; and there may be many more of which there is no trace. The largest Book in the *Registrum* is Book IX, containing 240 letters for the second Indiction (September 598–August 599). This is the most completely preserved, as there is a large overlap of two of our surviving collections, R and C, in it: the number of letters preserved only in the collection 'C' is 145. The remaining letters are found in the collection 'R', the principal collection extending throughout the fourteen years and containing the largest number of letters; some are both in C and in R. R thus contains 95 of the 240 existing letters in Indiction II, approximately 40 per cent. If the same proportion were to hold throughout the Register, 60 per cent of the total would be missing. We cannot, of course, assume that the same proportion would hold, or that the 240 letters in Book IX represent the total correspondence for the year. The total number of letters lost could therefore be much higher than around 1380 (the *c.* 860 existing letters, + 60 per cent).[2]

Nevertheless, incomplete and impressionistic as any result must be, the numbers of letters sent to different destinations gives some clue to the range of his concerns and the relative frequency of communications. Among the uncertainties involved in compiling a table of such numbers

---

[1] See Pitz, *Papstreskripte*.
[2] The estimate by Pitz, *Papstreskripte*, 252, of 20,000 'possible' letters, based on the estimated productivity of the *scrinium* (see chapter 1, n. 67) seems to me far too high; though I would think a few thousand possible.

are the following: what constitutes a letter? what constitutes more than one letter (when several copies of a single example preserved in the *Registrum* were sent to different recipients)?[3] and, especially, how far the incompleteness of what has survived of the *Registrum* may mislead. Riding roughshod over these and similar problems, I have made the estimates summarised in the Table.[4]

The following comments seem obvious: (1) the very high concentration of letters to destinations within the metropolitan province of Rome, *Italia suburbicaria*, though not unexpected, is striking. (2) So is, within this area, the high proportion of letters addressed to the officials of the Roman Church's lands, the *rectores patrimonii*, concentrated, especially, in Sicily and in Campania. (3) In the Northern part of the Italian peninsula, apart from Ravenna, the seat of government, Gregory's correspondence was very largely concentrated in the see of Milan, evacuated to Genoa. (4) The remaining greatest concentrations are with recipients in the cities which were seats of government: Constantinople and Ravenna, and to a lesser extent, Carthage.

Map 2 indicates destinations and the volume of correspondence addressed to them. Smaller towns, especially but not only in Italy, are not named, and, if close together, are not shown separately, but grouped together and indicated in a somewhat impressionistic manner.

Groupings of letters often provide a clue as to the circumstances of their despatch and the route taken: thus, for instance, most of the letters sent to Salona and other Dalmatian destinations appear to have been sent with correspondence to Ravenna, and presumably sent on from there. Similarly much of the correspondence with Antioch (one of whose bishops in Gregory's time was in any case resident in Constantinople much of the time) seems to have gone *via* Constantinople. The same was probably the case of correspondence with Alexandria, though some correspondence was carried on directly.[5] Obviously the letters sent to Britain were carried

---

[3] As a rough rule of thumb, I have counted identical letters sent to more than one correspondent (*a paribus*) as separate letters sent to each; not, however, letters sent to 'all the bishops' of Italy, or of Illyricum. I have excluded letters of dedication, which are not preserved in the *Registrum*. I have counted letters sent to Alexandria separately, but included those sent to Antioch, Jerusalem and beyond under Constantinople. To avoid the appearance of an exactitude which must be spurious, in the table I have rounded all figures up to the next multiple of 5.

[4] Pitz, *Papstreskripte*, 241–3 has undertaken a statistical classification on Gregory's correspondence in respect of their official type.

[5] *Ep.* vi.61: a letter had been sent to Eulogius by means of the *apocrisiarius*, Sabinianus; and timbers were evidently to be shipped direct to Alexandria (cf. *Ep.* xiii.43). *Ep.* X.21, however, suggests that some correspondence may have gone by sea *via* Naples. A Neapolitan youth also carried letters from Spain (to Rome?) (*Ep.* ix.229).

by Gregory's missionaries, together with letters to recipients along their route through Gaul; Jewish merchants travelled between Rome and Marseille frequently, and Marseille seems to have been on the route between Rome and Spain.[6] The comparatively small number of letters sent further North than the coastal areas is clearly accounted for by lack of contacts until they were established by the missionaries, with more distant sees and with the court and Syagrius, the bishop of Autun. In Spain, until the journey of his emissary, the *defensor* John in 603, Gregory's contact had evidently been confined to Leander of Seville and his immediate circle.

Any inspection of groupings of letters over more than short distances immediately reveals the very large extent to which Gregory had to avail himself of the opportunity of available carriers. Individual letters to the same destination separated by one, or very few, intervening letters in the Register were probably nevertheless sent with the others, but inserted in the *Registrum* by the clerks of the *scrinium* separated from them in the group. Quite frequently we find more than one letter addressed to the same individual being sent at the same time, with a batch of letters sent simultaneously to the same destination: this is almost certainly to be accounted for by one of the letters, already written, being held until the next post.[7] The letter (*Ep.* XI.56) to abbot Mellitus *in Franciis* (discussed in chapter 11) stands alone as one despatched by itself by a special messenger over a long distance.[8]

---

[6] See *Epp.* 1.45 for Jewish merchants; IX.209 and 212–30 for Spain.

[7] The most striking example is the batch of letters despatched to Constantinople in June 596 (see chapter 6), v.36–v.46. v.36 and 37 are both to the emperor Maurice, 38 and 39 to the empress; 41 and 42 both to Anastasius, the patriarch of Antioch (the former also sent to Eulogius, the patriarch of Alexandria).

[8] *Ep.* IX.218, *Aureliano in Franciis*, seems be so titled because Gregory did not know his exact whereabouts; similarly *Ep.* IX.222: they were sent by the bearer of the latter, Aurelius *presbyter Galliarum*, on his way to the patrimony of Provence.

Table *Gregory's Correspondence*

Destinations of letters	Numbers (percentages of total)		
Italia suburbicaria (south) (including the islands), of which:	500 (51.5)		
		Sicily	215
		Naples & Campania	105
		Rectors of patrimonies	130
Italia annonaria (North) (excluding Ravenna), of which	70 (7.2)	Genoa (Milan in exile)	25
Ravenna	70 (7.2)		
Dalmatia	40 (4.1)		
Illyricum and Balkans	35 (3.6)		
Constantinople	75 (7.7)		
Further East (Antioch, Jerusalem &c)	15 (1.5)		
Alexandria	15 (1.5)		
North Africa	40 (4.1)		
Gaul, of which	95 (9.8)	From Lyon North	30
Britain	5 (0.5)		
Spain	10 (1.0)		
Total:	970		

Glossary of terms for offices etc.

actor	agent
apocrisiarius	
(= *responsalis*)	representative (usually pope's)
comes excubitorum	commander of palatine troops
conductor	tenant farmer
defensor	originally of a city; here ecclesiastical administrative official
magister militum	military commander, general
notarius	notary: (papal) secretarial or administrative official, subordinate to *defensor*
pallium	scarf-like garment, signifying honoured (ecclesiastical) status
rector	generally: person in charge, superior, ruler; specifically: person in charge of church's lands
registrum	register of letters
responsalis	
(= *apocrisiarius*)	representative (usually pope's)
scrinium	writing office
tribunus	military officer
vir clarissimus	person of senatorial rank
vir gloriosus	person of high senatorial rank
vir illustris	person of highest senatorial rank

Sources

Details of editors and date are not given for works published in the standard series, *PL, PG, CSEL, CC, SC.*

Acta Conciliorum Oecumenicorum, IV/1 ed. E. Schwartz and J. Straub (Berlin, 1971); IV/2 ed. E. Schwartz (Berlin, 1914).

AGNELLUS
Liber pontificalis ecclesiae ravennatis, ed. O. Holder-Egger (*MGH SSRL* 1878, 265–391)

ANON.
Chronicon patriarcharum Gradensium, ed. G. Waitz (*MGH SSRL* 1878, 392–7)

ANON.
The earliest Life of Gregory the Great by an unknown monk of Whitby, ed. & trans B. Colgrave (Lawrence, Kansas, 1968) [*Whitby Life*]

ANON.
Auctarii Havniensis Extrema, ed. T. Mommsen (*Chronica Minora* 1. *MGH AA* 9 337–9)

AUGUSTINUS HIPPONENSIS
De civitate Dei (*CC* 47–8) [*De civ. Dei*]
Enarrationes in Psalmos (*CC* 38–40) [*Enarr. in Ps.*]
Epistolae (*CSEL* 34, 44, 57, 58, 88)
Sermones (*PL* 38–9; *PLS* 2)

BEDE
Historia ecclesiastica gentis anglorum, ed. B. Colgrave and R. A. B. Mynors (Oxford, 1969)

BOETHIUS
De fide catholica, ed. H. F. Stewart and E. K. Rand (London, 1926)

CASSIAN, JOHN
Conlationes (*CSEL* 13) [*Conl.*]
Institutiones (*CSEL* 17) [*Inst.*]

CASSIODORUS
Institutiones, ed. R. A. B. Mynors (Oxford, 1961) [*Inst.*]

Codex Theodosianus, ed. T. Mommsen & P. Meyer (Berlin, 1905) [*CTh*]

COLUMBANUS
Sancti Columbani opera, ed. and trans. G. S. M. Walker (Dublin, 1957)

Concilia Galliae, A. 511–A. 695 (CC 148A)

CYPRIAN
Ad Fortunatum (De exhortatione martyrii) (CSEL 3) [*Ad Fortun.*]

Epistolae Austrasiacae, ed. W. Gundlach (*MGH Epp.* 3, 110–53, [*Epp. Austr.*]

Epistolae Langobardicae Collectae, ed. W. Gundlach (*MGH Epp.* 3, 691–715) [*Epp. Lang. Coll.*]

EVAGRIUS SCHOLASTICUS
The Ecclesiastical History of Evagrius with the Scholia, ed. J. Bidez & L. Parmentier (London, 1898)

GELASIUS I
Epistolae & Tractatus, ed. A. Thiel, in *Epistolae romanorum pontificum* I (Braunsberg, 1868) 287–510

Gesta Collationis Carthagini habitae inter Catholicos et Donatistas anno 411, ed. S. Lancel (*SC* 194, 195, 224, 373)

GREGORY I
Dialogorum libri IV de miraculis patrum italicorum, ed. with intro. A. de Vogüé (*SC* 251, 260, 265) [*Dial.*]
Homiliae in Evangelia (PL 76, 1075–1312) [*HEv.*]
Homiliae in Hiezechielem (CC 142) [*HEz.*]; also: *Grégoire le Grand. Homélies sur Ézéchiel*, ed. and trans. C. Morel (*SC* 327, 360. Paris, 1986; 1990)
In Canticum Canticorum (CC 144) [*Cant.*]
In I Librum Regum (CC 144) [*I Reg.*]
Moralia in Iob (CC 143, 143A, 143B) [*Mor.*]
Registrum Epistolarum, ed. D. Norberg (*CC* 140, 140A, to which references are given, except when otherwise indicated. See also ed. by P. Ewald and L. M. Hartmann (*MGH Epp.* 1–2) which has been used where indicated. This edition has also been used for the dedicatory letter to Leander [*ad Leandr.*] prefixed to the *Moralia*, *Ep.* v.53a. The *Responsa* to Augustine [*Resp.*] are referred to in the version given by Bede, *HE* I.27.
Regula pastoralis, ed. F. Rommel, trans. C. Morel; intro., notes and index B. Judic (*SC* 381–2. Paris, 1992) [*RP*]

GREGORY OF NAZIANZUS
Apologia pro fuga, trans. Rufinus (*CSEL* 46)

GREGORY OF TOURS
Historiarum libri X, ed. and trans. R. Buchner, *Zehn Bücher Geschichten*, 2 vols. (Berlin, 1955) [*HF*]

ILDEFONSUS OF TOLEDO
De uirorum illustrium scriptis (PL 96)

JEROME
Epistulae (CSEL 54–6)

INNOCENT I
Epistolae (PL 20)

JOANNES DIACONUS[1]
Epistula ad Senarium (PL 59)

JOHN OF BICLARUM
Chronica (Chron. min. 2; *MGH AA* 11) [*Chron.*]

JOHN OF EPHESUS
Book of the Plague in the *Chronicle* of Pseudo-Dionysius of Tel-Mahre, trans. with notes and intro. W. Witakowski (Liverpool, 1996)

JOHN THE DEACON
Sancti Gregorii papae vita (PL 75)

JULIANUS POMERIUS
De vita contemplativa (PL 59) [*Vit. cont.*]

JUSTINIAN
Codex Iustinianus, ed. P. Krueger (Berlin, 1929) [*CJ*]
Novellae, ed. R. Scholl and W. Kroll (Berlin 1928) [*Nov.*]

Liber diurnus romanorum pontificum. Gesamtausgabe von H. Foerster (Berne, 1958) [*LD*]

Liber pontificalis, ed. L. Duchesne (Paris, 1955–7); E. Tr. (to 715): *The Book of Pontiffs*, trans. and intro. R. Davies (Liverpool, 1989)

PAUL THE DEACON
Historia Langobardorum, ed. L. Bethmann and G. Waitz (*MGH SSRL* 12–187) [*HL*]
Vita Gregorii, ed. H. Grisar, *ZKTh* 11 (188) 162–73; Stuhlfath, *Gregor I* (see below, under secondary works referred to) 98–108; Interpolated *Vita: PL* 75, 41–59

PELAGIUS I
Pelagii I papae epistulae quae supersunt (556–561) ed. M. Gassó and C. M. Batlle (Montserrat, 1956)

PELAGIUS II
Epistolae, ed. L. M. Hartmann (*MGH Epp.* 2, App. III, 442–7); also by E. Schwartz, *ACO* IV/2, 105–132. References to Hartmann's edition (page references in parentheses).

PETER CHRYSOLOGUS
Sermones (CC 24, 24A, 24B)

PROCOPIUS
Aedificia, in Works, vol. 7. (Eng. trans. H. B. Dewing and G. Downey. London, 1961) [*Aed.*]
Wars, ibid., vols. 1–6

Regula Benedicti (SC 181–2)

THEOPHYLACT SIMOCATTA
The History of Theophylact Simocatta, ed. M. and M. Whitby (Oxford, 1986) [*Hist*]

VENANTIUS FORTUNATUS
Carmina (MGH AA 4/1)

Vitas sanctorum patrum emeritensium (CC 116)

---

[1] Perhaps later pope John I (523–6)

Secondary works referred to

Allen, P., 'The "Justinianic" plague', *Byzantion* 49 (1979) 5–20
   Evagrius scholasticus the Church historian (Spic. Sacrum Lovaniense. Études et documents, 41. Leuven, 1981)
Arnaldi, G., 'L'approvvigionamento di Roma e l'amministrazione de "patrimoni di S. Pietro" al tempo di Gregorio Magno', *Roczniki Humanistyczne* 34 (1986) 63–74
   'Gregorio Magno e la giustizia', *Settimane* 42 (1995) 57-104
Aubin, P., 'Intériorité et extériorité dans le *Moralia in Job* de saint Grégoire le Grand', *RechSR* 62 (1974) 117–66
Auerbach, E., *Literary language and its public in late Latin Antiquity and the Middle Ages* (Eng. trans. London, 1958)
Banniard, M., '*Iuxta uniuscuiusque qualitatem:* l'Écriture médiatrice chez Grégoire le Grand', in: *Grégoire le Grand*, 477–87
   Viva voce. Communication écrite et communication orale du IVᵉ au IXᵉ siècle en Occident Latin (Paris, 1992)
Beck, H.-G., *Kirche und theologische Literatur im byzantinischen Reich* (*Handbuch der Altertumswissenschaft* XII II / 2. Munich, 1959)
Bélanger, R., 'Introduction', *Grégoire le Grand. Commentaire sur le Cantique* (SC 314. Paris, 1984)
Belkhodja, K., 'L'Afrique byzantine à la fin du VIᵉ et au début du VIIᵉ siècle', in *Actes du IIᵉ Congrès International d'Études Nord-Africaines* (*Revue de l'Occident Musulman et de la Méditerranée*, Numéro spécial, 1970) 55–65
Benkart, P., '*Die Missionsidee Gregors d. Grossen*' Diss., Leipzig, 1946
Berschin, W., *Biographie und Epochenstil* 3 vols. (Stuttgart, 1986–91)
Bertolini, O., 'Riflessi politici delle controversie religiose con Bisanzio nelle vicende del sec. VII in *Settimane* 5 (1958) 733–89
   'I papi e le missioni fino alla metà del secolo VIII', *Settimane* 14 (1967) 327–63
Blumenkranz, B., *Juifs et chrétiens dans le monde occidental, 430–1096* (Paris, 1960)
Boesch Gajano, S., 'Dislivelli culturali e mediazioni ecclesiastiche nei Dialoghi di Gregorio Magno', *Quaderni storici* 41 (1979) 398–415
   '"Narratio" e "expositio" nei Dialoghi di Gregorio Magno', *Bullettino dell'Istituto Italiano per il Medio Evo e Archivio Muratoriano* 88 (1979) 1–33
   'La proposta agiografica dei "Dialoghi' di Gregorio Magno', *Studi Medievali* series 3ᵃ, 21 (1980) 623–64

'Teoria e pratica pastorale nelle opere di Gregorio Magno', in *Grégoire le Grand*, 181–8

Boglioni, P., 'Miracle et nature chez Grégoire le Grand', *Cahiers d'études médiévales*, 1: *Epopées, légendes et miracles* (Montreal; Paris, 1974) 11–102

Bognetti, G. P.,
'Milano langobarda', in *Storia di Milano* 2 (Fondazione Treccani degli Alfieri per la storia di Milano. Milan, 1954) 57–295
'La continuità delle sede episcopali e l'azione di Roma nel regno longobardo', *Settimane* 7 (1960) 415–54

Bovini, G., 'Massimiano di Pola, arcivescovo di Ravenna', *FR* 74 (1957) 5–27.
'Giuliano l'argentario, il munifico fondatore di chiese ravennati', *FR* 101 (1970) 125–50.

Brandi, K., 'Ravenna und Rom: Neue Beiträge zur Kenntnis der römisch-byzantinischen Urkunde', *Archiv für Urkundenforschung* 9 (1924) 1–38

Brechter, S. *Die Quellen zur Angelsachsenmission Gregors des Grossen* (Beiträge zur Geschichte des alten Mönchtums und des Benediktinerordens, 22. Münster, 1941)

Brennan, B., 'The conversion of the Jews of Clermont in AD 576', *JTS* ns 36 (1985) 321–37

Brooks, N., *The early history of the Church of Canterbury. Christ Church from 597 to 1066* (Leicester, 1984)

Brown, P. R. L., 'Religious dissent in the Later Roman Empire: the case of North Africa', *History* 46 (1961) 83–101; reprinted in his: *Religion and society* 237–59
Review of Tengström, E., *Donatisten und Katholiken*, in *JRS* 55 (1965), pp. 281–283; reprinted in his: *Religion and society*, 335–8
Religion and society in the age of Saint Augustine (London, 1972)
'Eastern and Western Christendom in Late Antiquity: a parting of the ways', *SCH* 13 (1976) 1–14; reprinted in his *Society and the holy in Late Antiquity* (London, 1982) 166–95
'The saint as exemplar in Late Antiquity', *Representations* 2 (1983), 1–25 (the substance of which appears in a truncated form in *Persons in groups*, ed. R. C. Trexler (Binghampton, N., 1985), 183–94)

Brown, T. S., *Gentlemen and officers. Imperial administration and aristocratic power in Byzantine Italy, 554–800* (Rome, 1984)

Cameron, Averil, 'The Byzantine sources of Gregory of Tours', *JTS* ns 26 (1975) 421–6
'The early religious policies of Justin II', *SCH* 13 (1976) 51–67
'Byzantine Africa – the literary evidence', in *Excavations at Carthage*, ed. J. H. Humphrey, vol. 7 (Ann Arbor, Michigan, 1982) 29–62
'The language of images: the rise of icons and Christian representation', *SCH* 28 (1992) 1–42

Caspar, E., *Geschichte des Papsttums*, 2 vols. (Tübingen, 1933)

Chadwick, H., 'John Moschus and his friend Sophronius the Sophist', *JTS* ns 25 (1974) 41–74
'Gregory the Great and the mission to the Anglo-Saxons', in *Gregorio Magno*, 1, 199–212

Chadwick, O., 'Gregory of Tours and Gregory the Great', *JTS* 50 (1949) 38–49

Chavasse, A., 'Le calendrier dominical au VIᵉ siècle', *RechSR* 38 (1951/2) 234–46; 41 (1953) 96–122

Chazelle, C. M., 'Pictures, books and the illiterate: Pope Gregory I's letters to Serenus of Marseilles', *Word and Image* 6 (1990) 138–53

Clark, F., *The pseudo-Gregorian Dialogues* 2 vols. (Studies in the History of Christian Thought, 37–8. Leiden, 1987)

Collins, R. 'Mérida and Toledo: 550–585', in *Visigothic Spain: new approaches*, ed. E. James (Oxford, 1980) 189–219

Early medieval Spain (London, 1983)

Colorni, V., 'Gli ebrei nei territori italiani a nord di Roma dal 568 agli inizi del secolo XIII', *Settimane* 26 (1980) 241–312

Cracco, G., 'Uomini di Dio e uomini di Chiesa nell'alto medioevo. Per una reinterpretazione dei "Dialoghi" di Gregorio Magno', *Ricerche di storia sociale e religiosa* 12 (1977) 163–202

'Chiesa e cristianità rurale nell'Italia di Gregorio Magno', in *Medioevo rurale. Sulle tracce della civiltà contadina* (Bologna, 1980) 361–79

'Ascesa e ruolo dei "Viri Dei" nell'Italia di Gregorio Magno', in *Hagiographie. Cultures et sociétés, IVᵉ–XIIᵉ siècles* (Paris, 1981) 283–97

Cracco Ruggini, L., 'Grégoire le Grand et le monde byzantin', in *Grégoire le Grand*, 83–94

'Gregorio Magno, Agostino e i quattro Vangeli', *Augustinianum* 25 (1985) 255–63

'Il miracolo nella cultura del tardo impero: concetto e funzione', in: *Hagiographie. Cultures et sociétés, IVᵉ–XIIᵉ siècles* (Paris, 1981) 161–204

'Pagani, ebrei e cristiani: odio sociologico e odio teologico nel mondo antico', *Settimane* 26 (1980) 15–117

'Universalità e campanilismo, centro e periferia, città e deserto nelle Storie ecclesiastiche', in *La storiografia ecclesiastica nella tarda antichità* (Messina, 1980) 159–194

Cuoq, J. G. *Église d'Afrique du Nord du IIᵉ au XIIᵉ siècle* (Paris, 1984)

Dagens, C., *Saint Grégoire le Grand. Culture et expérience chrétiennes* (Paris, 1977)

'La fin des temps et l'Église selon S. Grégoire le Grand', *RechSR* 58 (1970) 273–288.

Damizia, G., *Lineamenti di diritto canonico nel "Registrum epistolarum" di s. Gregorio Magno* (Roma, 1049)

Deichmann, F. W., *Ravenna. Hauptstadt des spätantiken Abendlandes*. 6 vols. (Wiesbaden, Stuttgart, 1958–89)

Delehaye, H., 'S. Grégoire le Grand dans l'hagiographie grecque', *AB* 23 (1904) 449–54

Delogu, P., 'Il regno longobardo', in *Storia d'Italia 1: Longobardi e Bizantini* (Turin, 1980), 3–216

De Vogüé, A., 'De la crise aux résolutions: les Dialogues comme histoire d'une âme', in *Grégoire le Grand*, 305–11

'Grégoire le Grand et ses "Dialogues" d'après deux ouvrages récents', *RHE* 83 (1988) 281–348

'Les Dialogues, oeuvre authentique et publiée par Grégoire lui-même', in *Gregorio Magno*, 2, 27–40

Introduction, *Grégoire le Grand. Commentaire sur le Premier Livre des Rois* (*SC* 351, Paris, 1989)

'"Martyrium in occulto". Le martyre du temps de paix chez Grégoire le Grand, Isidore de Séville, et Valerius du Bierzo', in *Fructus centesimus. Mélanges G. J. M. Bastiaensen* (Instrumenta patristica 19. Steenbrugge, 1989) 125–40

'Les vues de Grégoire le Grand sur la vie religieuse dans son Commentaire des Rois', *StMon* 20 (1978), 17–63 (= 'The views of St Gregory the Great on the religious life in the Commentary on the Book of Kings', *Cistercian studies* (1982), pp. 40–64 and 212–232)

Diehl, C., *L'Afrique byzantine. Histoire de la domination byzantine (533–709)*, 2 vols. (Paris, 1896)

Dodaro, R., 'Christus iustus and fear of death in Augustine's dispute with Pelagius', in *Signum pietatis. Festgabe für Cornelius Petrus Mayer OSA zum 60. Geburtstag* (Cassiciacum, 40. Würzburg, 1989) 341–61

Duchesne, L., *Autonomies ecclésiastiques: églises séparées* (Paris, 1896)

L'Église au VIe siècle (Paris, 1925)

Dudden, F. Homes, *Gregory the Great. His place in history and thought*, 2 vols. (London, 1905)

Dufourcq, A., *Étude sur les* Gesta martyrum *romains*, 4 vols.(BEFAR 83, Paris 1900–10; reissued, with vol. 5, 1988)

Duval, Y., 'Grégoire et l'Église d'Afrique. Les "Hommes du pape"', in *Grégoire le Grand*, 129–58

Duval, Y.-M., 'La discussion entre l'apocrisiaire Grégoire et le patriarche Eutychios au sujet de la résurrection de la chair', in *Grégoire le Grand*, 347–66.

Eisenhofer, D., 'Augustinus in den Evangelien-Homilien Gregors d. Großen', in *Festgabe für Alois Knöpfler*, ed. H. M. Geitl and D. G. Pfeilschrifter (Freiburg, 1917) 56–66.

Étaix, R., 'Note sur la tradition manuscrite des Homélies sur l'Évangile de saint Grégoire le Grand', in *Grégoire le Grand*, 551–9

Fiedrowicz, M., *Das Kirchenverständnis Gregors des Grossen. Eine Untersuchung seiner exegetischen und homiletischen Werke* (Römische Quartalschrift für christliche Altertumskunde und Kirchengeschichte, 50. Supplementheft. Rome, 1995)

Fischer, E. H., 'Gregor der Große und Byzanz. Ein Beitrag zur Geschichte der päpstlichen Politik', *ZRG* Kan. Abt. 36 (1950) 15–144

Folliet, G., 'Les trois catégories de chrétiens', *Année théologique augustinienne* 14 (1954) 81–96

Fontaine, J., *Isidore de Séville et la culture classique dans l'Espagne Wisigothique* (Paris, 1959)

'Augustin, Grégoire et Isidore: esquisse d'une recherche sur le style des *Moralia in Job*', in *Grégoire le Grand*, 499–509

Frank, K. S. 'Actio und contemplatio bei Gregor dem Großen', *Trierer theologische Zeitschrift* 78 (1969) 283–95

Fredriksen, P., 'Excaecati Occulta Justitia Dei: Augustine on Jews and Judaism', *JECS* 3 (1995) 299–324

Frend, W. H. C., *The Donatist Church* (Oxford, 1952)

Fritze, W. '*Universalis gentium confessio*. Formeln, Träger und Wege universalmissionarischen Denkens im 7. Jahrhundert', *Frühmittelalterliche Studien* 3 (1969) 78–130

Fuhrmann, W., 'Studien zur Geschichte mittelalterlichen Patriarchate', I, *ZRG*, Kan. Abt. 39 (1953) 112–76; II, *ib.* 40 (1954) 1–84

Gillet, R., 'Introduction', to *Grégoire le Grand: Morales sur Job* (SC 32, Paris, 1948) 9–113

'Spiritualité et place du moine dans l'Église selon saint Grégoire le Grand', in *Théologie de la vie monastique* (Coll. Théologie, 49, Paris 1961) 323–51

'Grégoire le Grand', *DHGE* 21 (1986) 1387–420

Godding, R., 'Les Dialogues . . . de Grégoire le Grand. A propos d'un livre récent', *AB* 106 (1988) 201–29

Bibliografia di Gregorio Magno, 1890–1989 (*Opere di Gregorio Magno*, Complementi, I, Rome, 1990)

Goubert, P., 'Patriarches d'Antioche et d'Alexandrie contemporains de S. Grégoire le Grand', *REByz* 25 (1967) 65–76

Gray, P. T. R., and Herren, M. W., 'Columbanus and the Three Chapters controversy – a new approach', *JTS* n. s. 45 (1994) 160–70

Greenslade S. L., '*Sede vacante* procedure in the early Church', *JTS* n. s. 12 (1961) 210–26

Grégoire le Grand, ed. J. Fontaine, R. Gillet, S. Pellistrandi (Colloques Internationaux du CNRS. Paris, 1986)

Gregorio Magno e il suo tempo, 2 vols. (*SEAug* 33–4, Rome, 1991)

Grierson, P., 'The *Patrimonum Petri in illis partibus* and the pseudo-imperial coinage in Frankish Gaul', *Revue belge de numismatique* 105 (1959) 95–111

Grillmeier, A., *Christ in Christian tradition* 2: *From the Council of Chalcedon (451) to Gregory the Great (590–604)* Part II (Eng. trans. by Pauline Allen and John Cawte, London, Oxford, 1995)

Grillmeier, A., and H. Bacht, eds., *Das Konzil von Chalkedon*, 3 vols. (Würzburg, 1951–54)

Guillaumont, A. and C., *Evagre le Pontique. Traité pratique ou le moine*, 2 vols. (*SC* 170–1. Paris, 1963)

Guillou, A., *Régionalisme et indépendance dans l'Empire byzantin au VIIe siècle* (Rome, 1969)

'L'Italia bizantina dall'invasione longobarda alla caduta di Ravenna', in *Storia d'Italia* 1: Longobardi e Bizantini (Turin, 1980), 217–338

Hallinger, K. 'Papst Gregor der Grosse und der Hl. Benedikt', (*Studia Anselmiana* 42. Rome, 1957) 231–319

Hartmann, L. M., *Untersuchungen zur Geschichte der byzantinischen Verwaltung in Italien (540–750)* (Leipzig, 1889)

Harvey, S. A., *Asceticism and society in crisis. John of Ephesus and the Lives of the Eastern Saints* (Berkeley, Cal., 1990)

Heitz, C., 'Les monuments de Rome à l'époque de Grégoire le Grand', in *Grégoire le Grand*, 31–8

Hemmerdinger, B., 'Le "Codex" 252 de la Bibliothèque de Photius', *ByZ* 58 (1965) 1–2

Hodgkin, T., *Italy and her invaders*, vol. 5, 2nd edn (Oxford, 1916)

Holtz, L., 'Le contexte grammatical de défi à la grammaire: Grégoire et Cassiodore', in *Grégoire le Grand*, 531–9

Honigmann, E., 'Two metropolitan relatives of the emperor Maurice: Domitianus of Melitene (about 580–January 12, 602) and Athenagoras of Petra', *Patristic studies (StT* 173. Rome, 1953) 217–225

Hürten, H., 'Gregor der Große und der mittelalterliche Episkopat', *ZKG* 73 (1962) 16–41

Jenal, G., 'Grégoire le Grand et la vie monastique dans l'Italie de son temps', in *Grégoire le Grand*, 147–58.

'Gregor d. Grosse und die Anfänge der Angelsachsenmission', *Settimane* 32 (1986) 793–857

Italia ascetica et monastica. Das Asketen- und Mönchtum in Italien von den Anfängen bis zur Zeit der Langobarden (ca. 150/250–604), 2 vols. (Stuttgart, 1995)

Jones, A. H. M., *The Later Roman Empire, 284–602*, 3 vols. (Oxford, 1964) [*LRE*]

Kitzinger, E., 'The cult of icons in the age before Iconoclasm', *DOP* 8 (1954) 83–150

Kahl, H.-D., 'Die ersten Jahrhunderte des missionsgeschichtlichen Mittelalters. Bausteine für eine Phänomenologie bis ca. 1050', in *Kirchengeschichte als Missionsgeschichte*. Band 2: *Die Kirche des frühen Mittelalters*, ed. K. Schäferdiek (Erster Halbband. Munich, 1978) 11–76

Katz, S., 'Pope Gregory the Great and the Jews', *Jewish Quarterly review* 24 (1933) 113–36

Krautheimer, R., *Rome: profile of a city, 312–1308* (Princeton, New Jersey, 1980)

Landes, R., 'Millenarismus absconditus. L'historiographie augustinienne et le millénarisme du haut Moyen Age jusqu'à l'an Mil', *Le Moyen Age* 98 (1992) 355–77

Leyser, C., '"Let me speak, let me speak": vulnerability and authority in Gregory's Homilies on Ezechiel', in *Gregorio Magno*, 2, 169–82

Linder, A., *The Jews in Roman imperial legislation* (Detroit, 1987)

Llewellyn, P., 'The Roman Church in the seventh century: the legacy of Gregory I', *JEH* 25 (1974) 363–80

Lubac, H. de, *Exégèse médiévale. Les quatre sens de l'écriture* 1–2 (Lyons, 1959)

McCready, W. D., *Signs of sanctity. Miracles in the thought of Gregory the Great* (Pontifical Institute of Mediaeval Studies. Studies and Texts 91. Toronto, 1989)

MacIntyre, A., *After virtue: a study in moral theory* (London, 1981)

McShane, P. A., *La romanitas et le pape Léon le Grand. L'apport culturel des institutions à la formation des structures ecclésiastiques* (Recherches, 24. Tournai, Montréal, 1979)

Manselli, R. 'L'escatologia di Gregorio Magno', *Ricerche di storia religiosa* 1 (1954) 72–88

'Gregorio Magno e la Bibbia', *Settimane* 10 (1963) 67–101

Markus, R. A., 'Donatism: the last phase', *SCH* 1 (1964) 118–126; reprinted in *From Augustine*, VI

'Reflections on religious dissent in North Africa in the Byzantine period', *SCH* 3 (1966) 140–149; reprinted in *From Augustine*, VII

'Gregory the Great and the origins of a papal missionary strategy', *SCH* 6 (1970) 29–38; reprinted in *From Augustine*, XI

'Christianity and dissent in Roman Africa: changing perspectives in recent work', *SCH* 9 (1972) 21–36; reprinted in *From Augustine*, VIII.

'The cult of icons in sixth century Gaul', *JTS* n. s. 29 (1978) 151–157; reprinted in *From Augustine*, XII

'Carthage – Prima Justiniana – Ravenna: aspects of Justinian's *Kirchenpolitik*', *Byzantion* 49 (1979) 277–306; reprinted in *From Augustine* , XIII

'Country bishops in Byzantine Africa', *SCH* 16 (1979) 1–15; reprinted in *From Augustine*, IX

'Gregory the Great's Europe', *TRHS* 5th. ser. 31 (1981) 21–36; reprinted in *From Augustine*, XV

From Augustine to Gregory the Great (London, 1983)

'Ravenna and Rome, 554–604', *Byzantion* 51 (1981) 566–578; reprinted in *From Augustine*, XIV

'Justinian's ecclesiastical politics and the Western Church', in *Sacred and secular*, VII: English trans. of 'La politica ecclesiastica di Giustiniano e la chiesa d'Occidente', *Il mondo del diritto nell'epoca giustinianea: caratteri e problematiche*, ed. G. G. Archi (Ravenna, 1985) 113–124

'The sacred and the secular: from Augustine to Gregory the Great', *JTS* n. s. 36 (1985) 84–96; reprinted in *Sacred and secular*, II

Saeculum. History and society in the theology of St Augustine (Cambridge, 1970; 1988)

The end of ancient Christianity (Cambridge, 1990)

'Gregory the Great's *rector* and his genesis', in *Grégoire le Grand*, 137–46

'The Latin fathers', in *Cambridge history of medieval political thought, c. 350–c. 1450* (Cambridge, 1988) 83–122

'The problem of "Donatism" in the sixth century', *Gregorio Magno e il suo tempo*. I. Studi storici (*Studia Ephemeridis "Augustinianum"* 33. Rome, 1991) 159–166; reprinted in *Sacred and secular*, XIII

'Gregory the Great on kings: rulers and preachers in the *Commentary on I Kings*', in: *The Church and sovereignty*, ed. Diana Wood (Essays in honour of Michael Wilks, *SCH Subsidia* 9, Oxford, 1991), 7-21; reprinted in *Sacred and secular*, VIII

'Ravenna', *TRE* 27 (1997) 559–62

Sacred and secular. Studies on Augustine and Latin Christianity (London, 1994)

'From Caesarius to Boniface: Christianity and paganism in Gaul', *Le septième siècle: Changements et continuités / The seventh century: change and continuity*, ed. J. Fontaine and J. N. Hillgarth (Studies of the Warburg Institute, 42, London, 1992) 154–172; reprinted in *Sacred and secular*, XII

Signs and meanings. World and text in ancient Christianity (Liverpool, 1996)

Marrou, H.-I., 'Autour de la bibliothèque du pape Agapit', *MAH* 48 (1931) 124–69

Massigli, R., 'La création de la métropole ecclésiastique de Ravenne', *Mélanges d'archéologie et d'histoire de l'École française de Rome* 31 (1911) 277–90

Mayr-Harting, H. M. R. E., *The coming of Christianity to Anglo-Saxon England* (London, 1972)

Mazzotti, M., 'L'attività edilizia di Massimiano di Pola', *FR* 71 (1956) 5–30.

Meens, R., 'A background to Augustine's mission to Anglo-Saxon England', *Anglo-Saxon England* 23 (1994) 5–17

'Ritual purity and the influence of Gregory the Great in the early Middle Ages', *SCH* 32 (1995) 31–43

Menis, G. C., 'Le giurisdizioni metropolitiche di Aquileia e di Milano nell'Antichità', in *Aquileia e Milano* (*Antichità Altoadriatiche* 4, 1973) 271–294

Meyvaert, P., 'A letter of Pelagius II composed by Gregory the Great', in *Gregory the Great: a symposium*, ed. J. C. Cavadini (Notre Dame, In., 1996) 94–116

Benedict, Gregory and others (London, 1977)

'Bede's text of the Libellus Responsionum of Gregory the Great to Augustine of Canterbury, in: *England before the Conquest. Studies in primary sources presented to Dorothy Whitelock* (Cambridge, 1971) 15–33; reprinted in *Benedict, Gregory and others*, x

'The date of Gregory the Great's Commentaries on Canticles and on I Kings', *Sacris erudiri* 23 (1978-79) 191–216

'Diversity in unity. A Gregorian theme', *Heythrop Journal* 4 (1963) 141–62; reprinted in *Benedict, Gregory and others*, vi

'The enigma of Gregory the Great's Dialogues: a response to Francis Clark', *JEH* 39 (1988) 335–81

'Gregory the Great and the theme of authority', *Spode House Review* 3 (1966) 3–12; reprinted in *Benedict, Gregory and others*, v

'Le Libellus responsionum à Augustin de Cantorbéry: une oeuvre authentique de Grégoire le Grand', in *Grégoire le Grand*, 543–9

'Uncovering a lost work of Gregory the Great: fragments of the early Commentary on Job', *Traditio* 50 (1995) 55–74

Miller, D. H., 'The Roman revolution of the eighth century: a study of the ideological background of the papal separation from Byzantium and alliance with the Franks', *Medieval studies* 36 (1974) 79–133

Moeller, C., 'Le chalcédonisme et le néo-chalcédonisme en Orient de 451 à la fin du VIᵉ siècle', in Grillmeier and Bacht, *Chalkedon*, I, 637–720

Morini, E., 'Le strutture monastiche a Ravenna', in *Storia di Ravenna*, 305–21

Nelson, J., 'Queens as Jezebels: the careers of Brunhild and Balthild in Merovingian history', in *Medieval women*, ed. D. Baker (*SCH Subsidia* 1, Oxford, 1978) 31–77

Norberg, D., *In Registrum Gregorii Magni studia critica*, (Uppsala Universitets Arsskrift 1937/4; 1939/7)

'Style personnel et style administratif dans le Registrum epistolarum de S. Grégoire le Grand', in *Grégoire le Grand*, 489–97

Orselli, A. M., 'La chiesa di Ravenna tra coscienza dell'istituzione e tradizione cittadina', in *Storia di Ravenna*, 405–22

Paret, R., 'Dometianus de Mélitène et la politique religieuse de l'empereur Maurice', *REByz* 15 (1957) 42–72

Paronetto, V., 'I longobardi nell'epistolario di Gregorio Magno', in *Atti del 6⁰ Congresso internazionale di studi sull'alto medioevo* (Spoleto, 1980) 559–70

'Une présence augustinienne chez Grégoire le Grand: le *De catechizandis rudibus* dans la *Regula pastoralis*', in *Grégoire le Grand*, 511–19

Pasini, C., 'Chiesa di Milano e Sicilia: punti di contatto dal VI all'VIII secolo', in

Pricoco, S. and others eds., *Sicilia e Italia suburbicaria tra IV e VIII secolo* (Catania, 1991) 367–98

Petersen, J. M. 'Did Gregory the Great know Greek?', *SCH* 13 (1976) 121–34

The Dialogues of Gregory the Great in their late antique cultural background (Pontifical Institute of Mediaeval Studies, Studies and Texts 69. Toronto, 1984)

'Greek influences upon Gregory the Great's exegesis of Luke 15:1–10 in *Homelia in Evang.* II.34', in *Grégoire le Grand*, 521–9

'"Homo omnino latinus"? The theological and cultural background of pope Gregory the Great', *Speculum* 62 (1987) 529–51

Pietri, C., 'Clercs et serviteurs laïcs de l'Église romaine au temps de Grégoire le Grand', in *Grégoire le Grand*, 107–22

'L'évolution du culte des saints aux premiers siècles: du témoin à l'intercesseur', in *Les fonctions des saints dans le monde occidental (iiie xiiie-siècle)* (Coll. de l' École française de Rome 149, Rome, 1991) 15–36

Pietri, L., 'Grégoire le Grand et la Gaule: le projet pour la réforme de l'Église Gauloise', in *Gregorio Magno*, 109–28

Pitz, E., *Papstreskripte im frühen Mittelalter. Diplomatische und rechtsgeschichtliche Studien zum Brief-Corpus Gregors des Großen* (Sigmaringen, 1990)

Prinz, F., 'Das westliche Mönchtum zur Zeit Gregors des Grossem', in *Grégoire le Grand*, 123–36

Pringle, D., *The defence of Byzantine Africa from Justinian to the Arab conquest* (Oxford, 1981)

Ramos-Lissón, D., 'Grégoire le Grand, Léandre er Reccarède', *Gregorio Magno* 1, 187–98

Rebillard, E., *In hora mortis. Évolution de la pastorale chrétienne de la mort aux ive et ve siècles dans l'Occident latin* (*BEFAR* fasc. 283. Rome, 1994)

Recchia, V., *Gregorio Magno e la società agricola* (Verba seniorum n.s. 8. Rome, 1978)

'La memoria di Agostino nella esegesi biblica di Gregorio Magno', *Augustinianum* 25 (1985) 405–34

Riché, P., *Éducation et culture dans l'Occident barbare, 6e-8e siècle*₂ (Paris, 1962)

Rist, J. M., *Augustine. Ancient thought baptized* (Cambridge, 1994)

Rouche, M., 'Grégoire le Grand face à la situation économique de son temps', in: *Grégoire le Grand*, 41–58

Rousseau, P., *Basil of Caesarea* (Berkeley, 1994)

Rudmann, R., *Mönchtum und kirchlicher Dienst in den Schriften Gregors des Großen* (St Ottilien, 1956)

Savon, H., 'L'Antéchrist dans l'oeuvre de Grégoire le Grand', in *Grégoire le Grand*, 389–404

Schieffer, R., 'Zur Beurteilung des norditalischen Dreikapitel Schismas', *ZKG* 87 (1976) 167–201

Schindler, A.,'Afrika I', in *TRE* I (1977) 641–700

Shaw, B. D., 'African Christianity: Disputes, Definitions, and 'Donatists', *Orthodoxy and heresy in religious movements: discipline and dissent*, ed. M. R. Greenshields and T. A. Robinson (Lampeter, 1992) 5–34; reprinted in *Rulers, Nomads and Christians in Roman North Africa* (London, 1995) XI.

Sotinel, C., *Rhétorique de la faute et pastorale de la réconciliation dans la Lettre apologétique contre Jean de Ravenne*. (Collection de l'École française de Rome, 185, Rome, 1994).

Spearing, E., *The patrimony of the Roman Church in the time of Gregory the Great* (Cambridge, 1918)

Storia di Ravenna 2/2: Dall'età bizantina all'età ottoniana:ecclesiologia, cultura e arte, ed. A. Carile (Venice, 1992)

Straw, C., 'Gregory's politics: theory and practice', in *Gregorio Magno*, 1, 47–63

Gregory the Great. Perfection in imperfection (Berkeley and Los Angeles, 1988)

Stuhlfath, W., *Gregor I, der Große. Sein Leben bis zu seiner Wahl zum Papste nebst einer Untersuchung der ältesten Viten* (Heidelberger Abhandlungen zur mittleren und neueren Geschichte, 39. Heidelberg, 1913)

Testi-Rasponi, A., 'Annotazioni sulla storia della chiesa di Ravenna dalle origini alla morte di San Gregorio Magno', *FR* 33 (1929) 29–49

'Archiepiscopus', *Archivum latinitatis medii aevi* (1927) 5–11

Thompson, E. A., 'The conversion of the Visigoths to Catholicism', *Nottingham Medieval Studies* 4 (1960) 4–35

The Goths in Spain (Oxford, 1969)

Tuilier, A., 'Le sens de l'adjectif "oecumenikos" dans la tradition patristique et dans la tradition byzantine', *StPatr* 7 (*TU* 92, 1966) 413–24

Vaes, M., 'La papauté et l'Église franque à l'époque de Grégoire le Grand', *RHE* 6 (1905) 537-56; 755–84

Vailhé, S., 'Le titre de Patriarche Oecouménique avant saint Grégoire le Grand', *Échos d'Orient* 11 (1908) 65–9

'S. Grégoire le Grand et le titre de Patriarche Oecouménique', *Échos d'Orient* 11 (1908) 161–71

Van Uytfanghe, M., 'La controverse biblique et patristique autour du miracle, et ses répercussions sur l'hagiographie dans l'Antiquité tardive et le Haut Moyen Age latin', in: *Hagiographie. Cultures et sociétés, IVᵉ–XIIᵉ siècles* (Paris, 1981) 205–33

'Scepticisme doctrinal au seuil du Moyen Age? Les objections du diacre Pierre dans les *Dialogues* de Grégoire le Grand', in *Grégoire le Grand*, 315–26

Verbraken, P.-P., 'Les Dialogues de saint Grégoire le Grand: sont-ils apocryphes? A propos d'un ouvrage récent', *RBen* 98 (1988) 272–7

Vilella Masana, J., 'Gregorio Magno e Hispania', in *Gregorio Magno*, 1, 167–86

Von Simson, O., *Sacred fortress. Byzantine art and statecraft in Ravenna*, (Chicago, 1948)

Wallace-Hadrill, J. M., 'Rome and the early English Church: some questions of transmission', *Settimane*, 7 (1960) 519–48; reprinted in his *Early medieval history* (Oxford, 1975) 115–37, to which references are given

The Frankish Church (Oxford History of the Christian Church, Oxford, 1983)

Weiss, G., 'Studia Anastasiana I' (Miscellanea Byzantina Monacensia 4. Munich, 1965)

Whitby, M., *The emperor Maurice and his historian: Theophylact Simocatta on Persian and Balkan warfare* (Oxford 1988)

Wood, I. N., 'Frankish hegemony in England', in *The age of Sutton Hoo. The seventh century in North-Western Europe* (Woodbridge, 1992) 235–41

The Merovingian kingdoms, 450–751 (London, 1994)

'The mission of Augustine of Canterbury to the English', *Speculum* 69 (1994) 1–17

Index of Gregorian Texts

General Index

Acacian schism, 91
active life *see* contemplative life
Adaloald, prince, 138
adoratio, 175, 176, 177
Adriatic, 107
Aemilia *see* Liguria
Aethelberht, king, 82, 85, 178, 181–3, 187
Africa(n), North, 35, 51, 74, 95, 112, 113, 117,
	126, 188–202, 204, 209
Agapetus I, pope, 8, 10, 35
Agilulf, king, 99, 102, 103, 104, 105, 106, 137,
	139, 142
Agnellus, of Ravenna, 145–6, 147, 148, 152
agriculture *see* peasants
Aix, 178
Alexandria, 7, 93, 122, 161, 162, 179, 207, 209
	see also Eulogius
Alfred, king, 86
allegory, 45–7 *see also* scripture; exposition
Allen, P., 5
Ambrose, St, xii, 40, 60, 88
Amida, 5
Anastasius I, emperor, 88
Anastasius II, bp of Antioch, 12, 89, 161, 208
Ancona, 107
Andrew, St, 145
Andrew, *vir illustris*, 12
Andrew, *scholasticus*, 150
Andrew, St, monastery of, 10, 148
angels, 21, 178
Angers, 180
Angles, *Angli*, 178, 184
Anician *gens*, 8, 11
anniversaries, 59
Antichrist, 56, 57, 63
Antioch, 7, 93, 161, 162, 207, 209 *see also*
	Anastasius II, and Gregory, bps of
	Antioch
Antoninus, sub-deacon, 157, 158
Antony, St, 60
Apion, 11

Apollinare, S., in Classe, church of, 151
Apollinaris, St, 145, 151
Apollo, 184
Aponius, 28
'apostolic', 147, 162, 197
Apulia-Calabria, 112
Aquileia, 107, 126, 127–33, 134, 137, 139, 144,
	146, 147, 149
Aquitaine, 169, 171
Aratus, 38
Arab(s), 188, 200
archbishop(s), 145, 146, 147, 149, 160
archdeacon(s), 123, 148, 157
Aregius, bp of Gap, 174
Arian(s), 80, 106, 116, 165, 166, 191, 193
Arigius, *patricius*, 113
Aristobulus, *antigrafus*, 12
aristocracy, 6–7, 151, 168, 170
Ariulf, duke, 99, 100, 104
Arles, 75, 144, 169, 170, 171, 178, 179, 180, 185,
	190
Arnaldi, G., 90, 122
Arnobius the Younger, 11
ascetic, -ism, 53, 60, 61
Aubin, P., 58
Auerbach, E., 35
Augustine, St, of Hippo, xii, 17, 41, 192, 194,
	200, 201, 202, 204
	influence, 35, 37
	on active and contemplative life, 18, 19
	on authority, 30
	on carnal and spiritual, 58
	on Christian rulers, 57
	on Church and society, 58
	on created world, 49
	on diversity, 75
	on eagles, 53
	on episcopal office, 30, 94
	on eschatology, 51, 53
	on exegesis, 45, 48
	on martyrdom, 60

233